D0273090

WILD GIRLS

Wild Child

ALAN CROGHAN

PENGUIN BOOKS

PENGUIN BOOKS

Published by the Penguin Group

Penguin Books Ltd, 80 Strand, London WC2R ORL, England

Penguin Group (USA) Inc., 375 Hudson Street, New York, New York 10014, USA

Penguin Group (Canada), 90 Eglinton Avenue East, Suite 700, Toronto, Ontario, Canada M4P 2Y3
(a division of Pearson Penguin Canada Inc.)

Penguin Ireland, 25 St Stephen's Green, Dublin 2, Ireland (a division of Penguin Books Ltd)

Penguin Group (Australia), 707 Collins Street, Melbourne, Victoria 3008, Australia
(a division of Pearson Australia Group Pty Ltd)

Penguin Books India Pvt Ltd, 11 Community Centre, Panchsheel Park, New Delhi – 110 017, India

Penguin Group (NZ), 67 Apollo Drive, Rosedale, Auckland 0632, New Zealand
(a division of Pearson New Zealand Ltd)

Penguin Books (South Africa) (Pty) Ltd, Block D, Rosebank Office Park,
181 Jan Smuts Avenue, Parktown North, Gauteng 2193, South Africa

Penguin Books Ltd, Registered Offices: 80 Strand, London WC2R ORL, England

www.penguin.com

First published as *Disorganised Crime* by Penguin Ireland 2013

ISBN: 978–0–241–96852–9

www.greenpenguin.co.uk

MIX
Paper from
responsible sources
FSC
www.fsc.org   FSC® C018179

Penguin Books is committed to a sustainable
future for our business, our readers and our planet.
This book is made from Forest Stewardship
Council™ certified paper.

I dedicate this book to my mother.

Without her support and love I wouldn't have what I have today:
hope, faith, love and belief.

Contents

Chapter 1   A Problem Child   1

Chapter 2   My Criminal Niche   21

Chapter 3   Becoming a Hard Man   41

Chapter 4   Writer in Residence   57

Chapter 5   Actual Bodily Harm   66

Chapter 6   The Big Boys' Jail   87

Chapter 7   Protection   95

Chapter 8   Portlaoise and After   115

Chapter 9   Trying to Go Straight   121

Chapter 10   On the Run   129

Chapter 11   The Key   141

Chapter 12   Access All Areas   148

Chapter 13   2,800 Pesetas and an Envelope of Cocaine   157

Chapter 14   The Homeless Journalist   171

Chapter 15   In the Control Tower   190

Chapter 16   Isolation and Madness   199

Chapter 17   Rock Bottom   209

Chapter 18   Trying to Stop   216

Chapter 19   The Miracle Man   223

A Problem Child

In April 1968, while heavily pregnant with me, my mother boarded a plane in Vancouver, along with my father and their two sons and twin daughters.

My parents had emigrated from Dublin to Canada three years previously, hoping to pursue a better way of life than the one they left behind. They lived in a log cabin in Burns Lake, not far from Vancouver. My mother, who to this day has a beautiful singing voice, hitched up with a local band and recorded her own version of the Irish song 'The Spinning Wheel'. My father used to say that my mother's pregnancy with me was the sole reason they decided to return home to Dublin. My Ma's version is that they had to return because my dad missed his mother and had become really homesick. I'm inclined to believe the latter.

Halfway through the flight, at 35,000 feet, my mother suddenly went into labour. She believed, as did everyone else, that I was going to be brought into this world on board the aircraft, but somehow she held out. After the plane had touched down at Dublin Airport, my step-grandfather ushered her into his car and set off towards St James's Hospital, where he worked in the kitchens.

As he sped along a dark country road at the back of Dublin Airport he suddenly swerved to avoid a parked truck and ran into something solid – a pig! The car was wrecked, and with no houses nearby there was no way for them to call an ambulance. The farmer who owned the truck offered to drive my mother to the hospital. In the back of the truck were dozens of squealing pigs on their way to the slaughterhouse.

My mother was lifted from the car into the cab of the truck and the farmer got my Ma to the hospital, where I was delivered safely. To this day my mother still says to me, 'Alan, you were a problem child even before you were born.'

*

My mother was born in Co. Wexford in 1940. Her mother was only fourteen. At that time it would have been seen as a disgrace if it were known that a child had given birth, and that the father was in his thirties. So my grandmother moved to Dublin, and my mother was fostered off to a married couple by the name of Jordan.

When she was aged seven, her foster father passed away. One morning not long after Mr Jordan's death my Ma was taken by a priest, placed into a car and handed over into the care of the Sisters of Mercy convent in Ferns. (Some six years later my grandmother gave birth to another girl, who she abandoned in the Legion of Mary's Regina Coeli Hostel near the Four Courts in Dublin, and subsequently fled to England for fear of ending up in a home herself.)

My Ma suffered terrible physical abuse at the hands of the nuns. Because she was left-handed, the nuns whipped her hands so much that they bled, telling her, 'You sit at the right hand of the Father, so you will eat with the right hand.'

My mother eventually escaped from the convent in 1953, at the age of thirteen. She does not have any recollection of how she got to Dublin, but she remembers standing on a cold wet street – hungry, alone and tired. She changed her name from Christina to Diana and managed to get a job in a small café called The Rainbow. There she met Sylvia Costelloe, who was to become her lifelong friend.

When she was nineteen, she met Liam Croghan. He was two years younger than herself. Raised in the Liberties, he worked as a kitchen porter in the psychiatric hospital in Grangegorman. When they got married, a chap my mother knew called Vincent (who happened to be the brother to the later infamous criminal John Gilligan) gave her away, because she was not in touch with her own family.

It wasn't until 1993 that my mother eventually located her biological mother. My grandmother had married in Manchester and had three children from that relationship. After my Ma learned her mother was dying, she made great efforts to travel over to see her.

Minutes after my mother arrived at her bedside, with her dying breath she whispered, 'I'm sorry for everything. Find Teresa.'

My Ma as a young woman

Teresa turned out to be the younger sister my mother never knew she had. She had been abandoned in the Regina Coeli at the age of two, and was subsequently committed by the Courts for fourteen years. As a result of that visit, my Ma also learned about many other siblings she never knew she had.

*

My parents named me Alan Henry Croghan – Henry after my step-grandfather, a German who was a soldier in the Waffen SS during the Second World War. As a child I remember being told the unlikely story of how he ended up meeting May Croghan, my father's mother. Towards the end of the war, somewhere in Germany, he was caught in an ambush with a group of fellow soldiers.

I recall Henry telling me, 'I was not sure if the soldiers who surrounded us were Russian or American. I ordered my unit that if they were Russians we were to fight to the death – because if we were captured by the Russians we would have been tortured and killed! But if they were Americans, we'd surrender.'

It turned out that the soldiers who ambushed them were Americans, and so Henry's unit handed themselves up. He was en route to a POW camp in Arizona when orders came for the boat to divert to the UK and offload the POWs there.

Meanwhile, May was working in a flax factory nearby, and regularly brought linen into the POW camp. With my Croghan grandfather no longer on the scene, she had emigrated from Ireland in order to get work – and left her three-year-old son, my father, to be cared for by the Christian Brothers in Rathdrum, Co. Wicklow. He remained there until the age of nine. (My father has never spoken of his experience while under the care of the Christian Brothers, and I never pried.)

Henry could not speak English when he arrived at the English POW camp and May could not speak German, but a fellow internee of Henry's served as an interpreter after he noticed them exchanging smiles. Henry was a fine strapping German, and May was a petite and attractive brunette. Love can blossom in the strangest of places. Henry was released after nearly six years in the POW camp. They got married and moved to Dublin, where Henry found work in the kitchens of St James's. My grandmother took my father back out from the Christian Brothers in Rathdrum.

On my family's return from Canada we all moved in with May and Henry, my Nanna and Granddad, in Lisburn Street off North King Street in the north inner city. We stayed there for about six months until we got a Corporation house on Macroom Avenue in Coolock, a few miles north-east of the city centre.

For me, growing up in Coolock, no two days were ever the same. I ran wild – but if anything went wrong, the only thing on my mind would be to get home as quickly as my legs could carry me. Reaching the safety of my home was paramount, even though I knew I'd face the wrath of my mother. I always felt I could handle anything I got from her.

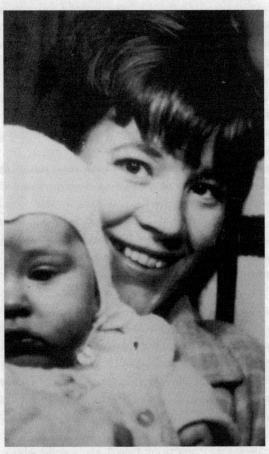

My mother and me

I distinctly remember one Christmas morning in the house in Macroom Avenue. I woke up very early in the morning and heard something in the living room. I went downstairs to investigate, and there were my twin sisters, Julie and Michelle, sitting beside the old radiogram where our mother hid all the chocolates and other goodies. The two of them had opened everything, and their faces were covered in chocolate. They would tear open a bar of chocolate, take a bite out of it and then just throw it to one side before starting on another – they were greedy and wanted the lot! I ran back upstairs and told my Ma. When the rest of the family came charging down the stairs, my twin sisters (wearing only their nightdresses) bolted out through the front door, each with a bag of sugar in her hands. Without thinking, the whole lot of us, bare-footed and only half dressed, pursued them up the road in the snow. I'm sure it would have been a strange sight if any of the neighbours had looked out through their windows to see if it was a white Christmas.

Another event that I recall from my early years was more disturb-ing, and for a long time I thought I would never disclose it to anyone. But with the passage of time I was eventually able to talk openly about it to people I trusted – starting with Dr McCormack, the prison psychiatrist in St Patrick's Institution for teenage offenders. At the time of the incident I was no more than five years of age. I don't remember anything that led up to it, and I can't recall any-thing after it. All I can see in my mind's eye is the event itself taking place. I know I was in my bed and it was dark out, so it must have been the middle of the night. There was a man who lived in our neighbourhood who sometimes slept over in our house. I remem-ber this man being in my bed; I don't know how he got there, I just remember him being there beside me. I remember him pulling down his underpants and exposing himself and then telling me to 'feel him' and to 'suck him', which I did. The other thing I can still clearly remember is his awful stench.

Do I hate him? I don't think I do. I was a child who was taken advantage of by a much older person. He is the one who has to live with the fact that he abused a child. I don't dwell on it, I don't carry it on my shoulder like a cross – it happened, and that's it. It just happened. I definitely don't hold any member of my family responsible. It makes me feel really uncomfortable even writing about it. I just want to forget the whole bloody thing.

My father had a collection of knives in his bedroom – everything from little daggers to bowie knives and large hunting blades. He would keep a knife on the floor beside his bed and another under his pillow; he also used to carry one in a sheath strapped to his ankle. I suppose when I was a small child I didn't think of this as strange. To be honest, I was really impressed by knives – and the more dangerous they looked, the cooler I thought they were. Sometimes I'd take some knives from my Da's wardrobe, go to the tree in our back garden and stick them in it to see how strong the blades were. Or I'd practise throwing them into the tree. All of this might have had some influence on my relationship with knives later in life.

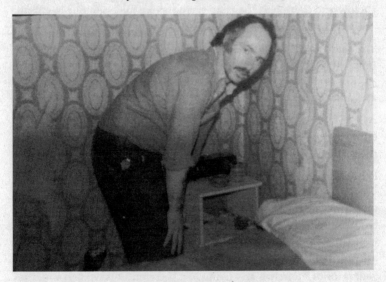

My father never worked. He just got drunk and started arguments. Once, when I was about twelve, my Da called me into the sitting room. He pulled a red-hot poker from the fire, said, 'I want you to see this,' and pressed the poker against the inside of his arm. Another time, when my Ma got a bit of work on the side and was paid cash in hand, he rang up the Social Welfare and grassed on her.

My mother went out to work, paid the bills, cleaned the house, washed the clothes, cooked the meals, got everyone out to school. She did everything, and to this very day she still does. I honestly do not know where my Ma gets her energy from. She's an amazing woman.

From as far back as I can recall, my Ma never turned anyone away from her door. People very often knocked up to our door freezing, sometimes in the middle of the night, saying they'd been kicked out of their home and had nowhere to go, and my Ma would say, 'Come on in, throw your head on the couch and I'll do you a bit to eat.' I remember my Ma taking in a sixteen-year-old kid who was addicted to drugs; his family had just kicked him out. She woke in the middle of the night, looked down over the bedroom banisters to our hall below and there was the chap trying to wedge open our payphone with a knife to get the money.

As cool as a cucumber, my Ma simply said, 'Rob, put the knife back in the kitchen and go back to sleep.'

Rob looked up and said, 'I'm sorry, Mrs Croghan,' and he did exactly as he was told.

She never saw bad in anyone. She would say, 'It wasn't Rob trying to steal the money – it was his drug addiction.' She refused to believe that people were evil. No matter who you were, my Ma always said, 'There is good in everyone, life just didn't give them a good start.'

At my Ma's seventieth birthday party in 2010 I was chatting to two family friends, John and Liz, who were in their mid-fifties. They are lifelong friends who were always around when I was growing up. Out of curiosity I asked John and Liz how they got to know our family. It turned out that when I was a baby and they were teenagers, both homeless and living in a battered Volkswagen van, they approached my Ma one day as she was making her way home from work. It turned out that Liz's parents had told her to leave the family home after finding out that she was pregnant. John then left his own family home in order to be with Liz. It was coming up to

Christmas and the young couple only had a small drop of petrol in the van, which they were trying to save for when it got really cold so that they could start the engine and knock on the heater for a short time. My Ma told them to come out to her house and they could park their van in our garden. At least they'd be safe.

Later that night, my Ma couldn't sleep for thinking about them. She got up and moved me and my elder brother, William, down on to the sofa, then went outside and told John and Liz to come into the house. Liz was put into my room and John joined myself and my brother in the front sitting room. Their first child was born at our home and they ended up living with us for about two years until they got their own place.

I could sit here and write a whole book just about my mother. I love her more than life itself.

My first school was Clonshaugh primary school – and from the very beginning, I hated it. I was not comfortable and did not fit in. I lasted four days before I was kicked out for smoking in the yard.

I was always nicking smokes on my Ma. As she slept at night I would sneak into her bedroom and rob three or four smokes from her handbag. Whenever any of my friends wanted a cigarette, they would ask me and I'd always manage to rob some from my house. It made me feel good that I was part of a group who saw me as 'sound'.

After I got kicked out of the school in Clonshaugh, my mother sent me to school in Marlborough Street in the inner city. It was just as bad as the last school. One day I put my hand up and asked if I could go to the toilet. The teacher told me I would have to ask in Irish before she would let me go. I couldn't speak a word of Irish, I was bursting to go and my bladder felt like exploding. So I just stood up and said, 'Fuck you!' before marching out of the classroom. Everyone in the class began clapping, and I got a great buzz out of defying an adult and gaining recognition from my classmates.

I ran out of the school building and down to the bus terminus on Gardiner Street, where I sat on the steps waiting for the bus home.

As I sat there having a smoke, I looked up to see my mother and my twin sisters getting off a bus. I nearly died – there I was, sitting on the stone steps with a fag hanging out of my mouth! I tried explaining what the teacher had done, but I couldn't get a word in edgeways because my Ma was running riot on me for smoking. She took me by the hand and led me straight back up to the school. My sisters had big smirks on their faces.

When we arrived at the school, the teacher told my mother that I had made no effort to speak to her in Irish and that I was not allowed to go to the toilet until I learned how to ask properly. That was enough for my mother. She took me out of the school, and I was then put into St John Vianney's in Coolock.

The school was close to my home and I could relate to a lot of the guys in my class. We all smoked and we all liked doing the same things: skipping school, robbing trays of cakes from the back of bread vans, stealing car stereos, sniffing tins of Newport lighter fluid that we'd buy in six-packs. Sometimes we'd go to a petrol station, purchase a gallon of petrol and sniff that. We'd wait for a truck to slow down before turning a corner and then we'd jump on to the back of the trailer, holding on in any way we could, and let the truck drive us down the road while holding on for dear life. (I think fear of this sort of carry-on was why my mother originally didn't want me going to a school close to our neighbourhood!)

The only thing I didn't do that the rest of the guys did was fight on the bridge near our school. I hated fighting. There were a few good street-fighters in our group, and we used to get together with other little gangs so that our best fighters could go up against their best fighters. Tomo Duffy, who was my mate, was a great boxer and he'd fight the Devil himself if he stepped on to the bridge.

One night, when I was six or seven, I woke to the sound of my mother screaming at me to get out of bed. We all ran out on to the landing, and I can clearly remember seeing the stairs and hall in flames, and feeling the intense heat on my face. My mother rushed us into the front bedroom. She got my three brothers, my three sisters and myself out of the bedroom window and on to the porch above the front door. The porch was supported by two steel poles, and we slid down one of the poles and into the front garden. I can't place my father at the scene – I don't know where he was. If it weren't for my mother we probably would have all burned to death. It turned out that the fire was started by a neighbour who was always having run-ins with the police.

Julie, Frieda, Will, myself, our mother and Michelle

After the fire on Macroom Avenue, we moved to a new house in a newly built estate called Fairfield. We all thought we were moving miles away, and myself and the rest of my brothers and sisters all clambered into the back of the removal truck singing silly going-away songs. The truck took off from the house, turned one corner, then another, and suddenly stopped. The shutters at the back of the truck were pulled up and the driver said, 'OK, we're here.' Our new house in Fairfield was literally just around the corner. I was gutted!

At this stage the family consisted of my mother and father, my eldest brother, Declan, my twin sisters, Julie and Michelle, my elder brother, William, my good self of course, then my little sister,

Frieda, and my younger brother, Glen. Emmagean, my youngest sister, was born in 1979, and that completed the family.

We were the first family to move into the estate, and I remember our first neighbour. Her name was Patty, and she came from England. Every so often this well-built guy called Cyril used to come up to visit Patty, driving a big white Ford Zephyr. My mother knew Cyril to see – he was a gangster/pimp from the south side, and Patty was one of his 'girls'.

Patty used to head into the city centre every day with stolen cheques and bounce them. She would often come home with bags of food and clothing and give my mother a lot of the stuff she had 'purchased'. One of her tactics was to go into shops with a friend, the two of them using identical pull-along tartan shopping trolleys. Patty would go in and draw attention to herself while she was going around filling up her trolley with expensive goods. Then, when she knew she was out of the floor-walker's view for a few seconds, she'd switch trolleys with her friend. As Patty walked out of the shop the security guard would stop her, thinking the trolley was full of stolen gear. As a delaying tactic Patty would refuse to open her trolley to allow it to be searched until the police came. In the meantime, her friend with the full trolley would be long gone. When the police finally arrived and Patty's trolley was opened, the trolley would be empty. Patty even got compensation after suing some of the stores she conned.

She was a great neighbour – down to earth, kind and genuine. One day she just disappeared overnight, leaving a fully furnished house behind her. Rumour has it she went back to England to escape from Big Cyril.

In the run-up to Christmas one year I recall my Ma telling Patty that she was in the process of buying bikes for myself, my brother William and my younger sister, Frieda. When I heard we were getting bikes, I was over the moon!

We were all packed off up to bed early on Christmas Eve, and on Christmas Morning the three of us came booting down the stairs. But there were no bikes to be seen. Ma told us that Santa (in whom

Frieda still believed) was running late and he'd get the bikes to us as soon as he could.

A few days later, at about ten o'clock at night, three Triumph 20 pushbikes arrived at the door. I'll never forget how happy I was. With the three of us dressed in our pyjamas and the road covered in snow, we jumped on the bikes and raced each other up and down the road to the point of exhaustion. In the darkness we thought the bikes were red in colour. The following morning we realised the bikes were not red, but pink! But I didn't care what colour it was – I had finally got my bike, and I was content.

Me, my bike and someone else's Saab

If you ask guys do they remember the time they lost their virginity, they always remember. I'm not sure when I lost mine, but I do remember the first car I ever drove: a blue Volkswagen Beetle. I was about seven years old, and a Traveller friend of mine, Tommy Joyce, showed me how to drive it. Tommy always had plenty of cash. When he wanted money, he'd go into the bedroom of his caravan where there were bundles of cash stuffed in a pillowcase. We would buy basically anything we wanted – gas or petrol to sniff, smokes and sweets, second-hand cars from other Travellers. Or we'd go into the inner city and buzz around the shops.

I was about eight years of age when I had my first experience with alcohol. A group of teenagers had robbed a pub and they gave me four bottles of Carlsberg Special. I remember drinking two of them. One of the guys who gave me the beer ended up carrying me home and telling my mother he'd found me passed out. So that was the beginning of my drinking career – and it may not be a coincidence that it was not long before I was caught behind the wheel of my first stolen car. As I began to drink I felt more alive, more like the person I wanted to be. Alcohol gave me the courage to do things that I otherwise thought I was incapable of.

The first car I ever stole was a brown Ford Escort Mark I. The car was parked outside a Post Office. I knew the owner was inside paying his rent so I tried his car door to see if it was unlocked – it was. I jumped into it and put my front-door key into the ignition and began to jiggle it: moving the key rapidly up and down, in and out, while trying to turn the key clockwise. I got the turn on the key and the red lights appeared. Bingo! I was in. Looking to the Post Office door, I started the engine and I was off. Once I'd got the car started, I wasn't sure if I could drive it, but I was very familiar with cars so I knew the basics. I was sitting on the spare wheel, but still I could barely see over the dashboard.

After about fifteen minutes, the police came blowing up behind me with sirens blaring. I put my foot to the floor and wrapped the car around a garden railing – narrowly missing a car that turned out to be carrying the wife-to-be of a serious armed robber to their wedding. With the Escort sitting on top of the garden railing, a police officer, baton in hand, screamed at me to open the door.

I shouted out to him, 'No! Read me my rights. Read me my rights.' I don't know what made me say that. Maybe I'd heard it on TV?

Anyway, he put his baton through the window and dragged me out by the ears. As I was only eight years old I was given a 'JLO' (in other words, a lecture by a juvenile liaison officer). The lecture would have had no effect on me – even at that age, I wanted to be the little hard man.

Starting when I was nine or ten, I used to visit my Nanna and Granddad in Lisburn Street every Saturday. Armed with my little shopping trolley, I would get the bus to the city centre, then make my way through the fruit and vegetable markets and past the courthouse on Green Street. My Granddad would load up my little trolley with meat that he'd nicked from the kitchens of St James's.

Every week my grandparents gave me a pound for myself. One week I brought my younger sister, Frieda, up with me and, to my surprise, she was also given a pound. I became enraged with jealousy – I had thought I was the only person privy to this generosity! As soon as we left our grandparents' house I pushed my sister up against the wall around the corner and demanded she hand over the pound. I told her that my grandparents really wanted to give me that extra pound and it wasn't meant for her. She tried to protest, but I confiscated the money. (To this very day my sister Frieda still denies that she ever handed over the pound.)

I decided then and there that I would no longer allow Frieda to come up to visit my Nanna and Granddad – instead, I would bring either my twin sisters or my little brother, Glen. They were less argumentative and would hand over the money without complaining. Every week we all got a pound each, which I seized from them as soon as we got around the corner.

My favourite car around that time was the Ford Escort Mark II RS 2000. In my estimation they were the best cars on the road, and everyone who knew me knew about my obsession with the RS. I remember one of my mates telling me about a red RS 2000 parked up at the shopping centre. I was halfway up the road before he even had the last syllable out of his mouth. When I arrived, there she was – a beautiful dark-red model. I went up to that car every single day and sat across the road just looking at it.

There was building work going on at the shopping centre, and one night I watched one of the workers drive the RS into the building site and then lock the gate. I went over to the builder and asked him what he was doing; he said that he was locking it up for the night. I couldn't believe what I was hearing. I told the guy that he couldn't leave the RS parked in there on its own, that it would be stolen. The guy told me that a security guard would be on duty at ten that night and he'd watch the car.

After the builders had all gone, I stayed watching that car for nearly four hours until the security guard arrived, just to make sure the RS was not stolen.

The next day, when I went up to stalk my RS, one of the builders came out at the end of his working day and asked me why I was so concerned about the car. I told him how much I loved those cars and I mentioned that I'd kept watch on it the night before. It turned out that the guy I was talking to was the owner. He then asked me would I like to go for a spin in the car with him. I nearly died!

When I got in the car, I asked if we could drive to where all my mates hung around. The builder hammered the RS down the road and on to Glin Drive, aka 'The Glin' – a curved road where stolen cars would frequently perform handbrake turns. Every night my mates hung out there drinking. The builder began pulling hand-brake turns and I was hanging out of the passenger window, waving and screaming. My mates all assumed that I was in a robbed RS 2000 because of the way the builder was driving it. We pulled up beside my mates, and Redser Bradley and Robbie Cullen jumped in. The builder brought us on a long spin and then dropped us off outside my house. I was thrilled that my days of stalking the car had paid off.

There were two guys in my area, Nada and Dottie, who drove RS 2000s. They both palled around with my elder brother, William. Nada used to come up to my house and tease me with his car – for a long time he wouldn't even let me touch it. One night, the car was parked outside my house. So to get my own back, I robbed his four hubcaps (which had the 'RS' emblem on each of them) and hid them in my bedroom.

A couple of days later, when Nada came up to me and asked did I know who'd robbed his hubcaps, I told him that I hadn't got a clue.

He said that if I heard of anyone who took them, or if I was able to get them back, he'd let me drive his RS. I met him later and told him that I had been unable to get his hubcaps back, but that I had managed to rob four hubcaps from another RS 2000. Nada stuck to his part of the deal and allowed me to drive his RS for about 300 yards, to the top of my road. For me to get a drive in the car of my dreams was like a man sleeping with the five top models in the world at the same time. That's how much it meant to me – that's how much I enjoyed it.

I became obsessed with cars, and car parts. Whenever a stolen car was going around my area, I found myself taking parts as souvenirs. It started with an RS 2000 the guys had dumped in a field. I took off the steering wheel, the gear knob, the coil wire, the ignition and the net head restraints from the seats. Over the years I was to accumulate miscellaneous parts from various different cars: spare wheels, rotary arms and coil wires, even a driving seat from a 7-Series BMW. I kept all this stuff in my bedroom. A lot of robbers in the area got wind of me collecting the car parts. Because they liked me, the guys got into the habit of taking something from each car they'd stolen and bringing it home to me as a souvenir. I was chuffed at this recognition from well-respected robbers.

There was one serious armed robber, Pete Cosgrave, who had a white Porsche 911 Turbo fully equipped with a body kit. He let me take the hubcaps from the car, but no matter how much I begged him he wouldn't bring me on a spin in it. This car was good for at least 150 mph, and it was going around my neighbourhood for months. When the police tried to chase it, they couldn't even get the colour of it – never mind the fuckin' reg. That car was later used in an armed robbery on a Coca-Cola bottling plant. Pete was nicked at the scene and sent to jail for many years because of it.

During the 1970s and early 1980s there were always a lot of people from Northern Ireland coming and going from our house. Some mornings there would be sleeping bodies all over the place. I recall one morning walking down the stairs and into the kitchen. There were a number of cool-looking guys from West Belfast sitting there with a member of my family, who will have to remain nameless, cleaning guns.

My family member roared at me to get out of the kitchen and back up to bed.

But one of the Belfast guys cut in and said, 'No, leave him alone,' and he asked me to make them a pot of tea.

As I was making the tea I realised there was no sugar, so one of the Northern lads put me on the back of one of the four high-powered motorbikes that were parked in the back garden and we sped up to Mr Green's shop. A short time later that morning I heard the four motorbikes kicking into life. That was the last I saw of the Northern guys – for a while anyway.

A week later, armed Special Branch officers raided the house and my family member was arrested. They also found a sawn-off .22 rifle underneath the floorboards. My family member was eventually convicted of possession of a firearm and was sentenced to eighteen months.

The family member I've referred to was involved with the Provisional IRA, and my mother was a member of the Cumann na mBan colour party, but our household was also connected, through my father, with the Official republican movement. Pat McCartan, a friend of our family, and his adviser Paddy O'Keeffe used to hold Sinn Féin/Workers' Party meetings in our house around election time, and on numerous occasions I was roped into putting flyers into envelopes. McCartan used to dress like a cowboy, with big boots and a frilly suede jacket. Paddy O'Keeffe was a heavily built Cork man. When he walked into the room, with his customised walking stick, he made his presence felt. No one ever questioned what Paddy said: his word was law. Why? Well, because no one knew the law better than Paddy O'Keeffe – even though he didn't have a formal qualification.

Because of these connections, the Special Branch continually raided our home. Whenever there was a raid, my mother would detail each of us to follow a police officer to make sure he didn't plant anything in our house. One time, I remember my mother watching a detective open a matchbox and look into it. 'I don't think you'll find any guns in there,' she said.

My mother worked as a waitress in the Burlington Hotel. When there were late functions, she often worked into the early hours of the morning and then cycled several miles home. As my father would be always out in the pub and then fall in the door drunk, my mother very much depended upon my eldest brother, Declan, to babysit us.

Often when my father arrived home, he would start arguments. I remember him saying that my brother William's real father was Dickie Rock, who my mother used to date before meeting my father. He attributed all of us (with the exception of my twin sisters) to other men; my real father was supposed to be a Canadian.

I never recall my father working. He used to go out to the pub and mix Valium with his drink; sometimes he forged prescriptions so he could get more. My dad gave the impression that he loved seeing me get into trouble – it gave him something to brag about to his mates in the pub. I used to wonder what his tablets were like, so one day when I was eleven or twelve I asked him for some. To my surprise, he gave me a handful of Valium and told me not to say anything to my mother.

For a while after that, every time my Da got his prescription he'd give me some tablets. It suited me, because I was getting stoned for free! But soon my father told me that if I wanted any more tablets I would have to buy them from him. I was by this stage addicted to them, so I ended up giving my father £5 for thirteen Valium 10. When I didn't have the money to buy them and my father wouldn't give me any, I would steal them by sneaking into his bedroom and breaking into the locker where he had them hid. I used to do crazy things when I was stoned on the tablets. When I came down off the Valium, I wouldn't remember a thing. My mates used to tell me what I had done.

Another substance that I used to get stoned on was nutmeg – it had to be Goodall's, or else it was no good. I used to empty the entire contents into a cup of warm tea, stir it and then swallow it back in one. It was revolting but worth it.

In the years from age five to twelve I had my introduction into drinking, drug taking, sexual abuse and a criminal way of life. Not for one minute did I think anything I was doing was abnormal. I knew I was breaking the law, and I had no problem with that. The thought of school made me laugh. As for getting a career or a job, that was a million miles away from my thinking. I lived totally in the day, I didn't think about tomorrow. I had ultimate freedom: my Da spent his days and nights in the pub and he didn't give a bollox, and my Ma was too busy working, shopping, cooking and cleaning to keep me under control.

2

My Criminal Niche

As I progressed into my early teens, stealing cars became my main occupation. My mother would constantly lecture me about it, and my brothers would slag me. But I liked being the centre of attention, so I didn't mind. During this time I was becoming more and more dependent on drink and on my dad's Valium and Mogadon sleeping tablets.

I wanted to be accepted by the older guys – in their late teens to early twenties – who used to hang around drinking in the middle of a field not far from where I lived, but they didn't give me much respect. There was one guy in particular who made it his goal in life to give me a hard time. I'll call him 'Billy', though that was not his real name.

I remember a sunny day when the gang were all sat in the field drinking bag-in-a-box cider. Billy called me over. There must have been about ten of them sitting there. I was always hoping that they would allow me to hang around with them, and that was what I was thinking as I walked over to them. But when I got there, they jumped on me, held me down and stripped me naked. They took my clothes and told me to fuck off. After much pleading for my clothes (to no avail), I ended up walking home in the nude. I still remember people looking and laughing at me.

When I got to my house, there was no one at home. My brother's motorbike was in the hall. For some reason I pushed the bike out into the garden. It was a Yamaha 80 and there was no baffle in the exhaust pipe, so you'd hear me before you'd see me. I started the bike up in the garden and, still naked, drove the bike back up to the green to ask for my clothes back. Probably somewhere in my mad thinking I reckoned that doing something so 'off the wall' might make the older guys accept me. When they saw me driving up on to the green, they were so amused that they decided to give me back my clothes. I thought I had finally earned their respect! I even thanked them as I made my way back home.

But my nude motorbike gambit did not change Billy's view of me. Every time I crossed his path, I got a hiding. I would just stand there and take the punches to the face – I would never try to fight back, or even hold my arms up in defence. I felt humiliated, small and insignificant. I joined a boxing club, and after training for eight weeks I had my first ever real boxing match. But on the night of the fight I lost my nerve and didn't turn up. I never darkened the club's door again.

It wasn't long before other people began following Billy's lead. The others would often call me over and slap me across the face and laugh. Then they'd make me run, not walk, all the way to the shop to buy them cigarettes. At that time I was what criminals would term a 'windy bastard', a 'fool', a 'gobshite'.

I started hanging around with a guy called Jimmy 'Dimmers' Deans. His dad used to scrap cars, and his eldest brother, Willie, was a serious criminal and a great fighter; he was also a good friend of my family. Willie was in his mid-twenties and a very smart and snappy dresser: white Versace shirt, black Armani suit, trilby hat and Crombie coat thrown over his shoulders. He liked his few drinks and his bit of coke, loved the women, was a great scrapper, had nerves of steel and was very hygienic. He used to drive a silver Mark II Cortina 16E with a Lotus engine: that car was fast.

Dimmers and myself became really good friends. I was about twelve or thirteen and Dimmers was about fourteen, but he was one of the best drivers around. A lot of people wanted to 'get in' with Dimmers – even some members of Billy's gang – but Dimmers wouldn't have any of it, and that made me feel proud. The thing about Dimmers was nobody would touch him because of his brother Willie, and that gave me a sense of security. Willie was feared. I began 'babysitting' for Willie Deans. I wasn't actually minding his kid – I think Willie just liked to have me looking after his flat in Ballymun when he was out with his wife, Ronnie.

I loved Willie's place. From the outside it looked like any other flat. But when you walked in, it was like a palace – decked out in the most expensive gear money could buy. He had big black leather armchairs and a massive TV and sound system; the carpet was thick and deep red in colour. Willie had a three-foot bronze statue of a rearing stallion on a stand. There was an old antique wooden clock on the wall, with a samurai sword hanging each side. His kitchen was beautiful, and full of fancy appliances.

One night when I was 'babysitting', Willie arrived home at about two in the morning and gave me £20 to get a taxi home. Instead of getting a taxi I decided to save the money and walk the four miles.

It was raining heavily, so I tried to hitch a lift. I noticed a blue Datsun 120Y estate coming in the opposite direction. The driver did a U-turn and pulled up alongside me. I opened the passenger door, and the guy offered me a lift. He then offered me a cigarette, which I took and lit up. The rain was coming down hard. At some point I realised that the driver's hand was resting on my thigh. I didn't take time to think; I just shoved the lighted cigarette into the guy's face and pulled up the handbrake of the car. With the car sliding all over the wet road, I opened the door and jumped out. The blue Datsun sped off with its passenger door still swinging open. I stood up, uninjured but panic-stricken.

A red Fiat X19 with two women in it had stopped dead on the road.

I dived on to the bonnet of the car, screaming, 'Help, help, rape, rape!'

The two ladies in the Fiat X19 powered the car and drove off at high speed, leaving me on the ground. I suppose you couldn't blame them. (I don't know if my earlier sexual abuse had anything to do with how dramatically I reacted – as a child, I never once thought about it.)

I walked all the way to the nearest police station and reported the incident. The police asked did I want them to take me home, but I declined the lift. Number one, I didn't want my mother to find out what had happened. And number two, I didn't want anybody from my area to see me getting a lift home in a police car. I would have been regarded as an informer.

The following day, I was with Dimmers outside his house when

Willie pulled up in his car. I told Willie I had hitched a lift home to save the £20 and been picked up by a pervert. Willie started giving me a hard time because I didn't get the taxi home like he told me to. About a week later, I was with Willie in his car and we were driving through a housing estate on the north side of Dublin. I can't remember what we were up to – Willie was always going somewhere to see somebody or to get something, and he would always throw me some money. Out of the corner of my eye I saw the guy who'd given me a lift getting out of his blue Datsun 120Y estate and walking into his house.

I said, 'There he is, Willie – the pervert!'

Willie swung his car around and sped up to the front gate of the guy's house, grabbed a small bottle jack from his car, ran up the driveway of the house, kicked in the front door and started bouncing the base of the steel bottle jack off the guy's face and head. There was blood everywhere. Willie proceeded to kick the shit out of him; the guy's wife was screaming and crying, and I actually began to feel sorry for him.

On another occasion, myself and Willie were walking through a shopping centre. Willie had a plaster cast on his left arm – the result of a fight that broke out when he tried to rob a pub in Birmingham.

As we walked through the shopping centre, out of the blue Willie said to me, 'Here, Alan, hold this.'

He handed me his trilby and bent his knees so I could remove the Crombie from his shoulders. I hadn't a clue what was going on. Before I knew it, another guy who also had a bad reputation, Gerald Lee, walked up to Willie. His girlfriend was with him.

Gerald pulled out a knife and said, 'Right, Deans, let's have ya now.'

I didn't know what to do. I considered running away, but the thought of what Willie would say about me was enough to prevent that.

There were about six security men there, and they were pleading with Willie not to start anything. But Willie ignored them, walked over to Gerald and kicked him in the face, busting his nose. Willie then grabbed the knife from Gerald's hand and stuck it into his forehead. Gerald's girlfriend jumped on Willie's back and started pulling his hair; Willie grabbed her by the hair and smashed her face into the back of his own head, busting her face open.

While Gerald and his girlfriend lay on the ground bleeding, Willie coolly walked over to me. He put his Crombie over his shoulders and fixed his trilby neatly on his head before casually walking through the crowd of onlookers and out of the shopping centre, with me hotfooting it close behind him. I stuck to Willie like glue. I felt really safe with him.

If I'm being totally honest, I think Willie was everything I wanted to be at that time – brave and feared – and I was happy to follow in his shadow.

There were four main joyriding/ram-raiding gangs in my area: the Belcamp gang, the Bunratty gang, the Senior gang and our gang. We were the youngest of the four gangs – most of us were about thirteen. Most nights, after drinking cider or bottles of Old Cellar wine, we'd head off to steal a car. We'd then drive up to our estate and do a few handbrake turns just to show off before heading down the country to do a few ram raids or smash-and-grabs.

The guys in the other gangs were older – ranging from their mid-teens to early twenties – and we used to have terrible problems keeping our cars safe from them. I had to hide from them if they became aware we had a very fast car because I knew they'd beat me up to find out where I had the car hidden. We used to do the same to them: if we heard where they had a stolen car parked up, we'd go down to where it was and steal it.

Apart from the four joyriding gangs, there were the real big boys, the serious armed robbers, the ones you wouldn't cross – well, not face-to-face anyway. We called them 'The Lads'. The main man was a guy we knew as 'The Basher'. Another member was Mick 'Hatchet Man' Doyle, who visited our house on a number of occasions. My Ma used to say to me that he was a very dangerous man, made of 'different stock'.

I recall one time he turned to my Ma and said, 'Mrs Croghan – look.'

When my Ma looked, he snapped a fly on the wall and then ate it.

He got his nickname 'Hatchet Man' after he got tired waiting for a guy who was using a public payphone to finish his call. He produced a hatchet from the inside of his jacket and smashed it through the perspex and glass of the phone box into the guy's head. He was a close friend of the Fuscos, the Belfast IRA family. (Whenever they travelled from Belfast to Dublin, they would stay in our house.) A guy I know once told me how himself and a number of serious armed robbers, including Mick Doyle, went to Kerry for a weekend of fishing and camping, and none of them dared go to sleep until the Hatchet Man was asleep.

My brother William, who was three years older than me, knew that I was robbing cars. He was always warning me that if he ever caught me in a stolen car, he would punch my head in. But that didn't stop me. It was a well-known fact that if you were a good driver, people looked up to you; I was a shite driver and I was always crashing cars that I stole. Some of the crashes were very serious and I was lucky to walk away. I tried so hard to be a good driver, but any time I ever lost the police in a car chase I put it down to sheer luck.

At home one night, I was drinking and watching *The Driver* starring Ryan O'Neal. My Ma was in work, my Da was in the pub and my brothers were out – so basically I had a free gaff. Fascinated by the driving skill in the scene in the underground car park, I left my house with a screwdriver, intending to steal a car. Within the hour I had got myself a Vauxhall Cavalier. I drove up to my area and, just like in the film, I opened the two doors on my side of the car and reversed them into a telegraph pole – but the doors did not fall off like in the movie. Then I tried it with the opposite doors, and they too didn't fall off. Nothing was working the way it did in the film. Disgusted, I drove the car to the nearest field and dumped it.

I was always trying to find my criminal niche, if you like, in the hope that I would gain some sort of recognition from the gangs, and eventually I found it. I was able to hot-wire cars very, very quickly – more quickly than anyone else around.

I remember asking a mate of mine to time me stealing a car. He started his watch. I placed the tip of the screwdriver between the rubber and the fly window, snapped the screwdriver down and shattered the window. Then I jumped into the back of the car and dived into the front. I slid the screwdriver into the gap where the indicator handle is, placed the bar of the screwdriver underneath the ignition and forced the screwdriver downwards, removing the casing from the steering column. I removed the screw from the back of the ignition, which released a small barrel. Then I placed the tip of the screwdriver into the centre of the barrel, turned it and started the car. Finally, I jumped into the passenger seat, braced my foot securely against the steering wheel and pressed hard, snapping the internal lock and freeing up the wheel. It took me forty-seven seconds from start to finish.

Fellow thieves allowed me to go off robbing with them because I was quick. I was dead chuffed I was good at something.

Myself and Dimmers would often find out where the serious robbers used to hide their stolen cars that were to be used in armed raids later on in the week. One time, we revealed to our mates that we knew where The Basher had a top-of-the-range Opel Commodore 30i parked up. When we suggested that we should go down to where it was hidden and rob it on them, they got very worried. Many of the guys in our gang lost their bottle and didn't want to go near the car, but myself and Dimmers did manage to get four of our mates on board.

It was a hot day as the six of us made our way down to The Basher's car. Dimmers tried to hot-wire it, but the car wouldn't start. He had a look under the bonnet and removed the distributor cap. The rotor arm was missing, so we decided to try to get a replacement. To ensure that the car would still be there when we got back, we removed the coil wire from the engine. I ran down to a DG Vauxhall/Opel garage on the main road and priced a rotor arm for an Opel Commodore 30i; the service guy said it would cost £3.75. With not a penny to our name and time being of the essence, we ran around to everyone we could possibly think of, trying to bum some money. In less than half an hour we had got the money together. I ran as fast as I could back down to the garage with my two hands full of pennies and shillings, and we got our rotor arm.

When we got back to the Commodore 30i, a couple of younger lads came over and told us that 'The Lads' had been at the car, trying to start it. When they couldn't start it, they too opened the bonnet and then walked off. We opened the bonnet, installed the rotor arm and replaced the coil wire.

As we slammed the bonnet shut, we heard a shout: 'Look behind you, lads!'

Coming over the brow of the hill, less than a hundred yards away, were The Basher, Gerald Lee, Pete Cosgrave, Hatchet Man Doyle and Dennis. They were carrying pickaxe handles.

Panic kicked in, and we all dived into the car while Dimmers tried to start it. But the car wouldn't start. The Basher and company were now running towards us. There was absolute mayhem in the car: I was screaming at Dimmers to get the fucking car started, while our mates were shouting, 'Let's run for it!' Dimmers was shouting that the car had an automatic choke. He put the car into reverse, took his foot off the clutch and began turning the engine over in gear. Just as The Basher and company reached us, the Commodore 30i kicked into life and we burned rubber backwards away from them. The lot of us in the car cheered as Dimmers locked the wheel, swung the nose of the car around and pulled away. In the distance we could see The Lads hurling bricks and poles at us – all to no avail.

We saw, to our delight, that the car was full of petrol, so we took it for a long spin to see what speed we could get out of it. On the nearest dual carriageway we brought the car up to 122 mph. I suggested we head back to our estate to give the lads a flash – in other words, show the car off by doing handbrake turns and other stunts. As we got up to our neighbourhood, we hammered around a corner to find The Basher and his gang standing there armed with bricks and pickaxe handles. The Basher ran out into the middle of the road with a cavity block in his hands. All of us ducked – Dimmers included! A brick bounced off the front window, cracking it, then the side window exploded after a rock was hurled through it.

Dimmers sat back up and put some distance between us and The Lads. We decided then and there that it would be best if we just dumped the car. We drove up on to the back roads, crashed through a cow gate and dumped the beautiful Commodore 30i in the middle of a field.

When we got back up to where all our mates were, the news was all over our area that The Lads were out looking for us. Then we saw them approaching. It was too late to run – and anyway, I was never a good runner.

The Lads proceeded to beat one of our mates with baseball bats and left him in bits on the ground. They then turned to me and Dimmers and said, 'You two consider yourselves very lucky. Ever go near any of our cars again, and you'll be found up the mountains.' The Basher and his entourage then wandered off.

Myself and Dimmers just looked at each other and breathed a sigh of relief. We knew why we had been spared a beating – because of Willie.

My mother knew that I was up to no good. But she was so busy working, as the sole breadwinner in the house, that she couldn't really keep an eye on me.

At this stage I was enrolled at Colaiste Dhulaigh secondary school, but I constantly played truant. I did not have the attention span for school. And no matter what school I went to, I always rebelled against authority figures. I didn't like being told what to do and when to do it, and I hated the teachers for talking down to me. When I played the hard man and disobeyed authority figures in front of other guys, I was looking for recognition.

At the age of thirteen I ended up getting kicked out of Colaiste Dhulaigh. I forgot to bring my gym gear in with me one day – in fact, I didn't know I had PE, and to be honest I didn't really care. The PE teacher told me to write 500 lines in my copybook – 'I must not forget my PE gear again' – knowing full well that I couldn't read or write. I got really angry and threw my school bag and a chair at the PE teacher.

I then sprinted out of the school and ran all the way home in tears. The school refused to take me back, and that was all right with me. In the two years I was registered at the school my attendance record was fifty-one days.

My mother got me into another secondary school, the North Strand Tech, near the then notorious Sheriff Street in the city centre. On my first day I met a load of guys who were up to the same kind of antisocial behaviour as myself – they were doing it in their neighbourhoods, and I was doing it in mine.

There was this fat guy in my class. One day when we were out in the yard, I gave him a hard time about his weight. When I went back into class, a guy who was sitting next to me warned me that I'd better get out of the school fast, because the fat guy I'd slagged off was related to the infamous Hutch family. A gang was going to get me outside the school and kick the shit out of me. Well, that was enough for me. I asked the teacher could I go to the toilet, then I grabbed my jacket from the wall outside, left my school bag in the classroom and jumped on the bus home. When I got home, I knew I had to twist the story to my advantage. So I told my mother that all the guys from the city centre were going to beat me up because I was from a different area than theirs.

It worked, and my Ma allowed me to leave school permanently. My wish had finally come true. I was free.

I thought I was going to have the life of Riley – no more school, and free to do whatever I wanted – until a friend of my mother's suggested that she would be able to get me a job with a window-fitting company called McMahon & Nagle. The boss, Paul Nagle, was a personal friend of hers. I wasn't keen. But rather than listen to another one of my Ma's never-ending lectures, I decided to give the job a go.

My birth certificate was altered to make me sixteen years of age, the legal minimum to take the job. I went out for the interview and – surprise, surprise – I got a job as an apprentice window fitter out in the vans. I honestly had good intentions when I started. But helping the fitters put new weather-glaze windows into fancy houses, I could not help but view each house as a little gold mine. Top-of-the-range TVs and videos, stereos, you name it – most of these houses had it all. I would note exactly where the house was, and that night myself and my mates would head out in a robbed car and relieve the owners of their possessions.

But my great little earner wasn't to last long. One of the drivers I worked with, in order to make another apprentice who worked with us jealous, told me to take the keys of the van and bring it for a spin. So I got into the Ford Escort van and I burned rubber out of the driveway of the house we were working on. I drove like a mad-man up and down the road, pulling handbrake U-turns at speeds of 60 or 70 mph. Not surprisingly, my bosses moved me off the road crew, and I found myself stuck in the warehouse.

I got on well with the lads in the warehouse, but I hated the work and handed in my notice. Shortly after I had done so, one of the guys in the warehouse asked me would I like to buy some LSD for 75p a tab. I asked him could he give me ten, and I'd fix him up after I got my wages on Friday. He didn't know I was leaving. When I got my wages, I told the guy I would look after him after lunch. Come midday I walked out of the gate with my wages in one pocket and the ten LSD in the other. I was gone.

I had never taken acid before, but I knew you got stoned on it – a 'trippy' kinda stoned. Later that night, I met up with my mate Tomo Duffy. I was after buying six cans of Newport cigarette-lighter gas to inhale and some two-litre bottles of cider. The two of us took one tab of acid each.

We both started freaking out. People who walked past us didn't look right, and we thought they were talking about us.

Tomo said, 'Let's go around to my brother's. He's taking acid years, he'll know what to do.'

When we got to Tomo's house, his brother Derek and Bomber Walsh were there. We told them what was happening. They said that they were also on acid and that we could chill out with them for the night. As we sat with Tomo's brother and Bomber, we started to relax, and very soon we were in stitches of laughter. It ended up being a great night.

The following day, we nearly died when Bomber said to us, 'We weren't on acid. We just told you we were, so you both felt relaxed and enjoyed it.'

I then became a bit of an expert when it came to taking acid. You couldn't take it every day. You had to give your body time to get it out of your system, and the kick was better the longer you waited for the next one. So on the days I wasn't taking acid, I'd sniff either gas or petrol, take Valium by the handful, Triazolam (which we called Upjohns), DF 118s, purple hearts, speed, Dalmane 15s or 30s, magic mushrooms – you name it, I did it – and I always took everything with alcohol, be it lager, spirits, cider, Old Cellar wine or whatever else was available. Once my system would be clear of the LSD, I'd then look forward to taking my next tab.

At this stage I was robbing cars nearly every single night, and most of the time I'd be tripping out of my head – either drunk or stoned on tablets. The car park of the local shopping centre was nearly always my first port of call. I recall spotting a lovely Ford Capri 2.0 S there; it had no alarm or chain on it, so it was begging to be stolen. It was a nice summer's day and I was on my own, tripping out of my head on acid. I had the Capri started in no time at all. After taking it for a nice leisurely spin, I parked it up in a local housing estate and decided that I would use it later that night to get me to the long-term car park at Dublin Airport, where you were always spoilt for choice on top-of-the-range motors. That night, when I went back to get the Capri in the estate where I'd parked it, I was delighted to see it was still there. But when I opened the car door, there was a chain and lock wrapped around the steering wheel, and this confused me. Then this lunatic came running out of a house towards me. I nearly slipped in my own shite, I was gone that quick. It turned out that I had actually parked the fucking car right outside the home of its owner!

One night, as I was making my way home with a friend and his girlfriend, a police van pulled up alongside of us. A copper by the name of Anthony Gannon got out and asked me my name.

When I told him, he said, 'I'm arresting you for a car you stole two weeks ago.'

I didn't have a clue which bloody car he was actually talking about.

He opened the back door of the police van, and sitting in the back also under arrest was one of the guys from the Senior gang. Unbeknownst to me, my friend went straight down to my house and told my mother that I'd been arrested. Gannon didn't take us straight down to the police station. Instead, the copper cruised around the area, looking to see if he could arrest anyone else.

I was only just inside the door of the station when my mother came in behind us. Because I was just fourteen, my mother told the police that she had a right to be present with me during questioning. A sergeant told my mother to come back in a few hours and they would talk to her then, but she refused to leave. Another officer walked out to the public area and pushed my mother so hard through the doors that she fell down on to the steps. My mother got to her feet and walked right back in again, at which point the officer swung around and punched her in the face. Then he grabbed hold of her and threw her out through the doors again.

I saw red. I ran over to the hatch separating the public area from the area where I was being held, and jumped up on to the counter. From the opposite side of the hatch the officer who had assaulted my mother ran to meet me and tried to push me back. I grabbed him by the ears and tried to pull him through the hatch. The sergeant grabbed me from behind and began whacking me across the back with his baton. When he got me on the ground, he kicked the shit out of me. Kicking and screaming, I was carried down to the cell. Once they had me there, the sergeant and the other copper took up from where they had left off and beat the living daylights out of me.

A couple of minutes later, my mother was brought down and put into the cell next to mine. They had arrested her for being drunk and disorderly, committing a breach of the peace, resisting arrest and assaulting three police officers. My mother had never been in a cell in her entire life. She has never been before a court on criminal charges, and she never drank alcohol.

The police tried to get me to make a statement admitting to stealing a car, but I denied it; I still didn't know which car they were on about. My Ma was released on station bail to appear in the District Court the next day. I was held overnight and escorted to the children's court the following morning.

When I got to court number 12, Judge Sean Delap was sitting on the bench. Judge Delap was a headcase, but I admired him. If he caught a copper lying, by God he'd let the copper have it and would throw the case out of court. By the same token, when sentencing a criminal he loved the word 'consecutive'. I was entitled to free legal aid, and I nominated Kieran O'Reilly from Lawlor O'Reilly & Co. Solicitors to represent me.

The police officer who had attacked my mother requested a two-week remand and objected to me being granted bail.

Judge Delap then said, 'Remanded to St Patrick's Institution for two weeks with no bail.'

When the realisation hit me that I was going to prison for the first time in my life, I nearly died.

My solicitor jumped up and objected on a number of counts: that I could not be remanded for two weeks without my consent; that I was too young to be remanded to St Patrick's Institution; and that I had a constitutional right to bail.

Well, Judge Delap didn't like to be dictated to in his own courthouse. He screamed at Mr O'Reilly, 'This is my court! And as long as it is my court, I'll continue to do what I want. Now get out of my court!'

Mr O'Reilly retorted that he would take the matter to the High Court. He then stormed out of the courtroom.

I was placed into the holding cell at the Bridewell. Two hours later, I was taken back before Judge Delap. It must have been around lunch hour, as Judge Delap was still chewing when he came out from his chambers and sat on the bench.

Delap said, 'Released on a surety of his own bond, and remanded for two weeks.'

As quickly as he had sat down, he was up out of his chair and back into his chambers to finish off his lunch. A High Court judge had got straight on to Judge Delap and ordered him to release me immediately. A couple of weeks later, the police had to ask that the car-theft charge be struck out: they had no evidence.

The charges against my mother were a different story, though. The three coppers were adamant that she was going to be convicted. But my mother had other plans. Paddy O'Keeffe, the big man from Cork, recommended that she get Pat McCartan to represent her. When the case came to trial, P. V. Doyle – owner of the Burlington, where my mother had worked as a waitress for the previous thirteen years – went to court and gave a character reference for her. Mr Doyle spoke very highly of my Ma, and told the court that he had never known her to drink alcohol or to be violent. My mother got into the witness box and told the court how she had been assaulted; she even had photographs of her black eye and of the bruising on her ribs. After listening to my Ma, the judge told her that he was not going to strike out the charges but dismiss them, so the police could not re-enter them. The judge then recommended that my mother take criminal proceedings against those concerned. It was a right kick in the arse for the police.

My mother later made out sworn affidavits against the three police officers concerned, and legal proceedings were set in motion to prosecute them. Paddy O'Keeffe was by my mother's side every time she went to court, and that made her feel safe. But on the day the trial was due to start, Paddy was stuck down in Cork on business. He told my mother how to get the case put back for one day.

When my Ma and I walked into the courtroom, Pat McCartan approached us and said, 'Diane, if you don't drop the charges against them, they will harass Alan for the rest of his life.'

I didn't want my Ma dropping the charges, but she felt intimidated by the police and ended up dropping the charges against the three of them.

When Paddy got up to Dublin that night, he was so disgusted with my mother that he didn't talk to her for well over a year. The dropping of the charges didn't change a thing: the police still raided the house, still continually arrested me and still stopped and searched me every time they saw me.

*

Not all the coppers in my local police station were bad. There was one we really respected; I'll call him 'Starsky', though that isn't what we called him at the time. When Starsky was on a shift, very few stolen cars came into the area, because if you got chased by Starsky, you knew you would have a hard time trying to lose him. He didn't care what he had to do to catch you – if you drove through a brick wall to escape from him, Starsky would follow suit. He loved a good car chase.

One night, Starsky got out of the car and searched me and my mates.

Then he said, 'Alan, you don't have a screwdriver.' He went over to his car, opened the glove compartment and threw me a screwdriver and said, 'Listen, I'm on till ten tonight, so make sure you get a car before then.'

In other words, he wanted a chase before he finished work that night.

He once got a chase he wouldn't forget for a long time. Across the road from my house there was a sort of pedestrian promenade, with six big flower beds surrounded by walls. In order to walk through it, you had to go through a gap in the wall, walk for twenty yards then go through another gap, down some steps, and finally walk another twenty yards and out through the last gap. The gaps were very tight and you would only fit a small car through them, such as a Ford Fiesta, an Escort or a Vauxhall Astra.

When we got chased by the police, we'd sometimes drive stolen cars towards the promenade, manoeuvre the hundred yards or so through the three sets of gaps and then out on to my road and away. It was a great way of losing the cops – their cars at that time were Vauxhall Cavaliers and Mark 5 Ford Cortinas, and they wouldn't fit through.

On this particular night, there was a Ford Escort going around and there must have been around thirty or forty lads all congregated in the area of the flower beds. The lads were hoping the guy driving the Escort would get chased because they had piles and piles of bottles and bricks all stacked up to stone the police with. The lads were all ready for a good night and they weren't going to let the Ol'

Bill spoil it by not turning up and chasing the car. The Escort was giving a 'flash' by speeding from one corner to the next corner, pulling handbrake turns.

Out of the blue, with lights flashing and sirens blaring, Starsky roared up in his Cavalier. Dozens of bricks were hopped off the police car, but only one window smashed. The driver of the Escort then came swerving in to drive through the flower beds. Starsky tried to follow suit. Everyone standing around the flower beds stood their ground and began lashing bricks and bottles off Starsky's car. The Cavalier's wing mirrors and door handles were all ripped off as Starsky wedged his way through the first gap. By this stage the driver in the robbed Escort was well through the third gap and was gone. But Starsky was not giving up. As the police car was bombarded with missiles, Starsky drove hard through the second gap, and the third, before the Cavalier died a death in the middle of my road.

Starsky got out of the car, with the thirty or more lads all stood there silently, looking at him. He coolly walked around to the back of the car, where there was only one little parking light that was not broken.

Then he looked over at everyone and shouted, 'You dirty shower of bastards, I'll get you all!' He kicked in the last little parking light, smashing it.

Everyone just laughed and cheered. Moments later, vans came from everywhere with police in riot gear, and the area around the flower beds was cleared in a matter of seconds.

As I stood in my driveway, which faced the flower beds, about ten of my friends walked into my front garden. A police car pulled up outside my gate, knocked on a spotlight and shone it on my house.

A copper in the car said over the megaphone, 'Get out of that woman's garden.'

I knew if any of the lads walked out of my front gate, they would be arrested.

A copper got out of the car and shouted, 'I said get out of that garden!' He moved towards my driveway.

I kicked the gate shut and informed him that he was trespassing and needed a warrant to come in. Then I opened my front door and said to my mates, 'Come on, lads. Let's all go inside and have a nice hot cup of tea.'

The spotlight stayed on my house for about five minutes before it was switched off and the police car drove away. Later, we all headed up to the field to drink more alcohol, before heading off to get up to no good.

Most days, myself and my mates would cycle or walk up to Dublin Airport to suss out the long-term car park. We'd make a note of which car we liked best, then go back up that night and rob it. For a long time the airport police could not twig how the hell we were getting the cars out of that particular car park, as it was surrounded by six-foot wire fencing and protected with steel barriers at the exits. The airport police put more and more patrols around the big wire fence, but we would sneak in under the cover of darkness and I'd hot-wire our chosen car. Then we'd drive up to the fence real slow. As soon as the bumper was touching the fence and the coast was clear, we'd literally power the car through the fence – it would spring up and then back down neatly into place as if it had never been touched, and there wouldn't be a mark on the car. It took the airport authorities a very long time to figure out exactly how we were doing it; eventually, they put steel bollards all around the outside of the fence.

One time, we spotted a brand-new Ford Sierra XR4i – a proper high-performance car. Four of us went back up that night to take it. My job was to hot-wire the XR4i while a mate of mine was the designated driver. I got it hot-wired in no time at all, and by Jaysus could that car move! I remember we were driving down a small stretch of road that runs through a housing estate and we were doing 115 mph. We drove into a cul-de-sac to show it off to some of our mates, and who do you think drove right in behind us? None other than the copper Starsky, in a Granada.

We floored the XR4i and got the hell out of the cul-de-sac as quickly as we could, and we were all taken aback when Starsky didn't even make an attempt to chase us. No matter how many police cars we came across that night, not one of them would chase us. We were baffled by this, but eventually we put it down to the fact that they realised they would have got nowhere near the car. Knowing all we wanted was a chase, they weren't going to give us the satisfaction. Killjoys!

All the guys I palled around with were getting served at a local bar and nightclub long before me, and I developed a bit of a complex about it. The first time I went down to try to get served was a complete joke. My mates told me that I had to look like a real hard man or else I wouldn't get in. So they put a black Crombie coat on me, turned up the collar and got me to wear black leather gloves. Here I was – fifteen years of age, pimples all over my face and trying to look hard. My mates told me that I should throw some shapes and put a mean look on my face. The plan was that I should walk into the nightclub part of the hotel ahead of them and that they would follow behind.

As I tried to get into the club, I came face to face with about six bouncers. I said, 'Hi, guys!' and went to walk past them into the club.

Well, the bouncers just pissed themselves laughing. They told me if I went back home and changed my clothes, they would let me in. They knew I was under age, but they admired my gall and how I'd gone to all the bother of trying to convince them I was a hard man.

Now that I could get served in the bar of the hotel and in the nightclub, I quickly became one of their biggest customers. The owners ran a cabaret night every week, and one night, full of Dutch courage, I got up on stage in front of a packed pub and told a funny story. It went down very well. After I was finished, the bar manager came over and fed me free drink all night. He asked me if I would try to turn it into something on a regular basis, but I declined the offer because I was not that confident – I thought I'd just been lucky the first time.

The following week, I went down and there were only a handful of people scattered around the large seating area of the pub. One of the band members introduced me to the tiny scattered audience and called me up on stage. I hadn't a clue what the hell I was going to do or say, and I was nowhere near drunk.

I got up on stage and tried to tell jokes, and immediately heard heckling: 'Get him off the stage – he's brutal!'

It was a classic disaster – the feedback from the microphone rang out loudly, the thirty or so customers in a darkened pub that would hold up to 200 people began to engage in casual conversation with each other, and I didn't know where to look or what to do. I just put the mike back into its stand and walked over to my mates, thinking I'd get some support from them. But all I got was a barrage of abuse. Fair play to the barman, he came over and gave me a free pint.

That was the last time I chanced my arm at stand-up comedy. Although I knew I would never make it as a comedian, I was sure I was going to do OK as a thief.

3
Becoming a Hard Man

Between the ages of eight and sixteen I accumulated approximately thirty-five criminal convictions, all for stealing cars and various misdemeanours. I was constantly before the children's court, but by the time I turned sixteen I had still never been to prison. I began to notice that some of my friends were treating me with contempt. I was convinced that they believed I was informing to the police, simply because I never got locked up on any of my charges. (It is only now that I wonder if my mad mind was imagining all of this.) I knew I wasn't a rat. If I was caught in a stolen car, I would make a statement admitting my guilt, but I never mentioned anyone else. It got to the stage where I thought some of my mates were withholding information from me for fear of the police finding out.

One night, shortly after I turned sixteen, totally inebriated and with no other thought in my head than to simply stagger home and sleep, I saw Starsky driving past. I found myself running into the middle of the road and flagging him down. I told him that I had robbed a Ford Escort XR3 and an Audi Coupé some nights previously and I wanted to be charged. Starsky happily placed me in the back of the car. I was taken to the local police station, where I made a full statement. I knew that I was guaranteed to be sent down on these charges, as I was now old enough for St Patrick's Institution, the youth prison in the grounds of Mountjoy.

I made out to my friends that the police had lifted my fingerprints from the XR3 and the Audi Coupé after receiving confidential information. The lads believed it, and were certain I was going to get locked up.

When my case was heard in court, Starsky got into the witness box and spoke up very well for me. This certainly wasn't the way I wanted things to be going! I wanted to hear him saying that I was a menace with a long list of previous convictions, not that I was a good decent kid who was easily led and always polite.

The judge said she was going to give me a chance, and my solicitor turned and gave me the thumbs up. The judge went on to say that if she received a favourable probation officer's report, she would apply six months' probation. My Ma was delighted that I wasn't going to prison, the judge felt she was giving a child a chance, Starsky was smiling at me and the solicitor thought he'd done a good day's work.

But I jumped up in the middle of the courtroom and shouted, 'No!'

The judge asked me what I was doing.

I said, 'Your Honour, I want to go to prison!'

The judge put the case back for a second calling to allow me time to think, and for my family and solicitor to consult with me. No one could understand why I wanted to be sent to jail, and I certainly couldn't tell them the truth. I just said I wanted to stop robbing, and a spell in jail might deter me from a life of crime.

My solicitor went back into the court and, with my Ma begging me not to go through with it, told the court that I wanted to go to prison. The judge reluctantly agreed and sentenced me to three months' detention at St Patrick's Institution. She also recommended that I see a psychiatrist. I was handcuffed, and kissed my tearful mother goodbye.

I was brought across the road to the Bridewell police station and placed in a large holding cell with about ten other guys. Some of them were older than my dad, others were in their mid-twenties and thirties. There were two or three drug addicts who continually banged on the steel door, screaming for a doctor to give them medication to stop them suffering from withdrawal symptoms. My nerves were gone and I clearly remember sitting there in this cold stone cell, feeling terrified. I actually thought that this was where I was going to serve out my three-month prison term; I didn't realise I was still to be transported to St Patrick's.

Then a voice outside the cell door shouted, 'Stand back!'

The door was kicked open, and I could see another prisoner

standing there with a big smile on his face. (I later learned that this prisoner, Brendan Lambe, had been allocated a single cell because of his violent tendencies towards anyone who stood in his way.)

Lambe said, 'Come on, lads. We're gettin' the hell outta here!'

Everyone else seemed delighted. But I didn't know what to do. If I stayed in the cell, what would the other prisoners think of me, or do to me? And if I went along with their attempted escape, what punishment would I receive from the authorities? I decided to go with the prisoners, as I was riddled with fear at not being seen as 'one of the lads'.

As I reached the cell door, an alarm went off.

Lambe shouted to us, 'Right, lads! Let's get ready. Let's get stuck into these bastards!'

Before I knew it, dozens of police officers wearing helmets and carrying riot shields came storming up to our floor. Lambe charged at the police, expecting everyone else to follow him, but nobody moved. Lambe was dragged to the ground. The rest of the riot police ran for us and, to my relief, everyone just retreated back into the cell. Lambe was carted off by the legs and arms, and the rest of us were separated. Sitting in my cell, I could still hear Brendan Lambe calling the police 'bastards' and 'pigs'. I wished I was as brave as him.

Later that evening, I was taken from the cell and lined up with the rest of the prisoners. I didn't have a clue what was happening. Everyone else seemed very much at home, laughing and joking, but I wanted to go home. A steel door was opened, and I saw a police prison truck parked about four inches from the doorway. Thoughts of my Ma, my family, my house – even my dog, Pedro – were running through my mind. I wanted to see them now more than anything else in the world.

Each of us was marched into the van and locked in a steel cage just big enough to hold one person. It wasn't possible to sit down, and it was almost completely dark. The van kicked into life and all the other prisoners were shouting out through their doors to each other. I could hear the voices of girls in the van, too, laughing and joking. But I was a nervous wreck.

There were tiny air holes in the side of the truck, above the level of my head. I stood on the fixed steel seat and peeked through. It was raining and I could see people – free people, walking and going about their business, going home, meeting their friends, going to the pub or maybe just going to the shop to buy the paper – unaware that they were being looked upon and envied by another.

'Please God in Heaven,' I thought, 'don't let this be real.'

Eventually, the van came to a halt and the doors were opened. We were all marched into the front hall of St Patrick's Institution and told to stand in single file and not to speak. I was then called into the front office and had all my details taken from me. I was informed by the chief prison officer that I would be called before the prison governor the following morning. I was then escorted down three flights of stone stairs. All I could see were cell windows with steel bars.

When I got down to the bottom of the stairs, there were about eight burly prison officers standing behind a counter, with a massive logbook in front of them. Most of the officers had their shirtsleeves rolled up over their hairy arms, and they had fags hanging from their mouths. Here I was, underground, surrounded by well-built men whose sole purpose in life was to punish people like me. To my right were naked guys showering and to my left were other prisoners getting dressed.

A prison officer barked at me, 'Croghan, Alan! Step forward.'

I was told to strip and hand my clothes to another officer. After I'd stripped naked, my body was searched: under my feet, between my toes. I had to lift up my testicles so they could look behind the bag. Then I had to turn around, bend over and spread the cheeks of my arse. I was then checked for scars and tattoos, given a towel and a bar of soap and told to shower.

I was terribly conscious of the fact that my penis was all shrivelled up. I tried to hide it, and I was hoping that no one else would notice my tiny penis. All the other inmates didn't seem to be hiding theirs – in fact, the other prisoners were laughing, acting and chatting as if they were showering after a football game. I had the quickest shower of my life. I was then handed a pillowcase with sheets, some toiletries, a pair of bell-bottom jeans, a horrible checked shirt with a massive collar, a pair of Y-fronts, a vest, a V-neck jumper and a pair of black crocodile shoes. Once dressed, I was given my cell-door card with my date of release, my name, sentence and religion written on it. I was then escorted up into the main prison circle.

I had been through a lot of things on the outside, but the first experience of prison was something completely new and unexpected. Even though I knew guys who had done time, even though I was getting up to things that were inevitably going to get me locked up, and even though I had heard stories of prison, I'd never really thought about what it would be like. On the outside, I always felt I could avoid danger if necessary. But in prison, I had nowhere to go, nowhere to run, no one to back me up.

I tried to take in my new surroundings: the stone walls, the tiled floors, the noise of doors slamming shut, keys being jangled, inmates shouting to other inmates, officers barking orders. My mind was going a million miles an hour. The heart of the prison building was the Circle: a circular space, surrounded by wire mesh, where the governors and prison officers stood to observe the goings-on. Three wings (B, C and D) radiated out from the Circle, and each had three landings. B1 and B2 belonged to the females and were sectioned off from us.

As I stood in the Circle, feeling like a fish out of water, I heard someone shout, 'What's the story, Alan?'

I looked up to see my mate Tomo Duffy looking down at me.

I thought, 'Thank you, God, for a familiar face – I love you.'

I was brought up on to a landing called C2. Tomo was there to meet me.

The first thing he said to me was, 'Alan, if the screws ask you if you want to go to the Training Unit, say no. Because you're better off staying here with us. I'll get you around on to my landing, D2, tomorrow. You'll be all right, we'll look after you.'

A prison officer then told Tomo to move along. The screw led me to my cell and opened the heavy steel door.

The cell was in bits: the back of the cell door had tea bags stuck to it; the chamber pot was mouldy green and stank; and a little wooden locker that sat in the corner was rotten and covered in graffiti. There was dried toothpaste plastered all over the eggshell-coloured walls. (I later found it was used as a substitute for Blu-tack to hold up posters on the walls.) The prison officer told me to clean up my cell, make my bed and that I'd be let back out in about an hour to go down for my tea.

I walked into the cell. Before I had a chance to turn around and ask the prison officer any questions, the door was slammed shut and locked.

I was alone.

I said to myself, 'Alan, keep it together! *Please* keep it together.'

I remembered watching a prison film about an infamous bank robber called John McVicar, and I recalled how he had made his bed: he had his blankets and sheets all folded neatly into the shape of a triangle. He also had his bed positioned in the middle of the cell floor.

'Right,' I said, 'I'll do the same and show everyone that I know what prison is all about.'

I tidied up the cell the best I could, and it took me ages to get the blankets and sheets into the shape of a triangle. When the cell door opened, I was standing there as proud as Punch with a big smile on my face. The screw and Tomo were standing outside the door, and they both broke into laughter.

The screw upended the bed, turned to Tomo and said, 'Duffy, show him how to make a bed.'

It turned out the blankets and sheets had to be folded in the shape of a rectangle and placed at the foot of the bed. As for the bed itself, it had to be tight against the cell wall and not in the middle of the floor. I felt such a fool.

Tomo gave me cigarettes, a radio and some good tips about prison life. Before long it was teatime, and the screw told Tomo to get back to his own landing. I didn't want Tomo to leave, but I dared not say that to him. The prison officer told me to grab my tray and follow the rest of the inmates down to collect my tea. This consisted of two sausages with beans, a few slices of bread and some milk (which I had to drink out of a stainless-steel teapot because I had no cup). When I got back to my cell, I was so hungry I wolfed it down. Then I sat back and enjoyed a nice smoke. I was delighted that I could smoke – I had thought the prison officers wouldn't allow it.

As I sat in my locked cell, I could hear a lot of activity outside – as if prisoners were getting out of their cells. The spyhole in my door was slid open and I could see an eye peering in at me

Then I heard a country accent shout, 'Would you like to go to the Training Unit?'

Remembering what Tomo had told me earlier, I nervously replied, 'No, no thanks.'

The officer outside then roared down the landing to someone else, 'Excuse me, Mr Noonan. Is that the Training Unit or Shanganagh open prison?'

I could hear another voice shout back, 'No, no, that's Shanganagh.'

The officer then said to me, 'Would you like to go to Shanganagh?'

I thought to myself, 'Well, anywhere has to be better than here,' so I said to the officer, 'Yeah, I'll go.'

I was then told to pack my kit, put all my blankets and sheets into my pillowcase and turn my bed on its side up against the wall. I was further instructed that when my cell door opened, I was to walk straight down with my kit to the Circle, where I would be collected. As the spyhole fell back into place, I thanked the officer.

About ten minutes later, my cell door opened, and I hurried down to the Circle. Along the way I met Tomo and a few other lads from my area. I told them I was going to Shanganagh open prison. They told me I was lucky: once I got down there, I'd be out in a matter of days.

I had been standing in the Circle for about a quarter of an hour when Chief Officer O'Sullivan asked me what was I waiting for. I told him that I was going to Shanganagh. Mr O'Sullivan looked at me and laughed. He said there were no inmates being transferred out of St Patrick's and that I had just fallen victim to one of the oldest prison wind-ups. I looked up and saw Tomo and the rest of the guys from my area standing on the second-floor landing, looking down at me through the wire mesh and pissing themselves laughing. I realised that the so-called officer at my door had actually been my mate Tomo, putting on a country accent. I was gutted, and I couldn't get back up to my cell quickly enough.

At seven thirty, I was locked up for the night. I lay on the bed and my mind began to flood with images and thoughts of my home, my mother and my friends. I cried my heart out – I don't think I have ever cried as much as I did that night. I was missing my mother so much that I believe if I had been let out of jail that very same night – the 'sharp shock' treatment – I might never have reoffended.

The following morning, all the lads were around in my cell first thing, making sure that I was OK and that I had everything I needed. They knew what the first night was like for an inmate – it was one of the best-kept secrets of prison life, and now I was in on it. That same day Tomo asked his class officer, Mr Brohan, if I could move on to his landing. D2 was known as the best and the cleanest landing in St Patrick's Institution, and all the inmates housed on that landing were either from the inner city or from the north side of Dublin. Mr Brohan allowed me to move on to D2, where I got a spotless cell next door to a guy called Peter Mitchell, who became a good friend. On the other side of me was Peter Mitchell's brother Jeff. The lads gave me posters – Bo Derek, a Lamborghini Countach S – to stick up on my wall.

Now that I was on a landing with guys I knew, prison was not such a fearsome place any more. I thought to myself, 'I can do time – no problem.'

On my first visit from my mother, I put on a brave front and assured her that I was OK. She was a worrier, and I didn't want her to know the truth. She left me money so I could buy smokes, sweets and anything else I might need. It was a good visit. As she left, I felt more and more confident about jail. I knew, too, that my Ma was not going to abandon me.

The Travellers and the culchies pretty much kept to themselves, and we didn't have much trouble with them. But when there were problems, they were settled very quickly and out of sight of the screws. Most of the fights would take place behind closed cell doors, and I was always terrified of getting into a fight – simply because I couldn't fight.

I was only in the prison about four weeks when Peter Mitchell, Larry Reilly and Tomo Duffy came up to me and said that a certain individual on another landing was going around saying that I was grassing to the chief prison officer, Mr O'Sullivan.

The lads were very insistent: 'Get around there to his cell at tea-time and kick the shit out of the cunt. We'll stand guard outside his cell and make sure no one goes in to help him.'

I was shitting myself at the thought of having to go around to his landing, walk into his cell and fight him. This guy was much taller than me and he was well built. But I had no choice. If I didn't do it, I would lose face with all the lads – and they would have to do it for me, because D2 had a reputation to uphold.

Myself, Peter, Larry and Tomo hid down at the toilets at the bottom of the guy's wing, waiting for him to come back. Meanwhile, I was trying to figure out what to say to the guy and how to start the fight. Then the guy appeared. The four of us surged towards his cell. The others stood guard while I, terrified, pushed the door open and marched in. One of the lads outside then pulled the door closed behind me. The big guy turned to face me and, to my surprise, there was nothing but shock and horror written all over his face.

The second I saw his fear, I got brave. 'Who's a rat?' I said as I swung a boot and tried to kick him in the balls. I missed, but he cowered into the corner.

Wailing like a baby, he begged, 'Please don't hit me, please don't hit me. I'm sorry, I'm sorry.'

I was delighted at his reaction. He was a 'fizzbag'; he was exactly like me. My heart went out to the guy. He was just a harmless bloke who'd spoken out of school.

I whispered to him, 'Listen, I won't touch you. I'm just going to trash your cell and I want you to scream so the lads outside think I'm giving you a hiding. Right?'

The guy nodded in agreement, and I began to wreck his cell. I hopped his locker off the wall and upended his bed. And as I did, he played his part well and screamed out loud.

I shouted, 'I'm no fucking rat! And watch what you say in future – you hear me?' As I left his cell, I kicked his pisspot across the floor, just to make some more noise.

The three lads were saying, 'Fair play to ya, Alan. Did you lash him out of it?'

I casually told them, 'Ah, I just gave him a few slaps.'

The reality of it was, if he had had any bottle at all, I would have come out the worse.

There were two prison jobs I was told to avoid at all costs.

One was the 'bomb squad', where you were given a wheelbarrow and a shovel and you had to walk along the drainage channels that ran along the grounds below the cell windows. Your job was to shovel up human excrement, which inmates would throw out of their cell windows wrapped in newspaper rather than have it smelling the cell out. That was a horrible job, and I got picked to do it on a number of occasions.

The second job to avoid was working in the 'block shop', where bricks and slabs were made (I never knew for what purpose) – by Jaysus did you do hard labour down there! But prisoners from the country who were built like brick houses themselves and had hands like shovels used to love the block shop. They were welcome to it.

To avoid getting picked for the bomb squad or the block shop, I decided to put my name down to go to school. I could just about spell my name and address, and I thought I'd kill two birds with one stone – avoid the dreaded jobs, and learn to read and write. I found I actually enjoyed going to prison school, even though I had spent my entire childhood playing truant and getting kicked out of every school I went to. This was my kind of school, full of my kind of people, and I enjoyed it.

While I was sitting in school one day, a screw told me that the two-bar chief, Mr Kane, wanted to see me. Mr Kane was a ringer for Manuel from *Fawlty Towers*; we used to call him 'The Mexican'. He asked me did I want to go to Shanganagh open prison – and this time it was for real. I jumped at the chance! I was told to get up to my cell, pack my kit and head down to reception to change back into my own clothes. I didn't even have a chance to say goodbye to any of my mates.

Shanganagh was located in south Co. Dublin. There were no steel locked doors, none of the screws wore prison uniforms, and it was all very informal. I was shown around the prison by the chief officer, Mr Mannix. I remember he brought me out to the back of the prison grounds, across a football pitch where the screws and inmates were playing football with each other, and showed me a little wall no more than three feet in height.

Mr Mannix said to me, 'Alan, if you step over that wall, you'll be out of the prison and you'll be free. So if you want to go, why don't you save us both some time and run now? I won't even try to stop you.'

I told him I didn't want to escape, that I just wanted to finish my sentence and go home when I was allowed. That was the answer Mr Mannix wanted to hear.

But the knowledge that freedom was to be had so easily was hard to forget. As I lay in bed in my dormitory, I kept visualising that three-foot wall. I jumped up out of the bed and slipped out through the back door on to the football pitch. I ran across the field, and in the blind darkness I tripped and fell. When I got to my feet, I realised I had fallen over the wall. I was free.

I ran like a madman until I reached train tracks. I wasn't sure which way I ought to follow the tracks, but my sense of direction turned out to be correct. I followed the track for about fifteen miles before I got to Raheny village, not far from where I lived. It was just getting bright, and I decided not to go home – I didn't want my Ma running amuck on me for escaping. I went instead to the house of a friend of my mother's who we all called Auntie Sylvia. I knocked her up out of bed and told her I had escaped from jail.

Auntie Sylvia gave me some breakfast and told me not to leave her house; she was going up to collect my mother. She asked her two daughters, Yvonne and Altona, to look after me. (Yvonne was a former Miss Ireland, and I think Altona was even better looking.)

When Auntie Sylvia arrived back with my mother, the two of them proceeded to talk me into handing myself up.

That evening, we went to the gates of St Patrick's Institution and explained the situation. The officer on the gate said they didn't have a warrant to hold me and couldn't take me in. Then we went to Mountjoy police station, and they told me that there was not a warrant in existence for me and that I would have to go down to Shanganagh. So that night, we drove to Shanganagh, where they took me back. A mattress was placed on the floor outside Mr Mannix's office, and I spent the night there.

The following morning, the governor added fourteen days on to my jail term and sent me back up to St Patrick's Institution. All the lads in St Patrick's gave me stick for handing myself up, but they were delighted to see me. And for some insane reason it felt good to be back.

The loss of remission meant that I was now due to be released on 26 December 1984. On Christmas Eve, just like every other day, everyone was locked up from twelve to two for dinner – so the screws could go and have their bit of grub. After I had eaten mine, I decided to have a wank. As I sat on my hard plastic chair, with my jeans and jocks down around my ankles, pulling the stomach out of myself, my cell door suddenly opened. I fumbled and fell on the floor, bare-arsed. I tried to pull up my jocks and jeans while the screw, who was nearly choking with laughter, told me to get my kit: I was getting out on temporary release.

I couldn't believe it! What a day to get out on – Christmas Eve. I ran around the landing, telling all the lads through their spyholes that I was getting out. Loads of lads asked me to do favours for them, such as asking their girlfriends to bring drugs up to them. I said yes to every one of them. But by the time I was taken down to reception and had changed into my own clothes, I couldn't remember the details of anything I had promised to do – or who I had promised to do it for.

My personal belongings were returned to me at the front office, and I was handed £36, which I had accumulated from the £1 daily gratuity. I couldn't get out through the main gate fast enough. No drug could have given me the natural high I was on as I left that prison. Now I felt like a real hard man, I had a little bit of bumfluff on my upper lip, and I thought I was the business. I walked into an off-licence across the road from the prison and bought a £10 bottle of Pernod, a bag of cider and twenty cigarettes.

My little spell in prison didn't deter me from crime in any way at all. The night after being released from St Patrick's Institution, I robbed a total of seven cars – I was like a one-man crime wave. I was sixteen years old, sniffing gas and petrol, swallowing Valium by the handful, taking LSD, popping Ecstasy, snorting speed and drinking enormous amounts of alcohol. And I thought I was untouchable.

One night, I was celebrating my release in a local pub, the Black Sheep. My old nemesis Billy was there with some of his mates. I was with three other guys, one of whom I'll call 'David', and I saw Billy talking to David.

When he came back over to my table, David said he wanted to fight me.

I knew that Billy had put him up to it, so I said, 'OK – let's do it.' I couldn't show that I was afraid.

As I got up from my seat, David broke a pint glass right into my face. Spitting blood and bits of teeth everywhere, I grabbed another pint glass, smashed it on the edge of the table and went to shove it into David's face. He put his hand up to block it, and the glass went through his hand. The two of us went to hospital in the same ambulance. I lost my two front teeth and received eight stitches in the lip, and David received a number of stitches to his hand.

I vaguely recall the two of us making peace with each other after I bumped into him on the way home. I knew that Billy was using David to get at me, and I didn't want to be fighting him all the time. But I knew I'd have to get him back for attacking me.

Some weeks later, myself and a mate of mine, Mick Flanagan, were at a UB40 concert. As I danced, I happened to look up into the tiered seating area and spotted David. I was out of my head and my actions were very impulsive. There were a couple of discarded

Coca-Cola cans scattered around the floor. I picked one up, ripped it in half, felt the edge of the aluminium can with my thumb and thought, 'That'll be good enough to rip his face open.' I went up to the seating area and down the aisle directly behind where David was sitting. I grabbed him by the forehead, pulled his head back and ran the ripped can across his face. I had got him back.

After cutting David up, I got into the habit of carrying a small Bohemian razor blade on my person no matter where I went. The Bohemian blades were very small and compact, easy to conceal between your fingers covered by the palm of your hand. It got to the stage where I felt I couldn't leave my home without a blade – that was the only way I felt safe. The knowledge that I had a blade in my pocket gave me confidence and the sense of security I needed. I would use it only as a last resort. But once the idea came to me, I acted on it. I hated using a blade but felt I had to, because I couldn't fight – and I certainly couldn't walk away, as everyone would have seen it as open season and walked all over me.

People often said to me, 'Why don't you just use your fists?' The truth is that I had no confidence in myself, and to this day I don't know if I can fight with just my fists. I hated fighting, I hated confrontation, and I felt I had to protect myself. Fear is a horrible thing to live with – fear of making eye contact with a stranger who might say something smart to me. But when I had alcohol inside of me, I felt more confident. And if I was on LSD, I felt in total control. That terrified the shit out of me – because once I got started on a person, I was unsure how far I'd actually go. I seemed like a 'hard man'. In fact, I was the total opposite. I was afraid, so afraid.

I quickly accumulated a large number of new charges for stealing cars. Each time I was nicked I was released from the police station on my own bail, known as 'station bail'. Because I now had a lot of criminal charges pending, I knew I would eventually be found guilty and sent back to prison. The last place I wanted to be was in jail, so at seventeen I failed to turn up in court on the many different court dates I had to face. The police revoked my 'station bail' and the judge issued bench warrants for my arrest. I knew if I was nicked, there was no way would I get out on bail. So I decided I was going to enjoy the freedom I had left.

Myself and a friend of mine, Colm 'Rosser' Ross, drank two bottles of Old Cellar wine each and stole a Ford Escort in the city centre. Rosser was driving, and as we made our way back to our neighbourhood we were spotted by the police, who gave chase and rammed us off the road. Our car crossed a footpath and smashed through a garage door. Two detectives jumped from their car and were on their way to apprehend us when we sped out backwards from the wrecked garage, hitting the two cops. Rosser spun the nose of the Escort around and we were back on the road again. A uniformed policeman tried to run for cover, but Rosser accelerated after him and tipped him with the side of the car. The copper lost his footing at sprint speed and went tumbling right into a wall.

At this stage there were a lot of police cars on our tail. We raced through our housing estate, where we were again rammed from behind. The car spun sideways, and we ended up wrapped around the pole of a street light. The dash compartment of the car burst into flames, the side windows were smashed and we were both pulled out by the hair. The police proceeded to kick the shit out of us in the middle of the road.

I clearly recall three women walking past and saying to the policemen, 'I'm reporting you to the Minister for Justice.'

One of the coppers who was beating me turned to the lady and said, 'Fuck you! And the Minister for Justice.'

I was charged with allowing myself to be carried in a stolen car. Rosser was charged with driving the car, knocking down the three policemen and ramming two squad cars. We were brought to court the following morning, and the coppers objected to bail. Well, I knew I wasn't getting out because there were already bench warrants for my arrest. We were remanded in custody to St Patrick's Institution with no bail. The judge gave us free legal aid and I asked for Michael Hanahoe, who had done good work for a number of my mates, to represent me. Rosser asked for Dermot Morris to represent him. Dermot was well known and liked by most delinquents. His nickname was 'Danger Mouse' (because he had a tendency to go off on one in court, telling the judge what he could and could not do).

When we got to St Patrick's, we were the talk of the prison. Our joyriding incident was all over the front page of a national newspaper. The headline read: GARDAI SAVE CAR GANG.

We were delighted. We were 'famous' now.

My first appearance on page one

4

Writer in Residence

Back on D2 in St Patrick's, I once again began going to school. My reading and writing were still very bad, but I had learned a small bit from my previous jail term. Mentally and verbally I was very creative, but I was unable to translate that on to paper, and that was very frustrating for me. I wanted to write, I needed to write – it was like a compulsion. At that time, I understood my own spellings and what I was trying to convey. But no one else could, and that did my head in.

One teacher took a particular interest in me; I think her name was Phil. Phil brought in newspapers for me to read, and that meant a lot to me. She'd sit beside me and slowly read out a paragraph, and then help me read the paragraph aloud under her guiding finger. At the end of class she would circle some news stories for me to study in my cell that night and give me a list of questions that I had to find answers to. She was really interested in me and in what I had to say, and I wanted her approval. She would constantly encourage me to express my thoughts on paper, and she showed me how to change details so that no one would know I was talking about myself. I think one of the reasons why I liked Phil so much was that she wasn't like a 'real teacher' with rules and regulations, and she wasn't a screw either: she was up for the prisoner. This was generally true of the prison teachers, and that was a major factor in explaining why I enjoyed prison school so much.

Phil told me about a competition judged by the famous playwright John B. Keane at Listowel Writers' Week in Co. Kerry, and she encouraged me to write a short play and enter it in the drama section. I didn't know the first thing about writing a play, and I said so.

Phil got a blank piece of paper and wrote at the top of the page: 'Classroom; Teacher Phil and pupil Alan are sitting at a desk.' Then she wrote her name, followed by a question. Then she wrote my name and asked me what was my answer to her question.

So I told her, and she wrote down my reply.

Phil said, 'That is how you start.'

Then it twigged with me: the format was similar to the Q&A that would take place between a police officer and a criminal during interrogation. It would subsequently be typed out and put into a book of evidence for a criminal trial. I started using my own book of evidence, which I had retained from my pending trial at the Circuit Criminal Court, as a rough guide.

I started working on a short play called *A Start in Life*. It was a story about a young boy, a foul-mouthed chap whose father gets him an interview with a very important man from the USA who will fix him up with a job. When I read it today, some twenty-eight years on, I notice the non-existence of stage direction, position, action and so on. It's simply dialogue – the way I was first shown by Phil.

My teacher typed it up and sent it off to Listowel, and I forgot all about it. Three weeks later, I got a letter from John B. Keane awarding me second place in the drama section. I won a gold Cross pen and a cheque for £20, but I didn't care about that: I just couldn't believe that I had won second prize in such a prestigious competition. The prison governor and chief prison officers were really impressed with me, and I earned myself some brownie points with them – after all, it made the prison look good that the education system within the jail had churned out a writer. I didn't care who claimed credit, as long as it made my life easier in the nick.

I was kept in custody until the final day of my first ever trial at the Circuit Criminal Court, where I was sentenced to eighteen months' detention and banned from driving for life. The judge, Michael Moriarty, was known for being lenient and for listening to what you had to say. I dressed in black to show respect for the court and I entered a 'Plea of Mitigation', a personal letter to the judge telling him how sorry I was for my actions.

I was not really sorry – I was just playing the system to the best of my ability, and I did it every time I was in court. From the moment of my arrest I would start work on my defence. I would make sure my barrister was armed with as many mitigating factors as possible in relation to my life, my family, my mother. I would try to appeal directly to the judge, making good eye contact.

I was a master at playing for sympathy, and it worked: Mr Moriarty backdated my sentence to the time of my arrest. I had less than a year left to do.

By this time I was well settled into prison life. Prison was just like another housing estate. The eggshell-coloured stone walls, the barred cell windows, the green prison doors, the locked steel gates, the polished floors and uniformed prison officers were my daily view, and I got used to them.

I began going to Alcoholics Anonymous (AA) meetings with some of my mates – not because I wanted to get off the drink, but because it gave us something to do. We took the piss out of the AA members who gave up their free time to come in and pour their hearts out to us. Often when I turned up for the meetings, I was tripping on LSD or drunk on my prison hooch.

The hooch was very easy to prepare. We'd get a load of white bread from the kitchen and break it up into a basin of hot water. Then we'd tear up a bed sheet into squares and place the hot wet bread from the basin on to a square of bed sheet. By wringing it tightly over a second empty basin, we extracted the yeast from the bread. Then we'd throw in as many chopped-up apples and oranges as we could get, mixing in heaps of sugar. We'd shake the gas from a bottle of mineral water until it was completely flat and pour the whole lot into a gallon drum. The drum would then be placed on the hot pipe that ran through the cell, and every six hours or so I would release the gas from the gallon drum very slowly. After about two to three weeks, the hooch would be ready to drink. We always made as much as we could, and then hid the gallon drums all over the nick. We knew that some would be found during cell searches, but most of them weren't.

After winning second place with my play, I became known in the prison as a writer. Some of the inmates would ask me to write poems that they could give to their girlfriends, mothers and kids (pretending they'd written them). My price was a packet of tobacco per poem. I was writing poems for birthdays and Christmas, as well as love poems and 'missing you' poems. I was no good at poetry, and I used to copy the poems from the obituaries in the *Evening Herald* newspaper, just changing around a few words here and there. Apologies, lads.

The prison three-bar chief officer, Mr O'Sullivan, was a decent man from Co. Kerry. His dress was immaculate: you could see your face in his shoes, and he always gave off a strong smell of Brut 33. For some reason the chief had a lot of time for me. One day, he called me into the Circle and told me to make sure my cell was spotless and up to scratch. As I made my way up to my landing, I wondered what this was about – I knew I had the cleanest cell on the landing, as did Mr O'Sullivan and my class officer, Mr Brohan.

During lock-up, as I ate my dinner, the cell door opened. Standing there were the three prison governors – all the chief officers – with another man whose face I recognised. He turned out to be the Minister for Justice, Gerry Collins.

Mr Collins sat himself down on my bed and chatted to me for about five minutes. We talked about my crime, my family and the prison. Of course, I had nothing but positive things to say about St Patrick's, but in the background you could hear the diehards shouting out through their cell doors: 'The food is rotten!' and, 'We're living in dire conditions!' and so forth. I shook hands with the minister, and as the entourage left my cell Chief Officer O'Sullivan looked back at me and winked.

I thought, 'I should be out on temporary release soon.'

After dinner, my cell was stormed by all my mates. They had great suggestions as to what I should have said to Mr Collins. What, and shoot myself in the foot? I don't think so. I was in prison, and once there I worked on one thing and one thing only – getting back out. The thought of going straight upon my eventual release never featured in my thinking; there was never a long-term plan, and rehabilitation was as far from my mind as God is from the mind of the militant atheist.

That evening, while we were on recreation in the exercise yard, some of the lads on D2 decided that we were all going to refuse our dinners in protest against the quality of the food. Personally, I found the food to be grand. But if I didn't go along with their protest, I would have alienated myself from all of them. There were five lads, all mates of mine, who went around to everyone on the landing telling them to refuse the food. As we queued up for our dinner on the day of the protest, the five organisers walked up and took great pleasure in telling the screws what to do with their dinner. Then they turned around and marched back up to their cells empty-handed. I was the sixth guy in the queue. I picked up a plate and let the screw put some peas on to it, then turned around and walked away without comment. When I got up to my cell, I left the plate with the peas untouched outside my door. The rest of the prisoners behind me followed suit.

About twenty minutes after everyone was locked up, the five ringleaders were dragged out of their cells one by one and had the shit kicked out of them. They were then shackled and thrown down the Base (the twelve-cell landing for violent and unruly prisoners). My cell door was then opened and the two-bar chief, Mr Kane, asked me had I got a problem with the food. I told him the food was fine, and he asked me why didn't I eat it. I said I wasn't hungry and I hadn't refused any food. In anger, he slammed my door shut. Nobody else on the landing could be touched, simply because they had all taken some peas – none of them had refused food.

Every Sunday I served at the altar for Fr Willie Maher and for Fr Mick Cullen, the prison chaplains. I also used to clean the church twice a week. I loved doing the readings. It was a form of drama – I was up there and I had an audience, including the governors and chief officers, looking at me being a good boy. Pronouncing words such as 'Corinthians' and 'Thessalonians' was a challenge. Fr Mick and Fr Willie would help me; they'd break the tricky words up into syllables for me. I would rehearse my readings in the chapel until I was word perfect. After mass in the main prison, myself and the priest would then go down the Base to say mass for the inmates.

On the Sunday after the food protest, with my five mates from

D2 locked up in the Base, I was going to take a considerable amount of pleasure in going down there. But when I got down, the lads were not too impressed with me. They maintained that I should have told them to take some peas, instead of keeping the gambit to myself.

I got on really well with nearly all the prison officers, but there were a few exceptions. One of the screws really detested me. He was on gate control at the end of C1. Each day all the inmates who didn't have regular jobs had to line up on C1, where the assistant chief officer, Dan Fitts, would allocate them to their workplaces for that day. Nobody wanted to get on the wrong side of ACO Fitts. He was about six foot two and built like a brick shithouse, and if he didn't like you, you were guaranteed to spend your entire sentence in the block shop or on the bomb squad. Because of my two regular jobs – I was a cleaner on D2 in addition to working in the church – I didn't have to queue up to get work assignments from ACO Fitts.

One day, I was chatting to some mates who were lined up for the work party, after which I planned to have my daily chat with the females in their exercise yard. (That was another great thing about working in the church: the window overlooked the girls' exercise yard, and I was able to sit on the ledge and chat to the girls below. I loved it.) After chatting to the lads on the work party line-up, I had to pass through the gate at C1 manned by the screw who hated me. When I got to the gate, the screw refused to let me through into the Circle, and told me to get into line for the work party.

I explained that I was working in the church and I didn't need to go to join the work party. I spotted Fr Willie walking through the prison Circle, and I called out to him and explained the situation.

Fr Willie turned to the officer and said, 'Alan is a trusted worker in the church. You can let him through, Officer.'

With that the screw turned to the priest and said, 'No.'

Well, Fr Willie's face went as red as a tomato, and he hurried out of the Circle and into the main hall.

Soon I heard a massive roar coming from the Circle, aimed at the screw: 'Get over here to me *now*!'

It was Chief Officer O'Sullivan, and Fr Willie was standing beside him. The screw walked sheepishly over to his boss, and although none of us could hear what was being said, we knew the screw was being lifted out of it by the chief. I suppose the chief's spittle spraying into the screw's face gave it away. The screw then walked back over and opened the gate for me. As I walked through the gate, I turned to the screw and just smiled at him. That was one of the best victories I ever got over a screw. I went up to the church, grabbed a bottle of wine from the vestry and opened the window for my daily chat with the females. Fr Willie knew I dipped into the wine, and he was cool about it – just as long as I didn't advertise it.

After recreation, I went up to my cell to get my bucket for a wash. As I turned around to walk back out of the cell, there was Chief Officer O'Sullivan.

The chief closed the door and said, 'Alan, I saw you smoking hash in the Rec tonight. I don't want you to end up like the rest of the scum in here, strung out on drugs. I'll overlook this hash-smoking incident. But if I ever see you smoking hash again, me and you are finished.' He then walked out of my cell.

All my mates saw him leave and looked at each other in amazement. The Chief was never normally up on the landing, let alone in an inmate's cell. When I told the lads what had happened, they were shocked – the Chief barely said 'hello' to inmates, never mind hiding behind a cell door and waiting for an inmate to return to his cell to lecture him about drug taking. I don't know why Mr O'Sullivan and the governors showed such a keen interest in me – at the end of the day I was just another inmate, no different from anyone else.

On my first sentence, the judge had recommended that I see a psychiatrist, and so every week I would be called out to see the prison shrink. I got to know Dr McCormack really well and I opened my heart to him. I told him about being sexually abused, about my drink and drug addictions, and my feelings. I told that man almost everything about myself – he was the only person I felt I could confide in.

Dr McCormack recommended that I go to the Central Mental Hospital over a three-day period for a psychological evaluation. The doctors had me play silly games, such as putting plastic objects of different shapes and sizes into their right place on a board. They'd create a number of fictitious scenarios and ask me how I would deal with them. I was sent for a brain scan – an ECG, I think it was called. I must have passed the evaluation because I wasn't kept there, thank God – that place scared the shit out of me, with its dazed inmates walking aimlessly along the gleaming white-tiled floors. The food was lovely, though. When I got back to St Patrick's, I got the piss ripped out of me by all my mates.

I applied for three days' temporary release to go home for Christmas, but the Department of Justice refused me. On my first Christmas in prison I sat in my cell thinking of my family sitting at home, opening their presents, watching TV, eating and drinking together and going to parties. I missed even the smallest of things, such as the decorations and the tree. All the lads were up on their windows, singing Christmas carols, but I was too upset. I would have been lost without my class officer, Mr Brohan; he was a great character. He taught me how to play chess, and that game would take me away from myself and into a little world of tactics and forward planning. We would often sit in the recreation hall and play chess together, and he'd always beat me. But he would say, 'Alan, you're always better off playing someone better than yourself, you'll learn more.'

Every week, myself and Officer Hand from the gym brought all the gym laundry over to the female wing for the girls to wash. From my daily chats at the church window I already knew most of the girls, and I was writing to a girl called Catherina. The girls were always asking Mr Hand to give them five minutes with me in their cell or behind the press irons, but he would never let me out of his sight. He knew what would happen.

After serving my eighteen months, I went home. My Ma gave me a big lecture, saying she hoped I'd learned my lesson and this would be the last time I'd be inside. I agreed with her and filled her head with false promises. As for my mates, they gave me a nice 'welcome home' present. My mother woke me up and told me to look in the front driveway. I looked out of the bedroom window to see a yacht parked in the garden. It turned out the lads who were out robbing the night before had stolen a car with the yacht attached and decided to reverse it into my mother's garden. They even went to the bother of putting up the sails.

5

Actual Bodily Harm

After getting out of St Patrick's, I got straight back into robbing. Despite my promises to my mother, the thought of getting caught and going back inside didn't even feature in my thinking.

We often headed down the country at night to rob shops and break into pubs. Cigarettes were like cash; shop owners in our area would buy them from us. But driving down the country in a convoy of stolen cars was never easy. You very seldom got to your destination without getting chased at some point. Then, of course, there were the other robbers from various parts of Dublin who would also be heading down the country to do the same as us. I never made any real money from robbing – just a quick couple of hundred here and there – but I enjoyed it. I thrived on the adventure of stealing a car, driving into quiet towns, disrupting the place with smash-and-grabs or ram raids, and being chased by the police.

At this stage I was, to put it mildly, a bit of a nuisance to my neighbours with my constant joyriding up and down my road, getting chased by the police and drinking on the street corners. My antisocial behaviour was driving everyone up the wall, including my own family. But I never reflected on my actions, or how they made my mother feel.

When a handful of our neighbours congregated just near our garden gate, posing as vigilantes, I thought it was hilarious. There were two families that never joined the protest against me, nor did they sign the petition that was doing the rounds to have my family removed from the estate. (The petition was pointless, because we owned our home.) These two families were good people who never fell foul of the law. They never wrote me off; they just kept themselves to themselves and did their own thing. I can understand, though, why the others came out in protest. I was a little bastard, and I didn't care about anyone or anything. I did what I wanted to do, when I wanted to do it. It was as simple as that.

Most of my crimes served no particular purpose, but car and van parts could be sold for good money. If I got a diesel engine and gearbox from a Toyota Hiace van, I was paid £800 a pop. My friend Marko was good to work with: he could see money where no one else could, and he had contacts who'd buy the gear from us. Once, I was in the process of hot-wiring a Hiace when I looked in the wing mirror and spotted five or six women running towards the van.

Marko jumped out and started shouting, for their benefit, 'If I caught them, I would have fucking killed them. There were two lads on a motorbike, and they were trying to steal your van. As soon as they saw me coming, they jumped on their bike and sped off up the road.'

As Marko was spinning this yarn, a police car pulled up and one of the women blurted out, 'Officer, Officer! They're gone that way, two men on a motorbike.'

The sirens went on and the coppers burned rubber in the direction the lady had pointed. The woman thanked myself and Marko for saving her van and gave us £50 to buy ourselves a drink. We hopped into our own car and headed to the nearest pub. Happy days!

Myself and Marko were always out scouting the side streets and back roads of Dublin, looking for opportunities to make cash. We'd dress in overalls, so when we were up to no good in other people's yards and garages, we didn't look out of place. One day, we drove by what we assumed to be some sort of a truck-repair business, so out we got to have a little nose around the yard. We walked into a garage and a big fat guy, middle-aged with greasy hair, stuck his head out from under a truck and asked, 'What can I do ya for?'

Marko pretended to be a haulage company owner and told the gentleman that one of his drivers had to do a country run later that evening, but the starting motor in his 360 Hino was knackered. Would he know where we'd get a replacement – even a reconditioned one?

The mechanic scratched his greasy head and replied, 'Well, that's the brother's department. He looks after sales.' Then he thought to himself for a moment and said, 'Ah, sure, come on up here and I'll see what I can do for you.'

The greasy mechanic led us across the yard and up a green grass verge to a wooden shed behind a bungalow. He opened the back door of the bungalow, took a key off a rack, then walked to the wooden shed and opened the door. The shed looked like an old pigeon loft. But instead of pigeons, each hatch contained a brand-new 360 Hino starting motor.

We told the mechanic that we'd be interested in buying four or five starting motors from him, but we'd have to go to the bank first and would pop back in about two hours or so. The mechanic told us that his brother might be back by then, and he would look after us. We walked with him back down to the yard, said goodbye, got into our car, drove around to the driveway of the bungalow, ran up the driveway, opened the back door to the bungalow, took the key off the rack, opened the shed and took all nineteen of the 360 Hino starting motors. We knew we'd get £250 a pop for them – we had hit the jackpot. I don't know how the front of the car stayed on the ground with the weight in the boot. We drove straight up to our contact and got close to five grand for the starting motors.

There wasn't quite as much money in lorry tyres, but I used to enjoy taking them. Around lunchtime on weekdays the tyre centres would be virtually deserted, with the exception of maybe some young lad who would be there on work experience. Myself or Marko would keep the young guy occupied by engaging him in chit-chat, while the other would be wheeling lorry tyres out of the garage. We'd put one hanging out of the boot, another on the bonnet and the third on the roof of the car, and we'd actually drive like that through the city to another contact who had his own tyre centre. We weren't worried about being stopped by the police – before we actually robbed the tyres, our contact would issue us with a receipt to state that we had bought the tyres from him.

We had a few run-ins with a guy who owned breaker's yards around the city. We nicknamed him 'Jack the Hat', for the big J. R. Ewing-style hat he wore. Myself and Marko had been eyeing up a

68

360 Hino engine and gearbox in one of his yards. We went to Paddy, a Traveller friend of ours who owned a truck with a Hiab loader crane attached, and asked could we borrow it for a few hours. Paddy lent us his truck, and we parked it just outside Jack the Hat's yard in the heart of the city. I stood on the chain attached to the jib while Marko, who was operating the crane, lifted me up over the high steel fence and down into the yard. I hooked the chain around the Hino engine and gearbox until it was secure, and then Marko lifted me and the loot over the fence and down on to the back of the truck.

As I was undoing the chains, I heard a car screeching to a halt beside us. A tiny man wearing a big fuck-off cowboy hat jumped out from the car with a camera flashing and screamed, '*Gotcha!*' It was Jack the Hat, and he was snapping photos of us. In a panic, trying to hide his face from the camera, Marko let go of the controls. The steel jib swung to the left, hitting me in the chest and pinning me tight against the steel fence. As I screamed in pain, Marko ran away from Jack the Hat and his poxy camera.

By the time I managed to wriggle myself out from behind the jib, Marko had calmed Jack the Hat down. He told him he would pay him for the engine, as he had a buyer for it. Jack the Hat agreed to let us have the engine on the condition that if we ever wanted anything from his yards, we would give him a ring and he would cut us a deal. But there was no way he was going to get a penny from us.

One day, Marko and I were driving on a little country road just outside of Dublin. As we drove along the country road, we noticed what looked like a yard behind two big galvanised steel gates. When I looked through a small gap in the gate, all I could see were trucks and trailers – it was a little gold mine. There was a big house next door to the yard so, dressed in our overalls, we walked up the driveway of the house and into the yard. In the yard there were rich pickings: two cars that had been sanded down and were ready to be resprayed; three flatbed forty-foot trailers; one forty-foot box trailer full of house contents; six trucks, most of which had good tyres; and an old-fashioned Posts & Telegraphs van packed to the rafters with thick slabs of aluminium.

While we were rooting in the back of the box trailer, Marko pulled out a sign with the name of the yard owner on it – it was Jack the Hat. We nearly pissed ourselves laughing. Just then, an old man appeared from the house next door and enquired as to what the hell we were doing there.

Marko dropped the sign, jumped down and said, 'Ah, Jack sent us down to clean up the yard.'

The old man replied, 'Oh, sorry, lads. That's no problem, you work away, sorry to have disturbed you. If you want a cup of tea or anything, just give me a shout.'

As the old man walked away, we realised that this yard was now our yard. We drove to a hardware store and bought steel bolt-cutters and a lock. Back at the yard, we cut the old lock off the gate and replaced it with our new one. Now we had free and easy access.

We emptied the old P&T van of all the aluminium and loaded it on to a trailer attached to our car. Within the hour, we had sold the metal for £1,300. Then we went to see our contact who owned the tyre centre. We knew that if we told him the truth, he wouldn't touch the stuff from Jack the Hat's yard with a bargepole, so we informed him we had just purchased a yard. Would he be interested in buying the tyres from the trucks? Our tyre buyer came to Jack's yard and walked around with a piece of chalk. He marked each tyre that he wanted his men to remove – something like sixteen tyres. His two employees then reversed a Ford Transit van into the yard and went to work with their big power tools, removing the wheels from the trucks.

Half an hour later, Jack the Hat's trucks were all left on blocks, and myself and Marko were well over another grand richer. The two cars that were sanded down and ready to be resprayed were next to go: we sold them to a guy who owned a garage. The only things left to sell were the three flatbed forty-foot trailers.

We knew a guy (I'll call him 'Jay') who had his own trailer yard down at the docks on the North Wall, and he agreed to buy two of the trailers off us. Following myself and Marko back to 'our' yard in his truck, Jay hitched up one of the trailers and paid us up front for the second as well. We agreed that one of us would go with his driver to collect the second trailer that evening. At this stage Marko and myself were getting a little bit worried that before long some-one had to cop on to what we'd been doing in the yard. We decided to offer fifty quid to the boyfriend of one of Marko's sisters, whose nickname was 'Judas', to go with the truck driver and help him hitch up the trailer. We told Judas that as soon as he was finished, we'd meet him in a pub in the city centre.

We'd been in the pub for four hours, out of our heads on cocaine and drink, when Judas came in, covered in muck.

Out of breath, he said, 'When I got to the yard, I went to open the gate. Jack the Hat dropped out of a tree with a camera and started taking photos, so I just ran.'

We asked what had happened to Jay's driver.

Judas said, 'Oh, they have him. A couple of guys jumped on him, so I just got offside.'

Later that week, we drove past a Toyota Hiace van with the keys in the ignition. Realising there was £800 to be had for the engine and gearbox, I jumped into it and started the engine. The owner of the van walked out of a shop nearby.

As I reversed away from him, he smiled and waved his arm. 'Ah, come back and stop the messing.'

He realised that I wasn't 'messing' when I banged the van into first gear and sped off. I parked the van up in a housing estate for a few hours, just until the heat had died down. Later that evening, myself and Marko went back in our car and I drove the Hiace away. Marko was in front of me when we stopped at a set of traffic lights. Out of the blue my door was pulled open, and three big guys tried to drag me from the van. I accelerated away and ploughed into the back of Marko's car, which smacked into the back of the car in front of him. The guys dragged me out and pulled me to the ground. I jumped up and swung a boot at one of the guys, who grabbed my foot in mid-air and pulled off my runner. He then threw my runner back at me, busting open my nose.

Dazed, and wearing just one runner, I jumped over the roof of Marko's car and dodged through the heavy traffic into a residential side street, where I squeezed my body underneath a parked car.

As I lay under the car, with the driving shaft digging into my back, I heard the car door being opened, someone sitting down in the driver's seat and the door closing. I scrambled out, ran into a front garden and hid under some garden bushes. I could see and hear policemen running up and down the road, asking passers-by if they'd seen me. An old woman led a detective over to the garden where I was hiding. I was dragged out of the garden, bundled into the back of an unmarked police car and brought back to the crashed Hiace.

Marko was pretending to be a law-abiding citizen, taking down the owner's insurance particulars, and didn't even acknowledge me. When I was brought back to the police station, I found out that there was £5,000 worth of designer tracksuits and runners in the back of the van. In addition, £700 in cash was missing from the glove compartment. I was charged with the unauthorised taking of the van, and released on station bail.

After I got out of the police station, I knew that I'd have a few quid to fall back on from the money that Marko had taken from the glove compartment. But Marko denied taking the money from the van. He insisted that it was probably the owner of the van who took it himself and tried to claim it back on his insurance. I gave Marko a wide berth after that, and I went back to robbing with my other mates.

One day, myself, Dimmers Deans and two other guys headed down to Co. Wicklow, scouting for a car to rob. We travelled in what the police term a 'company vehicle' – a car that young delinquents purchase from members of the Travelling community for little or nothing. We came across a snow-white Vauxhall Astra GSI in a little Wicklow town. This was a proper car and would piss on any police car that gave chase. I had the Astra hot-wired in under sixty seconds, and we were off.

Almost immediately, we came across a police car – a scabby Renault 5. The coppers would be lucky if they got 80 mph out of it. As Dimmers accelerated away, I put on my Simon and Garfunkel *Concert in Central Park* tape, sat back and lit up a cigarette. Dimmers began toying with the cops, slowing down and letting the police car catch up with us, then powering away.

Eventually, Dimmers said to me, 'Alan, put your window up. It's time to say bye-bye to the filth.'

I flicked my cigarette out of the window, and off we went. But when Dimmers floored the GSI, the car wouldn't go past 75 mph. It turned out there was a governor on the car – a steel bar fixed into the floor underneath the accelerator that limits the speed. There was no way to remove it while driving, and here we were getting chased by the police in this piece of scrap that was keeping up with us.

As we drove on to the Stillorgan dual carriageway, all I could see on my left and right at each set of traffic lights we passed were police cars blocking off every alternative route. It was like a scene from the film *The Blues Brothers*, or *Heat*. As we passed the police vehicles, they fell in behind and joined the chase. Any time a police car tried to overtake us, Dimmers swerved at them and rammed them off the road. We made it as far as the city centre before a Special Branch car came speeding up behind us, got his right front wing level with the back end of our car, then pulled a sharp right into us, sending our car tailspinning out of control. We crashed into a little island in the middle of the road, where we were boxed in.

Dimmers reversed hard and pulled a handbraker. The nose of the GSI spun around and smacked into another police car. My passenger door was pulled open, and two detectives tried to pull me from the car. With half my body hanging out of the car I managed to let the handbrake down and Dimmers powered away, pushing another police car from his path. The detective let go of my jacket, I slammed the door shut and we hammered our way through the city centre. We drove the wrong way down one-way streets in the hope the police wouldn't follow us, but they did. We made it back to our neighbourhood and began driving around a large block of houses, hoping that our mates would stone the police. But there was no chance of that – one of our mates counted thirty-six police cars behind us. Dimmers finally crashed the GSI into a garden gate after a police car rammed us from behind.

I was dragged from the GSI and slung into the back of a detective's car. When we arrived at the station, Dimmers was already in the cell. I knew I was banged 'left to rights' on this, so I made a deal with the detective. I told him that I would make a full statement admitting to my part, thus saving the State time and money, but only if he wouldn't object to me getting my own bail when I appeared in court. The cop agreed and, the following morning, after appearing in court, myself and Dimmers were released from custody on our own bond.

After I got released, my mother, not for the first time, gave me a massive lecture. These lectures followed a familiar form. She would sit me down. She would be very composed. She'd remind me of how other people who chose the route I was choosing had ended up – in prison, on the streets, on the run, causing harm, ruining their own lives, keeping the police, the judges, prison officers and solicitors all in a job. And what about their poor mothers and fathers, having the police raiding their homes every week? My Ma would go on and on and on. Those lectures were worse than any hiding I got from the police. They drove me mad. I was wasting valuable time – all I wanted to do was get out of the house.

To keep my mother off my back, I let her get me a job as a kitchen porter in the Regency Airport Hotel, where she and my sister Frieda worked as waitresses. I was a general dogsbody, but mostly the job consisted of scrubbing pots and pans. The head chef, Pat, was always screaming for clean pots. It was a bloody nightmare.

One day, the head chef and managers were rushing around, fussing and panicking, because the hotel owner's son and his new bride were having their wedding reception. At one point a massive pot full of greasy water appeared on the steel table where dirty pots were put for cleaning. I emptied the pot, dumped the leftovers into a rubbish bag, cleaned the pot and put it back on to its shelf. A little while later, the head chef came over and asked me where the big pot had gone. I told him it was up on the shelf, ready and waiting to be used.

The chef stopped dead in his tracks. As if speaking to a child, he asked, 'Where's the stuff that was inside the pot, Alan?'

I told him I had dumped it into the skip out back.

He began screaming. 'The main course for the wedding was in that fuckin' pot!'

He sprinted out to the skip and retrieved the black bin bag. The contents of the bag were tipped into one of my two sinks. Among the dumped ice cream, vegetables and other bits of rubbish were nice chunky pieces of steak all cut up into neat cubes. Myself and the chef proceeded to pick out each and every piece of steak, and then we hand-washed them as quickly as we could. The bride and groom enjoyed their main course.

What the eye don't see, the chef gets away with.

There was a married woman who also worked as a waitress at the hotel. I'll call her 'Louise'. She was thirty-seven – more than twice my age – and extremely attractive. One night, when I had nearly finished work, Louise asked me did I fancy heading out to a club with her. As I was wearing a tracksuit and runners, I was a bit hesitant. I was also skint. But Louise wasn't bothered about how I was dressed, or the fact I had no money. She was very persistent, so I ended up jumping into a taxi with her.

We fell out of a nightclub at about three in the morning and went in under some bushes beside the entrance gates to St Stephen's Green. After we finished fucking each other's brains out in the bushes, we went to flag down a taxi. As we did so, I got this awful smell of excrement. I looked at Louise's jeans and jumper. She was covered in dog shit. I just went into convulsions of laughter – I thought it was the funniest thing ever. Smell or no smell, we needed to get home, so we flagged down a taxi. After we got into the confined space of the car, the smell got a hundred times worse. All the way home not one word was spoken between the taxi driver and ourselves.

Louise had five kids – four boys and a girl. She told me she was eager to leave her husband, who beat her, so I suggested that we move to England. To my delight she eagerly agreed. I wanted to go as soon as possible – I wanted everything to happen yesterday.

I purchased seven ferry tickets and bought new coats, jeans and even toothbrushes for the kids. Every day when Louise would go to work, she'd smuggle some of her own and the kids' clothes out of her home and leave them in my house. After a couple of weeks, she had all the clothes she and the kids needed at my house.

My Ma and family were well aware that myself and Louise were going to Manchester. None of them showed any sign of disapproval – not that it would have made any difference. They probably thought I was mad to be heading off to England with a much older woman and five kids in tow. On the flip side, I think my Ma thought that the relationship and the responsibility might settle me down.

I met Louise's kids for the first time when we boarded the ferry. The kids were mad with excitement, as was I – I couldn't wait to get to the bar. We bought the kids a McDonald's, and myself and Louise grabbed a table with our drinks. Then the kids were off, booting around the ship and driving everyone but me and Louise mental. I didn't think, not for one second, that I was taking on the role of 'stepfather'. In my mind, I had a girlfriend, and the kids were hers. Anyway, I had a great buzz with the kids. We got on great, so it wasn't going to be a problem.

We went to Wythenshawe in Manchester and registered as homeless. I was happy that Louise had finally got away from her husband. For my own part, I had jumped bail on the charge for the stolen GSI and was now on the run from the law. I saw this as a new start – as far as I was concerned, I was getting a second chance at life with Louise and the kids.

We were lucky enough to be housed straight away in a nice little flat, fully furnished. The kids sometimes missed their dad, which was to be expected, but they settled in well. Each day we'd all go to the park, and at night I would tell the kids stories and sing them songs. But after about four weeks, things began to go downhill. If the kids were acting up and I was watching TV, I couldn't even ask them to stay quiet. Louise would jump straight in and tell me that I had nothing to do with those children. She was right – they were her kids, not mine. By this time she was also in regular contact with her husband over the phone, and he was trying to talk her into going back home.

The final straw came when there was no food in the house and the kids were literally starving and crying with hunger pains. I ended up taking potato skins from the bin and frying them on the pan. It was then that we both decided that we'd go back home and split up. I was okay with the split, though I didn't think it was a good idea for Louise to go back into an abusive relationship. I've never seen her since. I have no regrets from that relationship – she was a good person, and we had a mad time together.

After I got back home, I knew it was only a matter of time before I got nicked. I was never any good at evading capture, but this time I was determined to give it my best shot. To alter my appearance I got a perm in my hair and dyed it jet black. I also put false tan all over my face and body. I looked like Michael Jackson! I felt really confident in my new disguise – until Starsky pulled up in the squad car and recognised me immediately.

I was remanded in custody with no bail. Dimmers was still on the run, and he never turned up for his trial. (Twenty-eight years on, Dimmers is still alive, working in a permanent job and married with children. Although still on the run, he has never reoffended.) I was sentenced to eighteen months in St Patrick's for allowing myself to be carried in the stolen car.

A mate of mine would come up to visit me in prison, and although he knew I didn't smoke hash (it made me feel sick), he'd bring some up every week. I'd either swap it for cigarettes or give it to my other mates in the nick. One week, there was this really cute-looking female screw called Miss Young monitoring the visit. We were waiting for the right moment to present itself so that my mate could throw the hash over the partition to me. When the moment came, I told him to throw it between my chest and folded arms, but the block of hash bounced off my arm and rolled out into the middle of the counter. I looked at Miss Young, Miss Young looked at me and we both looked at the block of hash. I then calmly picked it up, placed it into my mouth and swallowed it. Without saying a word, Miss Young got up and left.

Two minutes later, she came back with four screws. The visit was terminated, and I was taken into a room and strip-searched. Obviously, they found nothing. I was then thrown into the 'chokey' – a cold empty cell with nothing but a pisspot, a mattress on the floor and an itchy Indian blanket. I was stripped to my underwear and locked up in that cell for three consecutive days and nights. On the second day, I had a shit in the cell. I flattened out the excrement with my hand until I found the block of hash, and then passed it out through the spyhole to my mates. Later that day I climbed up on to my window and looked down into the exercise yard. Through the beaming rays of sunshine that almost blinded me, I could see all my mates sitting down, relaxing and smoking the hash.

Because of the violation, I lost fourteen days' remission and twenty-eight nights' recreation. Come five thirty in the evening, when everyone was being let out of their cells to play pool, watch a video, kick a football around or play cards, I had to sit in my cell twiddling my thumbs. But then I found myself getting stuck into my writing again – anything from letters to short stories, poems and the odd short play. Every night before lock-up, the lads would ask me had I any stories for them to read. I'd get the feedback the following day – and believe me, if the lads thought my stories were crap, they'd make no bones about saying so. They were my best critics simply because they didn't lie. I very quickly became addicted to writing; it's an amazing gift to have.

I had about four months of my sentence left to serve when I was transferred over to Mountjoy's Training Unit. The Training Unit was a complete shock to me. There were no bars on the big windows. You had a hand sink in your 'room' (which was not like a cell), a wardrobe to hang your clothes up in, and no more itchy Indian blankets. I had the luxury of a quilt and a built-in radio on my wall. Compared to St Patrick's this place was the Ritz. You could take a shower as often as you liked, and there was even a laundrette. You were unlocked from your room at seven thirty every morning and not locked back up until ten that night. If you didn't want to watch TV or a video, you could play snooker, pool, tennis, squash, basketball or football. Or you could go to night school. By day you were also spoilt for choice. You could go to the workshops and learn a trade in welding or making brass and copper buckets. I did a six-month course in vision mixing, which gave me a great insight into how TV programmes are made.

In the Training Unit at Mountjoy

The food in the Training Unit was top class. The screw who was in charge of the kitchen was nicknamed 'Scratch' because he was always scratching his balls. We used to tell him what *we* wanted for lunch. The governor, Mr Carling, was nice to talk to but completely unreliable – he used to promise inmates temporary release, and then they wouldn't get it. After prisoners had been refused temporary release, having been told by the governor that they were sure to get out, they would often get very depressed.

Life in the unit was easy. Everyone wore their own clothes, and the majority of the screws were sound. Visits were not supervised: you were put into a room and you and your family were left alone. I used to get my mates to bring me up naggins of vodka. There were cells above the visiting rooms. A friend would tie a piece of string to a plastic bag and lower it down to the window of my visiting box. I would then put my bottle of spirits into the bag, and it would be hoisted back up and into the cell above me. Unsurprisingly, you could buy any type of drug you wanted in the Unit.

The governors were proud of their jail and relished showing it off to VIPs. We were given two weeks' notice of a visit from the Minister for Justice, Alan Dukes. The chiefs had every prisoner out scrubbing the walls and windows; they even had inmates down on the floors with toothbrushes, cleaning between the tiles. I had got hold of some fake human excrement, and on the day of the visit I placed it in the middle of the floor, right in front of the doors that Mr Dukes would have to walk through. I threw some toilet paper over the fake shit and poured some cold tea over it to add to the effect. Ten minutes later, the Minister for Justice and his entourage, escorted by Governor Hayes and Governor Carling, emerged through the doors and nearly tripped over the mess.

The following morning, Governor Carling called me into his office and said that if I found out who had put the fake excrement there, he would guarantee me early release. I know he said the same thing to lots of other inmates, but I was never caught.

After my release, I went straight back off the rails. I was drinking every night and running amok. I had a heavy rainproof wax jacket, and I altered the inside pocket so that it could hold a machete. The blade on the machete was too long, so I cut half of it off with an angle-grinder and then sharpened it up.

One night, I met a guy from the area whose father had recently been in a fight with my friend Bomber Walsh. I made a remark about the guy's father. In the blink of an eye he jumped and caught me in the chest with a roundhouse kick. My head bounced off the pavement.

He taunted and beckoned me, saying, 'Come on, Croghan, let's have ya now. Do you think I'm afraid of ya? Come on, get up off the ground.'

As I lay on the road, I slowly unzipped my jacket. Then I jumped up to my feet, pulled out the machete and smacked him with the blade full force across the head before he ran away.

I walked home and sat in the kitchen alone. I placed the machete between my feet and buried my head in my hands. Soon I saw blue lights flashing through the window. Then I heard a faint knock on my kitchen door – it was Starsky.

'Listen, Alan,' he said, 'I just want to talk to you. Why don't you toss that ol' machete over to me, and we can both sit down and have a little chat.'

I trusted Starsky, so I kicked the machete across the kitchen floor to him. Starsky picked it up and, without looking, tossed the blade out towards his colleagues standing in the hallway behind him. He came into the kitchen and closed the door behind him. He told me that if I didn't walk out with him, there was a small army of police officers eagerly waiting outside who would love the opportunity to come in and drag me out. I didn't want any more hassle, and my mother was upset enough as it was. I agreed to walk out, and Starsky cuffed my hands behind my back.

As I walked out to the waiting police car, I could see crowds of onlookers standing behind police tape. There must have been at least ten police cars, and they had the whole road cordoned off. You'd swear there had been a murder. I was brought to the local police station, charged with actual bodily harm and released on bail the following day. The guy I'd hit with the machete had needed something like seventeen stitches to the head.

I now had an impending criminal trial ahead of me over the ABH incident, along with a number of outstanding summary charges currently before the district courts. I formed the conclusion that I had nothing to lose – I was definitely going to prison.

One night, out on a drinking binge, I met a girl I had liked for a while, called Geraldine Kinsella. I was surprised and happy when she asked me would I walk her home.

As we walked past a group of guys, one of them, whom I'll call 'Eddie', shouted out to Geraldine, 'Go on, Kinsella, you dirty slut!'

I walked back and told the guy to apologise. He refused, so I produced the bowie knife I had stuffed down the back of my jeans. I stuck it to his neck and told him if he didn't apologise, I'd run the blade along his throat. He quickly apologised to Geraldine. I told the guy I was sorry for pulling the blade on him, but added that he shouldn't have said what he did.

A few minutes later, Geraldine and I noticed this tall fat guy walking towards us.

The guy stopped and asked, 'Are you Alan Croghan?'

I immediately placed my hand on the knife in the back of my jeans and told him I was.

He said, 'Listen, mate, I'm just putting you wide. Eddie and about fifteen of his mates are waiting down the road to lash you out of it.'

I realised that Eddie and his mates must have moved quickly to muster the drinking gang that congregated in the flats complex. They would then have cut back across, ahead of me and Geraldine. I turned to Geraldine and told her that we should double back the other way in order to avoid them. As we did, I bumped into three of my mates. I filled them in on what was going down (conveniently leaving out the part that I was carrying a blade), and my mates said that if there was any trouble, they'd back me up. I told Geraldine not to walk with us – I would meet her at the other end.

As we approached a small field, I came face-to-face with Eddie and all his mates. I ran straight for him and head-butted him in the nose. Then I pulled out the knife and began stabbing him in the stomach, side and back. The minute his mates saw the knife, each and every one of them ran – as did my own mates. I stabbed him repeatedly and indiscriminately. He finally fell to the ground in a pool of his own blood, where I left him.

I wandered around my area, trying to clear my head and figure out what the hell to do next. I knew I couldn't go back home, because the police would come looking for me. I didn't know where I was going to stay that night. I ended up going over to the home of a girl I sometimes hooked up with and told her what had happened. She told me to come back at around 1 a.m., when her parents had gone to bed, and she'd sneak me in and let me stay the night. But I'd have to leave first thing in the morning. She was a lifesaver. I went over to a local park and sat in the darkness of the field to kill time before spending the night at the girl's house.

The night after the stabbing, I met up with all my mates in a pub in the city centre. One of my mates told me they'd heard Eddie was dead. I didn't feel anything. I didn't project my thinking into the future, nor did I think about my past actions. One of my mates, sensing that I didn't care, jokingly scrawled on the bar top: 'Alan Croghan is a Murderer.'

I began sleeping at different safe houses every night in order to avoid arrest. I found out that Eddie was alive: his heart had stopped for a time, but he was revived. He had a number of stab wounds to his legs, back and face, along with a punctured lung. The police were arresting friends of mine outside the local employment exchange, raiding the homes of friends and family members and questioning them as to my whereabouts. It turned out that not only was I wanted for the stabbing of Eddie, but also for a separate assault on the same night in the city-centre pub where we'd been drinking. Some guy had had a pint glass shoved into his face, suffering very serious injuries. Detectives investigating that crime found the scrawled inscription made the next evening by my friend on the bar top. After cross-checking my name on the police computer, they found I was already a wanted man for the Eddie incident. They now believed I was the perpetrator of both crimes.

My twin sisters' flat was raided, and detectives found a suitcase full of my clothing as well as a mountain knife with a six-inch blade. That week my mugshot was featured on the monthly TV programme *Crimeline*. Viewers were advised by detectives not to approach me, because I was armed and dangerous. By this stage I was running out of places to hide.

I thought, 'What better place to stay now than my mother's home? The police would never expect me to go back there.'

But on the second night there, I was awoken by my mother in the early hours of the morning: the police were knocking at the front door. I jumped out of bed, straightened out the quilt to make the bed look as if it had not been slept in, and kicked my clothes under the bed. Dressed only in my underwear, I climbed up into the attic and stepped into the water tank. As I sat in the frigid water there was only about three inches of my face exposed at the top of the tank. (Unbeknownst to me, the policeman leading the search,

Detective Sergeant Cathal Cryan, had pulled back the quilt on my bed and placed his hand on the bed sheet, which was still warm.)

I heard the attic door opening. The beam from a torch scanned the attic and eventually fixed itself on my face.

A copper's voice said, 'Alan, come down. I can see you in the water tank.'

I was thinking to myself, 'He's bluffing, he's bluffing. He can't really see me. If I don't answer him, he'll probably just go away.'

Then the copper shouted, 'Listen, Alan, if you want us to come up to get you and wreck your mother's attic in the process, that's OK with us.'

I got up out of the water tank and climbed down from the attic. I was allowed to quickly dress before being ushered out of the house into a waiting police car.

I made a full statement to the police about my part in the stabbing of Eddie. Then I was questioned about the guy who'd got the pint glass shoved in his face outside the pub. The police were actually starting to convince me that I had done that too, and I came very, very close to making a statement admitting it.

'We know that night was sketchy for you, but we're here to help you,' they said. And: 'We know you didn't mean it.' And: 'You're going to get done for it anyway, because you already have a serious trial ahead of you for one stabbing. So any jury will convict you. At least if you admit it, mitigate your role in it, we'll put in a good word for you, and you won't get any more time.'

There were rotating pairs of detectives, each with a 'good cop' and a 'bad cop'. The continuous questioning over many hours without breaks, without even a smoke, wore me down physically and psychologically. But fortunately I did not break down and admit to a crime I had not committed.

I was charged with actual bodily harm (ABH) on Eddie, and a file was sent to the Director of Public Prosecutions. After forty-eight hours in police custody, I was brought before the courts. Although Detective Sergeant Cryan objected to bail, the judge granted it.

At the exact same time as this was going on, I was meant to be up in another court for having no tax or insurance on a car. Unbeknownst to me, I was sentenced to six months' imprisonment in my absence, so I now had a six-month committal warrant out for my arrest. I was now twenty years old – old enough for adult prison. If I was stopped by the police at any time, I would be taken straight to Mountjoy to serve out my six months. With all of this hanging over me, I went even heavier on the drink. I was also taking speed, acid and Ecstasy on a regular basis. As far as I saw it, I was going to enjoy myself before I was sent to prison on my two ABH trials.

At the time, I couldn't believe that the two guys I'd injured had made statements against me and were willing to give evidence against me in court. It was not the done thing for anyone to get the police involved in anything that happened between guys from the 'wrong side of the fence' or who were considered 'rough characters'. When I look back at it now, I see that I deserved everything I got. I had no regard for the well-being of others. I acted like an animal, and I deserved to be sent to prison. I was lucky that no one had died.

Around that time, I was corresponding with our family friend Angelo Fusco, the IRA man. He was doing ten years in Portlaoise for escaping from Crumlin Road prison and another three years consecutive for trying to escape from Portlaoise in 1985. Angelo was also facing extradition back to Northern Ireland to serve a thirty-year jail term for killing SAS Captain Herbert Westmacott.

One night, while drinking at home and rereading the letters I had received from Angelo in Portlaoise, I got it into my head that I would love to kill a police officer. I began to form visions of the newspaper headlines, how the news on TV would cover it, what the reporters would say and write about me, how other criminals would view me, how much I'd be hated by the police, how much I'd be talked about. I pictured the police and army escort I'd get to the courts. Although I fantasised about getting caught and sentenced to forty years, I also fantasised about the crime itself, and how I might get away with it. My plan was to ring the police to come to the scene of a 'disturbance' at an old folks' home. When the copper arrived, I would be waiting behind the bushes with my crossbow in hand. I would stand up and silently shoot him in the back of the head at point-blank range, and then make good my escape over a wall.

I don't know what made me develop such an insane fantasy. Did I want to be like Angelo? Did I want to go down in history as a cop killer? Did I want to be 'infamous'? In any case, I decided I needed someone to give me a hand. So I left the house to knock up for some mates and see if they fancied it.

I had walked no more than 200 yards when a police car pulled up alongside me and an officer got out. He walked over to me and asked me my name. When I told him, he grabbed hold of me and pinned me face down on the squad car. He told me he had a committal warrant for my arrest. I was handcuffed, bundled into the back of the police car and taken to the police station. Later that same night, I was transferred to Mountjoy prison to serve my six-month sentence.

They say the Lord works in mysterious ways, and I believe that to be true. Would I have actually carried out my fantasy if I had not been arrested when I was?

6

The Big Boys' Jail

The following morning, as I snuggled under the covers of my warm bed, I was thinking about having a nice big fry-up, then knocking up for my mates, heading into the city centre, hitting the pubs and then maybe chatting up some bird and shagging her. When I opened my eyes, I was expecting to see the familiar surroundings of my bedroom, and perhaps my mother bringing me up a cup of coffee. But as I registered the eggshell-coloured walls, the dingy cold steel bed, the Indian blankets and the steel door with the spyhole, the reality hit me.

This was my first time in Mountjoy prison, and I didn't know what to expect. When my cell door opened for me to slop out, I was told that the doctor and the governor wanted to see me after breakfast. I stepped out of the cell with my green chamber pot full of urine, and walked down to the toilets. There were half a dozen guys, stripped to the waist, washing themselves over stainless-steel sinks. As I slopped out, I was consumed with regret: *Alan, you stupid, stupid bastard*.

After breakfast, I queued up to see Dr Teeling. When my turn came, I told him I was addicted to Valium and asked him to prescribe me some in order to wean me off them. The doctor told me that he would do no such thing. He just checked my breathing and then abruptly told me to get out of his surgery. I stood my ground and informed the doctor that if anything happened to me in relation to my health, he would be held fully responsible. He didn't like that very much, and barked instructions that I was to be placed in the 'green room'. Three medical officers grabbed hold of me and dragged me away, kicking and screaming.

I was made to strip down to my underwear and brought through two sets of steel doors to a cell whose interior was covered in green padding. There was no window, no bed, just a light fixture built into the twelve-foot-high ceiling and a toilet built into the floor. There was no toilet paper.

Later that afternoon, I was brought out to the visiting area. My mother had come to see me. I told her what had happened between myself and Dr Teeling, and how I'd been sent to the padded cell. She told me that she would contact the prison chaplain, Fr Mick Cullen, who I knew well from St Patrick's. After my mother's visit, I was brought back to the padded cell, where I became badly distressed from Valium and alcohol withdrawal.

The following day, I was brought to see Dr Teeling. He told me that I was being prescribed 10 mg of Valium three times a day for one week. That would be reduced to 5 mg three times a day for the second week, and eventually I'd be weaned off the drug completely. I was then told by one of the medical officers to get back up on to my landing: I would not be returning to the padded cell. It turned out that my mother had managed to contact Fr Mick, and this explained the change in approach. My medical file from St Patrick's was then checked, and the psychiatrist, Dr McCormack, confirmed that I had been on Valium while an inmate there.

In the Circuit Court I was sentenced to twelve months for the machete attack, and I got fifteen months for the stabbing of Eddie. In both instances the judge was made aware that the injured party had been the instigator of the violence, although that didn't excuse my actions. To my surprise, each sentence was backdated to the time of my arrest on foot of the six-month committal warrant. I had been expecting, if not consecutive jail terms, at the very least a heavy custodial sentence.

One of the inmates on landing C3 in Mountjoy was a middle-aged man by the name of Mick Boyle, who was doing fourteen years for kidnapping. Mick had his own typewriter, and he let me use it to type up things I had written. He wouldn't let me take the typewriter into my cell, so I had to go to Mick's cell each day to type up my work. We spent lots of time just chatting to each other. Mick was an ex-IRA man and a very learned criminal, and he taught me the best ways to pull off a kidnapping. Other inmates were surprised that Mick talked to me – he usually kept himself to himself – and were curious as to what he was saying.

I didn't understand until some years later why the officers and some inmates were so interested. It turned out that Mick had been George 'The Penguin' Mitchell's right-hand man. (Upon Mick's release from Mountjoy, he was contracted by the Penguin and sent over to London to assassinate an infamous East End gangster by the name of Tony Brindle. Unbeknownst to Mick, he was under surveillance by Scotland Yard's Serious Crime Squad SO19, and just as he ambushed Brindle and shot him, Mick himself was ambushed and shot five times by the police. Mick is now serving a life sentence in the UK.) I knew Mick was a hard nut and a professional kidnapper, but never in my wildest dreams did I think he was a contract killer.

In Mountjoy, for the first time ever, I felt myself attracted to a guy – another inmate on C3, who I'll call 'Tony'. I felt it was wrong to be feeling or thinking that way – it was dirty. And there was a big fear factor around it. But every time I saw or spoke to Tony, I would get a tingling sensation in my stomach. I didn't even think about trying to get it on with Tony, as 'queers' are a big no-no in prison. If I made a move and Tony reacted negatively and told everyone that I 'dropped the hand' on him, I knew I would have been kicked to bits and probably had my throat cut. I just had to settle for hanging around with him and being able to see him every day. But I thought constantly about what it would be like to be with him. I knew that was a little part of my life that I had to keep secret at all costs.

Myself, Tony and Larry Reilly – who I knew from St Patrick's – had our landing sorted. We recruited an English guy called Paul Kane into our circle. 'Kaner', who was English, had come over to Ireland to try to get a job, but he was caught shoplifting and sentenced to twelve months. Kaner had no family or friends in Ireland and had to survive solely on his prison gratuity of seven quid a week. Realising that he was weak, myself, Larry and Tony began to use him to our advantage. He became a valuable tool in making our life that little bit easier in prison. We forced him to make our beds, wash our pisspots and scrub our floors.

To scrub the floors you needed a deck brush, a bucket of hot soapy water, another bucket of clean hot water and two cloths. You had to remove everything from the cell and get down on all fours and hand-scrub the wooden floor. We used to sit on the landing railing and watch Kaner scrub our cell floors – our very own personal English slave. We saw it as an act of revenge against the English for invading Ireland 800 years ago. We also formed the conclusion that if we were banged up in an English jail, we'd be treated exactly the same way.

If any of us was expecting a visit, Kaner would have to wash our shirts with a small nail brush, and we always insisted that he particularly focused on the collars and armpits of the shirts. On shop order days we would tell him what to order. Poor Kaner would try to tell us he had no money and no visits, but that didn't matter to us. We'd make him buy biscuits, shaving foam and deodorant, and then we'd confiscate it all from him.

Kaner was a harmless bloke, but making him do things that he detested doing gave me a great feeling. It suited me to treat him the way I did. It made me look like a 'header' – a bloke who didn't give a bollox, who was up for a laugh, who was sound. Although I wasn't aware of it at the time, all I was doing was hiding behind a mask in an effort not to show the real me. It is only now that I can see it was pure madness and cruelty.

I was also manipulative in my dealings with the screws. Inmates were allowed only one shop order a week, and each wing was allocated a particular day for their orders. On one occasion, I ran out of tobacco two days before my shop order day. I walked down to the Circle, where the most feared and respected prison officer, Vincent Duffy, always stood. Duffy was a two-bar chief officer, but he had more power and influence than any of the three-bar chiefs, assistant governors and deputy governors. Only the governor himself, John Lonergan, was more powerful. Chief Duffy always stood in the middle of the Circle, resting his hands on the walkie-talkie strapped to his chest, rocking back and forth on his feet and giving off a powerful vibe that he was not to be disturbed.

Knowing it wasn't my shop order day, I decided to see if I could get some tobacco from the prison tuck shop. I walked across the Circle into the shop, but the ACO who was minding the shop ran me out. I walked back over to the Circle gate, and told my mates that I was going to go over the ACO's head and ask Chief Duffy. My mates strongly advised me against it, but this only made me more determined.

Nervous about approaching him for my very first time, I asked the chief could I see him for a moment.

To my surprise, he simply replied, 'What can I do for you, Alan?'

I was amazed he knew my name. My confidence grew. I explained I had no tobacco and I wasn't due to get my shop order for another two days. But was there any chance I could get some today? Mr Duffy called out to a female prison officer by the name of Ms Tierney. I liked Ms Tierney, who was attractive and a lovely person to talk to. Mr Duffy instructed Ms Tierney to accompany me into the tuck shop and allow me to get what I wanted.

When Ms Tierney told the ACO that I was to get a shop order, the ACO bluntly replied, 'No, he's getting nothing!'

Ms Tierney's face went bright red with embarrassment, and she stormed out of the tuck shop. She went straight over to Chief Duffy, and I could see that she was telling him everything that had happened. Chief Duffy then walked towards the shop, very slowly and coolly. As he stepped into the shop, he took off his cap. The ACO immediately fixed his clip-on tie to his shirt collar.

Chief Duffy shouted loud enough for everyone to hear. 'I'm telling you to give that young man a shop order and to do it now – *right now!* Do you understand me? This is a direct order from me to you.'

Five minutes later, I walked out of the shop with a crisp box full of goodies. My mates were gobsmacked.

I winked at them and said, 'Alan – one, ACO – nil.'

From that point on, Chief Duffy was an ally. I could approach him any time, and he never dismissed me.

I enjoyed attending school in Mountjoy, and my writing was getting better and better. I entered a public-speaking competition in the Training Unit and worked very hard on a speech arguing that nurses were underpaid – something I felt strongly about. I would not be up against other inmates, but against students from UCD, Trinity College and DCU.

I'll never forget the evening I was brought over to the Training Unit for the competition. I met the RTÉ newsreader Anne Doyle, who was one of the four judges, and found her to be a very caring and decent person to talk to. When you're an inmate in Mountjoy, you don't expect well-known people to treat you as an equal, but Anne Doyle did. I got up and delivered my speech, and then all the students got up and gave theirs. I wasn't too bothered if I won or lost – the fact that I was taking part meant more to me than any-thing else. I was there for the adrenalin boost. And, of course, it also made me look good in front of the governors, and might increase my chances of getting out of prison early on temporary release.

When Anne Doyle stood up and announced me as the winner, I was amazed. She presented me with a silver cup, and I was handed the microphone for my acceptance speech. I thanked the prison, the Department of Justice and the school. I also thanked the people from the outside for taking the time to come in.

I then turned and said, 'And as a token of my appreciation to Ms Anne Doyle for coming in here tonight, I would like to present her with this silver cup.'

For all my model behaviour – getting on well with other inmates and staff, winning the public-speaking prize – I got just twenty days off my sentence.

Upon my release, I made it my business to meet up with my friend Tony, from C3, and we went out clubbing together. I still fancied him. Even as I write this now, I feel my stomach churning with embarrassment and shame. But another part of me is saying, 'Don't be embarrassed, don't feel shame, he was an attractive bloke.'

That night, I had a free house and I asked him did he want to come back and stay over. I was delighted when he said yes, but my head was melted because I didn't how I was going to make a pass at him, and I didn't know what his reaction would be. What if he was not that way inclined, left my house and broadcast my sexuality to everyone? My standing in the community would be badly affected.

I wouldn't have had the courage to take the risk if I'd been sober. But I was not sober.

We were watching a video. I recall sitting at one end of the sofa, and he was sitting at the other end. There was a horribly uncomfortable silence between us, so I got up and grabbed a few beers from the fridge. When I sat back down, I sat right next to Tony; my right leg was against his left leg. I began to slowly move my right hand towards his left leg, and began to rub my little finger against his thigh. There was no reaction from Tony. Then I tried two fingers (no reaction) then three fingers (still no reaction). By this stage he had to know what I was doing, so I put my whole hand on his leg. To my delight, Tony looked at me then, and we kissed each other fully on the mouth.

I'd never felt so excited in my life. I also felt a real sense of relief. We didn't have intercourse with each other, just oral, which is what I enjoyed. Tony later told me that when we were in Mountjoy together, he often felt like making a pass at me. I couldn't believe it – we were both on the same page when in prison, but neither of us knew it. It wasn't long before Tony went his way and I went mine, but it was good for the very short time it lasted.

It wasn't long before I was back up to my old criminal tricks. On my way home one night, I spotted a drunken figure leaving my driveway. When I walked into my house, my sister Frieda told me that Eddie's elder brother had waved a knife under her chin and said, 'Tell your brother Alan that when I get him, he's going to get this through the neck.'

I ran upstairs to my bedroom, took out my knife and balaclava from under the bed, hurried out of the house and sprinted up the road in the direction that Eddie's brother had just gone in. As I reached a basketball court, I could see him walking ahead of me. I pulled down my balaclava, ran stealthily up behind him and tipped him on the shoulder. Then, as he turned around, I gave him a full-force smack of my head, busting his nose wide open. He went down. In a mad frenzied attack I began sticking the knife into any available part of his body, then spat on him and walked away.

As I walked across a small patch of green grass, I could feel that my right runner was soaking wet. I realised I'd been stabbed. I was trying to make it to the opposite side of the road when I met a mate of my brother Glen. I rolled the knife up in the balaclava and gave it to my brother's friend, telling him to get rid of the evidence. All I remember after that is lying on the ground, and two ambulance men trying to put a breathing apparatus over my mouth. Each time they tried to put it on my mouth, I pushed it off – I felt suffocated by it.

I awoke five days later in the intensive care unit of the James Connolly Memorial Hospital. I had been on a life-support machine, having lost seven and a half pints of blood. Upon my arrival in the hospital, my blood pressure was 70/40 and all my urine and excrement had involuntarily left my body. It turned out that I had sustained a stab wound just below my right knee, and the main artery in my leg was completely severed. For some reason the police saw fit to inform my mother and family that I was 'not going to make it'. In the end, I was kept in hospital for nine weeks

The police wanted me to make a statement against Eddie's brother. Only one knife was found at the scene, with his fingerprints all over it. I declined to make a statement.

After I got out of hospital, I settled back to enjoy one of the few Christmases that I spent out of prison during those years. I loved to see the excitement on the faces of my nieces and nephews, and I sat down with the whole family for the big dinner.

I was with my family and having fun. Christmas was in the here and now, I'd a few quid in my pocket and plenty of alcohol. It was time to party, party, party.

Or so I thought.

7

Protection

For as long as I live, I will never forget the night of 29 December 1989. My life took a very dark turn that night.

Myself and a former friend of mine, who I'll call 'Mr X', were drinking cans of beer in my bedroom. It was about 8 p.m. when my mother came into my bedroom and told me that Mr X's sister, who I'll call 'Miss X', was at the front door with a friend, looking for us. I went down and brought them up to my bedroom. They had their own cans of beer, and the four of us sat there drinking, listening to music and chatting. Miss X was a lovely-looking girl and we got on really well with each other. Mr X asked me would I mind if he went into the adjoining bedroom with his sister's friend. I was OK with that, and off they went.

Miss X and I began kissing and caressing each other. Eventually, we tried to have intercourse. But each time I tried to ease the head of my penis inside her, it became too sore for her. She suggested trying different positions, to see if it would make it any easier for us, but it didn't. We then carried on with sexual foreplay and had a few more cans of beer. After the other two were finished, they came back into my bedroom. Miss X and her friend left the house a short time later; they were heading off to a club.

Four days later, unbeknownst to me, Miss X went to the local police station and claimed that I had raped her. Three days after that, on 5 January 1990, Detective Sergeant Cathal Cryan and a team of police officers raided my home. I hadn't the foggiest idea what the police wanted me for, and when the detective sergeant informed me that I was being arrested for the rape of Miss X, I nearly collapsed on my bedroom floor. As I was handcuffed and led out of the house, my head was in a spin. After arriving at the police station, I told the police exactly what had happened between us that night.

Despite hearing my account, Detective Sergeant Cryan decided to charge me there and then, rather than prepare a file and send it off to the Director of Public Prosecutions. Deciding to make a gangster movie out of it, Cryan had me taken to court under police escort that day.

In court I was remanded into custody for one week with no bail. I was brought down to the holding cells underneath the courthouse and placed into a cell on my own. In the cell next to me were about twenty other prisoners, most of whom I knew. The only thing separating me from them was a wire-mesh fence. All the guys were asking me what I was in custody for, and how come I was segregated. I was completely devastated. I felt alone, deserted, hated, dirty, confused, numb and sick.

Out of embarrassment and fear I found myself lying to my friends, telling them that I had been nicked for robbing a car. I knew they would have turned against me if I'd told them what I was really in for – even if I also told them I hadn't done it. But in reality I made the situation much, much worse for myself by lying. Once the lads found out what I was really in custody for, they would naturally believe that I was guilty – because I had lied to them.

I was placed in the tiny cold steel cubicle of the meat wagon, separated from the other prisoners. They all had a look at me through the spyhole of the cubicle door. Then I could hear them mumbling.

'He's not in for a fuckin' robbed car.'

'There's somethin' he's not tellin' us.'

Then I began to really panic.

As we made our way towards Mountjoy, I overheard another prisoner shout, 'Hey, lads! We have a rapist on board.'

The guy had been sitting in the court, waiting for his own sentencing, when my case was called and the charge was read out. The prisoners began firing abuse at me from behind their doors.

'When we get you in the Joy, Croghan, we're going to cut you up!'

'You're nothing but a scumbag – you rapist bastard!'

I couldn't reply; I just sat down and silently cried my heart out. As the truck rocked its way through the streets of Dublin, I was cold, alone and full of fear.

Upon arrival at Mountjoy, I was taken out before the others and brought down to reception to give my details. I noticed that even the screws looked upon me with distaste. Some of the prison officers I'd had a good relationship with on my previous jail terms now had no time for me whatsoever. They spoke to me as if I was a piece of dirt. And, as a result, that's what I felt like.

I was escorted up on to C2 landing – the 'Protection Wing'. There I was to spend twenty-three hours a day, seven days a week banged up in my cell. Every night other inmates would be up on their windows, hurling abuse at me and calling me the most despicable names you could think of. During the day I would have prisoners banging at my cell door, issuing all sorts of threats.

Thankfully, I still had good friends in the Joy who knew I wasn't a rapist, and they stood by me. Those guys know who they are, and I will always be grateful for their support and friendship. They encouraged me to come off protection. They said I would be showing the others that I was not afraid of them, and that I was innocent. But I was feeling so vulnerable that I began to think that maybe it was some sort of plot – my supposed friends wanted to get me off protection so they could all get to me. I told the lads that the governor, for legal reasons, could not allow me to come off protection. (In fact, I had never asked the governor about it.) Although I detested my circumstances, I knew that – at least, twenty-three hours a day – I was safe.

The following week, when I went back up to court, the case was remanded for six weeks for the preparation of a book of evidence. Detective Sergeant Cryan again objected to bail, claiming that I was a 'flight risk'. He also said he suspected that I might, if released, interfere with his witness, Miss X. I was again remanded in custody with no bail. Miss X was the only witness he had – even her brother did not want anything to do with the case, and he declined to make a statement to the police. I was later to hear that he was going around telling people that he knew I did not rape his sister.

Back in Mountjoy, there was tension between inmates who

believed I was innocent and those who thought I was a rapist. As a result of this, I was taken from my cell in Mountjoy without any notice and transferred to Dublin's sex-crimes colony: Arbour Hill. My family were not even made aware that I was being moved.

The atmosphere at Arbour Hill was like nothing I had ever experienced. It smelled different, felt different, looked different; I could feel that this place had pure evil within its walls. I was afraid. People who had committed the vilest of crimes were walking around laughing, joking and playing football together – as if they didn't have a care in the world.

I remember the notorious sex offender dubbed the 'Northside Rapist' coming over to me with a group of other sex offenders and asking what was I in for. When I told him that I'd been falsely accused of rape, they all just looked at each other, laughed and said, 'Yeah, like the rest of us,' and then walked off.

After only a few hours in the place, I just wanted to be dead. That night in my cell, I can clearly remember listening to Elton John's latest release on the radio – 'Sacrifice' – and feeling that I had reached the very lowest ebb in my life. I thought about ways I might take my own life. Then I began thinking about my mother, my family and the effect my suicide would have had on them, and I cried uncontrollably. That night I turned to God, and I prayed to Him and Mother Mary, begging them to help me make my life normal again.

After spending six weeks in Arbour Hill, I was brought back before the courts. Detective Sergeant Cryan asked for more time to prepare the book of evidence, and the judge put the case back for another two weeks. Despite Cryan's strong objections, the judge granted surety bail of £2,000 cash. The judge may as well have put a million pounds on me, because no one in my family had that kind of money to put up.

I had been ten weeks in custody when, on a visit, my mother told me that she had got £2,000 cash from my brother's friend P. J. Loughran. I told her to lodge the money at the main prison gate to get me the hell out. I did get out of Arbour Hill that day, but they held me in reception for about four hours, just to mess with my head. I'll always be grateful to P.J. for putting up the bail money. He was a member of Martin 'The General' Cahill's gang; he used to sit me in his Ford Escort XR3i and advise me what criminals I should steer clear of. He believed in my innocence.

The case went on and on. Week after week, I went up to the District Court. And week after week, Detective Sergeant Cryan continued to ask for more time to produce the book of evidence. By this point he must have known full well there was never going to be one. My solicitor could have got the case struck out because of the delays, but he didn't want that: he wanted the State to admit that I had been charged in haste and then to withdraw the charge. Meanwhile, I was the one who was left to suffer with a rape charge hanging over my head, enduring the sleepless nights and the stigma surrounding the charge.

I frequented nightclubs on my own, knowing full well that there would be people in these establishments who believed I was guilty, that I was nothing but a filthy rapist. I wanted to show them that I didn't care what they thought, and I was not afraid of them. In reality I was riddled with fear, and I always made sure I carried my blade with me.

During this period, P. J. Loughran was shot outside a bank in Athy, Co. Kildare. The Garda Emergency Response Unit had been following P.J. and his gang for a number of months. So when they went to rob the bank in Athy, the ERU were waiting. However, the ERU made a balls of it. They formed a semicircle outside the bank, and when Austin Higgins – a member of P.J.'s gang – came out, they opened fire. They killed Austin, but they also shot the bank manager, another bank employee and some of their own guys. In total, seven people were shot that day, including P.J. The ERU said they believed that the raiders opened fire first. But as it turned out, not one raider fired a single shot.

I decided the best way to lose the stigma of the false rape charge was to go out and do an armed robbery. I got together with a mate of mine, Frank Sinclair, and armed myself with an imitation 9mm Bruni automatic handgun. We decided to rob a large Bank of Ireland branch on College Green in Dublin city centre (not the one housed in the former Irish House of Lords, but a branch that's not there any more), with entrances on College Green and Suffolk Street. I was far from a professional bank robber – it was more a case of pick a bank and rob it.

It was a Friday afternoon when we ran into the bank with balaclavas on our heads. There must have been about eighty customers in the branch at the time. One picture sticks in my mind from that moment: an old lady with grey hair and the fear of God written all over her face. I looked directly into her eyes as she got down on her hunkers, clinging to a radiator, and I could see her fear.

For a split second I thought, 'That could be my mother.' But as soon as the thought came into my head, it left. I went about my business of robbing the bank.

We vaulted the counter, ordered everyone to stay on the floor, and we grabbed bundles of cash from the drawers. As I glanced around and saw all the bodies lying flat on the floor, I felt a surge of confidence. I was the cause of all this, and that made me feel powerful.

I stuffed cash down the neck of my jumper, which was tucked into my waistband. When I felt we had enough cash, I called on Frank to make a move. We didn't head out of the front doors that led on to College Green. Instead, we took the back way that led out on to Suffolk Street. As we ran out through the big glass swivel doors, I could see armed police – guns drawn, flak jackets on – hiding behind their car doors for cover. They had Suffolk Street completely sealed off. We sprinted down a side street, and I threw my balaclava and windbreaker into a street bin. We then came out on to Dame Street. I veered left and bolted along the pavement, ducking and diving between the crowds, and sprinted across Dame Street into Anglesea Street.

As for my mate Frank, he split the other way and was throwing his money up in the air. He was hoping the crowds would start grabbing it, to create a diversion – he was seriously watching too much television! Most of the cops followed him, but one cop stuck with me.

As I sprinted down Anglesea Street, I could hear him shouting, 'Armed police! Stop, or I'll fucking shoot you!'

I didn't need a second warning. I stopped, knelt down and raised my hands.

I was pushed to the ground. The detective jammed his boot against the nape of my neck and began screaming over his radio.

'Assistance! *Assistance!* I need assistance, I've an armed raider here!'

With a gun stuck to the back of my head, I was dragged into the foyer of Bloom's Hotel and handcuffed to a radiator. I heard police sirens and cars screeching to a halt outside the hotel. It was like something you'd see in the movies. With my hands handcuffed behind my back, two detectives ran with me out of the hotel, continued running across the street and bounced my face full force into the back door of a police van. I was then thrown into the back, where I was greeted by four or five big brawny coppers. On the way back to the police station, the coppers danced all over me with their size-12 feet.

Upon arrival at Pearse Street Garda station, I was dragged from the van and frogmarched into a cell. I thought to myself, 'Now people will see me in a different light.' I wasn't thinking of the armed robbery charge or the jail time I would receive for it. I was more concerned about losing the stigma arising from the false rape charge. That was all that mattered.

As I sat in the cell, I realised I still had all the cash – I'd been rubbed down and my pockets emptied, but they never searched the front of my jumper. I tried to think of ways to hide the money. But then my cell door opened, and two detectives from the serious crime squad were standing there.

The detective who had arrested me, said, 'Let's go, Croghan. Time for your fifteen minutes.'

I was taken into an interrogation room and questioned about my part in the robbery. I knew if the police found out that I was already out on bail on the rape charge, I'd never get out. I'd be locked up for twenty-three hours a day in Mountjoy – or, worse still, sent back up to that hellhole, Arbour Hill.

I made a full statement to the police about my part in the bank robbery, but I also came up with a yarn I thought might get me out on bail. I told the detective that P. J. Loughran (who was under armed guard in Beaumont Hospital with a neck wound from the foiled bank robbery in Athy) was a personal friend of mine and that I would be able to get important information on Martin Cahill's activities.

The detective told me that if I could do that for him, he'd get me off on the armed robbery charge. Not only that, but if I was ever charged in future I could get the arresting officer to contact him. I took it that he was offering me a licence to rob in this town.

The detective went on to tell me that he would be up in the hospital that coming Monday night. That was when I should go up to visit P.J. in his sickbed. I jumped at the chance to get bail, and I was also pleased at the opportunity to thank P.J. for bailing me out of Arbour Hill.

As I was being brought back down to my cell by two detectives I didn't know, one of them warned me that no matter how much information I came up with for Greg Sheehan, I was going to go down for the armed robbery – he'd make sure of it. Just before I walked into the cell, the copper spun me around against the wall and poked me in the stomach with his finger. The two coppers looked at each other, and then they looked at me. My jumper was pulled out of my jeans and the cash fell out on to the floor – £7,980, as I later found out. The police were highly embarrassed – I could have had a gun up my jumper.

When Greg Sheehan learned of what had happened, he wasn't impressed with my little stunt. But I told him I still wanted to play ball with him. He had to laugh at my effrontery in trying to keep the money. And he still believed I'd come up trumps for him in the intelligence-gathering department.

Later that night, I was charged with the robbery of the Bank of Ireland and possession of an imitation firearm. I was then brought before a special sitting of the District Court. Detective Sheehan had no objection to a low-surety bail being put on me. The judge put me on a bond of £100 of my own bail with an independent surety of £250. My mother stood up and posted the bail for me – I was out. As I made my way home, news of the armed robbery was all over the radio.

The following day, a Saturday, the robbery made the papers, and I was named. On the Monday I went to visit P.J. in Beaumont. I made sure I brought along a mate, who I'll call 'Lar'. I brought Lar up with me for two reasons. Firstly, I wanted people to know that I was friendly with P.J. This might make them think twice about hurting me. Secondly, I wanted a witness to everything that was said between myself and P.J. If anyone ever thought that I was sniffing for Sheehan, Lar could set the record straight.

As arranged, Sheehan and two other armed detectives were there to greet me when I arrived at the door of P.J.'s private room. Sheehan didn't say a word to me; he just gave a slight nod as Lar and I walked past and into the room. I thanked P.J. for giving my brother the two grand to get me out of Arbour Hill, and we talked about the raid in which he'd been shot. I didn't try to get any information from P.J. about the General. Even if I had tried, P.J. would never have been foolish enough to tell me anything that would be of interest to the police.

About an hour after I left the hospital, Detective Sheehan rang me to arrange a meeting. I told him there was no point in us meeting up, as P.J. hadn't said a word about Cahill – or anything else, for that matter. I said that I felt very uncomfortable at the thought of giving him information, and I further told him in no uncertain terms what he could do with his 'licence to rob in this town'.

Sheehan wasn't happy. 'I'll have my day in court,' he said.

The phone went dead, and I felt relieved that my dealings with Detective Sheehan were over.

On 12 May 1990, after four months and one week, the State finally stood up in the District Court and withdrew the rape charge against me. Although I knew I would be going to prison on the armed robbery charge, my main concern was that the false rape charge was now history. People began to look upon me in a different light.

I wrote a detailed letter to the Chief State Solicitor, Mr Louis J. Dockery, requesting answers as to why Miss X was not being prosecuted for making false allegations against me. The Chief State Solicitor wrote back, telling me that the matters raised by me were more appropriate to the Director of Public Prosecutions, and I should write to him. I then wrote another very detailed letter to the DPP and, after nearly three months, I received a letter from a Mr Domhnall Murray. He stated that if I had evidence that some person had committed an offence, I should place that evidence in front of the police to enable them to investigate it.

I then wrote to the Police Commissioner, Mr Patrick Culligan, saying that fifteen months prior to Miss X making the false rape allegation against me, she had made an allegation of attempted rape and sexual assault against four youths. One of the individuals was later charged with sexual assault against Miss X, but the State subsequently withdrew the charge. I felt Miss X had to be made to realise that she couldn't just go around making dangerous allegations against people.

Four months later, I received a letter from the Police Commissioner. The letter stated that my case had been fully investigated and a file submitted to the DPP, who had not directed any criminal proceedings against Miss X. I didn't want my whole life taken up with the Miss X saga, so I decided to try to move on from it.

I made my Circuit Court appearance on the armed robbery charge and was sentenced to three and a half years. (My co-accused, Frank Sinclair, never turned up for his trial and absconded to the UK.) Because everyone in Mountjoy was aware that I'd been charged with rape, I was again put on the protection wing. I was first put into a double cell with a drug addict who was a suspected police informer. I used to hold the guy's tourniquet for him when he was banging up his heroin or cocaine. Every night, the guy would offer me a turn-on, and I considered it – I could have done with something to take my mind off how I actually felt. I knew if I stayed in that cell, it would be only a matter of time before I took that shit, and so I asked the governor if I could be transferred to a single cell. I was told I would have to wait a few days until one became available. Three days later, I got a single cell – and I thanked God that I'd had the sense to stay off heroin.

Most of the lads in the Joy were advising me to get off protection because I no longer had the rape charge. I saw the logic of this, but

I was still afraid I'd be attacked. My head was messed up, and I didn't know how to make a decision. But eventually, I informed the governor that I wanted to come off protection. The governor was not happy about this. He stressed that although many of the prisoners knew I was not a rapist, there would be some who would think otherwise and might try to get me.

Before I came off protection, I melted down the head of a toothbrush, then I broke up a few disposable razor blades and embedded them into the heated plastic. The plastic hardened and I had myself a makeshift knife. But my nerves were shattered, and my insides were in bits. I had to sign a disclaimer that I was coming off protection at my own risk. The reality hit home that no matter what happened to me, the prison was not responsible. The only person who had anything to lose was myself. When I came off the protection wing, I was literally shaking like a leaf.

Then, on my second day off protection, I got a tip-off from a friend of mine that a number of inmates from A-Wing were going to cut me up. That was enough for me; I approached Chief Duffy and requested to be put back on to protection. An hour after going back on to protection, I was told to pack my kit.

I was being transferred to Wheatfield Prison, in Clondalkin.

Wheatfield was a complete culture shock. The place was spotless. You had your own radio built into the wall, a hand sink with a mirror, and a proper toilet that you could actually sit on. You also had a built-in wardrobe, a long table that was fixed to the wall for eating and writing, and, joy of joys, quilts instead of Indian blankets. Wheatfield had a ground floor and a first floor, called G and F respectively. Each floor had ten landings, with twenty cells per landing. I was put on to G5. There were four protection landings up on F, and I was delighted that I wasn't put up there. I knew most of the lads in the prison, and I settled in very quickly.

My main difficulty in Wheatfield was my relationship with the three-bar chief officer, Dan Fanning. He was about six foot four and well built, with hands like shovels and forearms like tree trunks. He also had a massive head and was completely bald, and he had a bad turn in his right eye. I never did anything to annoy Mr Fanning, so I couldn't understand why he disliked me so much. I used to make drawings in my cell and then put them up on my wall – naked women, or portraits of Mikhail Gorbachev, the Krays, Saddam Hussein and armed IRA men wearing balaclavas.

One day, when I walked into my cell, I found all my drawings had been torn down from my wall and ripped to shreds. I asked my class officer what had happened, and I was told that Mr Fanning had done it. When I asked Mr Fanning why he'd done it, he told me that I was not allowed to put provocative, criminal or political pictures up on my wall.

I began to keep a diary. If I had an argument with Chief Fanning, I would write down exactly how I felt about Mr Fanning and the situation. It was a way of venting my anger; it worked as a release valve. If I had a bad visit, I would write down how I felt about the family member I'd had the argument with. Ditto if I had a run-in with an inmate. No one was exempt, and in my diary I was totally honest. But if an officer or the governor did something good for me, I would write about that, too.

In Wheatfield Prison

One day, I walked into my cell after coming in from the exercise yard and noticed that my diary was gone. I asked my class officer about it, and was told that Mr Fanning had confiscated it.

I thought to myself, 'When he reads what's in that diary, I'll be fucked!'

I was put on a P-19 disciplinary report – apparently, inmates were not allowed to keep a diary. I was brought before Chief Fanning and Governor McPherson. I told the governor that I kept the diary as a way of venting my emotions and anger. I told him that was the way I could release my tension, and I felt I wasn't hurting anybody. I said that although I was critical of Mr Fanning in the diary, I was also critical of my family and fellow inmates. I added that I also praised officers. Mr McPherson told me that he would take the diary home to read and would give me his decision on whether I could have it back or not in a few days' time.

Three days later, Mr McPherson called me into his office. We were alone. He told me that he and his wife had sat up in bed for most of the night, reading my diary from start to finish, and they had never got so much amusement from anything they'd ever read. However, he told me that he could not give the diary back because of my comments about Mr Fanning. He said he'd put the diary in my locker with my other personal belongings, and I'd get it back when I was released.

With Christmas approaching, but for no good reason, my mate Larry and I decided that we would try to escape from Wheatfield prison. We came to the hare-brained conclusion that if we both slashed our wrists, we'd be rushed to hospital. Then we could over-power the screws and make good our escape. That night, as I stood by my mirror with my makeshift blade, I could hear Larry from his own cell.

'We do it on the count of three, Alan.'

Larry counted to three, and I made a half-hearted attempt to cut my wrists. Meanwhile, Larry went for glory and opened his arms fairly deeply with the blade. We pressed the call bell in our cells, and we were rushed up to the medic's office. My wounds were only minor lacerations; after a quick rub of an antiseptic wipe, my arms were bandaged up and I was returned to my cell. As for Larry, he was rushed to hospital and did receive stitches. Of course, he did not try to overpower the screws and escape.

The following morning, which was Christmas Eve, the two gym officers that I worked for, Mr Foley and Mr Hand, gave me the height of abuse for cutting myself up. They couldn't understand why I would do such a thing. On Christmas Day, as I sat in my cell, thinking about my family and generally feeling homesick and sorry for myself, my cell door opened. Two prison officers ran in half drunk. One of them pulled out a bottle of whiskey from under his jumper and filled my mug. They smiled at me and wished me a Happy Christmas. That really cheered me up.

Fr Willie Maher, who I knew from St Patrick's Institution, was now the chaplain at Wheatfield, and so, as I had done at St Patrick's and Mountjoy, I did the church readings. The church at Wheatfield was massive. At one end was the altar, and at the opposite end was a stage with fantastic backstage facilities.

One Sunday, as the chiefs and governors sat down at the back of the church, looking up at me doing my reading, I lost my train of thought and said aloud, 'Ah, fuck.' I quickly realised what I had said, where I was and who was watching me. The inmates all broke out into loud laughter. I looked at Fr Willie, whose face was bright red with embarrassment. I tried to apologise over the microphone, but that just made things worse. Eventually, I pulled myself together and carried on. After mass, I met Governor McPherson outside the church, and he said it was the most amusing mass he'd ever attended.

Around this time, the Education Unit and the governor announced they were putting on a play in the prison: *Brownbread* by Roddy Doyle. It was a terrific play and, as usual, I was keen to get in the limelight. I was cast in the lead role, as a character called 'Ao', and I was totally geared up for it. The plan was to rehearse the play every day for six weeks, and then it would run for four nights. Before we began rehearsals, we had a full briefing. We were informed that on the opening night of the show, two members of our families would be allowed to attend. The Minister for Justice and other ministerial heads would be there as well.

I worked very hard at learning my lines, and I was off my script in the space of two weeks. Janice Jarvis, who was brought in from the outside to direct the play, told me that in all her years working as a director, she had never seen anyone learn his lines as quickly as me.

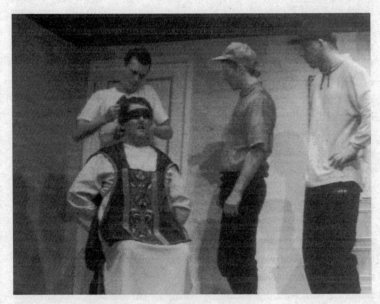

Blindfolding a priest in the Wheatfield production of Roddy Doyle's *Brownbread*

I loved acting – it gave me a real adrenalin boost. I thrived on the anxiety that went with going out on stage and performing in front of a packed auditorium. Prisoners are the toughest critics: if they think you're crap, by God they'll let you know about it then and there.

Although the only thing on my mind on opening night ought to have been the play, myself and my mate Larry (who was playing a character called 'Donkey') had arranged for our mothers to smuggle us in a bottle of Southern Comfort each for the after-show party.

All I could think about backstage was, 'God, I hope they get the Southern Comfort in!'

I was quickly snapped out of my daydream by the stage manager shouting at me to get on stage. I was the first person to enter and, despite all my previous arrests, interrogations and robberies, I was never so nervous as walking out on to that stage that night. But after a slight hesitation, I kicked into overdrive – and I loved it.

The play went off without a hitch, and we got a standing ovation. After the cast had washed and changed, we were brought down to the gym, where a big spread had been put on for our families and the dignitaries. There were plates of cocktail sausages, chicken pieces, spring rolls, sandwiches, cream cakes, biscuits, and tea and coffee. Naturally, there was no alcohol. Standing in the middle of the floor, watching my every move, was the bould Chief Fanning, who had detailed two officers to guard myself and my mate Larry while we were with our families – to make sure no contraband was exchanged between any of us. Then two other officers, who we got on really well with, came over and discreetly asked did we have any alcohol brought in. I'd known these officers since I first came into prison at sixteen, and I trusted them, so I took a chance and told them we had. The friendly officers then told the two other prison officers that they would keep an eye on us.

Myself and Lar mixed our Southern Comfort with red lemonade while the friendly officers kept watch. By the end of the night, well pissed, I was running around putting all the leftover cream cakes and sandwiches into a bag to give to the other inmates the following morning. Then Fanning decided to stick his nose in and told me that I was not allowed to bring anything back to my cell.

Mr McPherson intervened and said, 'Ah, come on now, Chief. It's only a few sandwiches. And they did a great job tonight, so the least we can do is let Alan have the few cakes.'

Success! Of course, now that I had the permission of the governor, I went overboard and took everything I possibly could.

A week or so after the play, a massive riot broke out in Mountjoy, and many of the prisoners climbed on to the roof. Two of my mates, Derek Murphy and Paddy Maples – who were serving twelve and seventeen years respectively – were involved in it. After the riot had ended, Derek and Paddy along with eighteen other rioters were transferred to Wheatfield and locked up twenty-three hours a day, seven days a week for punishment. When the rioters arrived, about sixty of us greeted them by singing 'Up on the Roof' by the Drifters.

After the rioters were placed on to their segregation wing, Derek and I worked out a method of communicating. Using shoelaces, Derek would lower a plastic bag from his cell window to the cell below him, and each week I would go to the cell and fill the bag with reading material, tobacco and sweets. Derek would then hoist his parcel back up into his cell. At one point, Derek passed a note asking me would I accept a visit from a female friend of his and take in a parcel of drugs for him. He told me I could keep half the drugs for myself and send the rest up to him.

Although I genuinely did not want to do it, for fear of being caught, I didn't want to let Derek, Paddy and the other lads down either. I knew that if I did take in the drugs, I'd be seen as an inmate who was 'well in' with some of the toughest prisoners around. Prison is a bit like a housing estate, where the local Residents Association might ask you to sign a petition. If you refuse to sign, you can become an outcast. In the same way, if I said no to Derek, I would have been seen as a gutless swine, unwilling to help out the rioters, who were now prison heroes. Another factor for me in deciding to accept the drugs was that it would help dissipate whatever remained of the stigma of the false rape charge.

When I met Derek's friend, she told me the parcel of drugs – £30 worth of grass, three morphine tablets and five microdot LSD tabs – was wrapped in cellophane in her mouth. When the screw handed Sandra her visiting docket to indicate the end of the visit, she leaned across and kissed me, passing the parcel from her mouth to mine. As I got up to leave the visiting room, my nerves were beginning to go. I could see four search screws waiting at the search room on the right.

Just as I got to the door, one of the screws barked, 'This way, Croghan! Strip search!'

As I was brought into the room, I somehow managed to swallow the large parcel. The screws then went through my clothes before I was allowed back into the main jail. I went straight to my cell, where my mates had me drinking shampoo and eating bars of soap to induce me to vomit the parcel back up. All I was doing was dry-retching and tearing the throat out of myself – it was a nightmare. I decided to wait until I went to the toilet.

About an hour later, walking down the prison landing to collect my tea, I saw my mate Larry walk past – and then I saw another four Larrys following suit, in a psychedelic kinda way. I knew then that the cellophane wrap the drugs were in had opened and I was coming up on five of the strongest LSD tablets on the market.

I rushed back to my cell to tell the lads what was happening. As I did so, the screws came along and banged us all up in our single cells for the night. I began to panic. My mates were shouting through their doors, telling me not to worry, to drink loads of sugar and water. But the trip got worse and worse. From experience I knew I wouldn't be able to handle the five LSD, so I pressed the call bell in my cell. The screws came down and I told them that I was overdosing on five acid, three morphine and £30 worth of grass. I was immediately bundled into an unmarked police car and, with sirens blaring, I was rushed to St James's Hospital.

When I got to the hospital, I was brought into a room and hand-cuffed to a bed. I said to myself, 'At least the doctors will know what to do.'

But I was wrong: the doctors hadn't a clue what to do. They were faxing off my symptoms to psychiatrists and psychologists in the hope that they could advise them on what course of action to take. By this time my brain was completely saturated with LSD. I was convinced that the hospital was really the Devil's waiting room, the screws were his disciples of doom and I was now just waiting to be called down through the corridor of Death to take me to Hell.

The two screws sitting beside me kept patting me on the arm and saying, 'Relax now. It won't be long.' I was reading that as, 'Relax now, the Devil will see you shortly.'

Then a nurse stuck her head in and asked the prison officers if the priest had arrived yet. That was enough for me: I began kicking and screaming, saying, 'I'm not dying, I'm not dying! I'm not going to the Devil!'

I was given a cigarette, and somehow the officers were able to calm me down. After twelve hours, the doctors said I could be taken back to the prison. But I was to be kept under constant supervision. And if I took a turn for the worse, I was to be rushed straight back.

When I arrived back at Wheatfield, I was stripped down to my boxer shorts and put into the padded cell. Standing outside, looking in at me with a big dirty smile on his face, was Chief Officer Fanning. The door was then slammed in my face, and I was alone with nothing but a blue flickering fluorescent light fixed into the ceiling. I suddenly got a nanosecond glimpse of reality, and I grabbed it. I began to pray: for hours and hours, I said the Hail Mary and the Our Father over and over and over. At that moment, prayer was the only thing that I knew to be true and real. It prevented my mind from spiralling out of control.

Prior to the acid overdose, I had just finished reading *A Season in Hell* by Jack Higgins. There was a professional hit man in the book called Jago, ex-SAS, expert marksman, eighth dan in martial arts – he was a real cool dude. In my army-green boxer shorts, I began to think that I was actually Jago. I believed I had been arrested and was now serving forty years in this padded cell for my crimes.

After two days and nights of tripping and praying, I was taken out of the padded cell and brought before Governor McPherson. Dan Fanning had me on a P-19 disciplinary report for taking in the drugs. The prison authorities knew that I didn't do drugs, and they also knew the drugs were for the rioters. But I had to be punished.

McPherson took fourteen days' remission from me and told me I was being transferred to Portlaoise. Fanning ordered two prison officers to watch me pack and to take me down to the holding area. While I was in the holding cells, McPherson came down to see me.

He said, 'Alan, Chief Fanning wanted me to shift you to either Cork or Limerick prison. I'm not going to do that. My brother is the number one governor in Portlaoise. If you play your cards right, he'll look after you. I will ring him later and let him know that you're on your way down. The rest, my friend, is up to you.'

8

Portlaoise and After

It was very late at night when I arrived at Portlaoise. As we drove along the outer walls, I could see the barbed wire and the high watchtowers, which were patrolled by the army rather than the prison service. The soldiers were wearing helmets and carrying automatic weapons. We had to go through three sets of gates to gain access to the grounds. I was taken to a cell and locked up for the night. I recall standing on my chair and looking out of my cell window. Every few minutes, big searchlights would sweep across the grounds and along the walls.

The next morning, I was brought before the governor. He informed me that I had spent the night in D-Block, rather than on E-Block where I was supposed to be housed. I was told that D-Block inmates had their jail terms automatically cut in half, because they worked as cleaners in the notorious E-Block. This housed paramilitaries and organised crime gangs who would not clean their own landings or toilets. The governor told me that, having spoken to his brother, he was willing to give me a chance and would leave me in D-Block. If, in three months' time, I was showing good behaviour, he would leave me there, and I'd get my 'half remission' – six months off my twelve-month sentence, rather than the three months I'd have been in line for ordinarily.

As it turned out, the Provos and INLA guys cleaned every inch of their landings first thing in the morning – but only three days a week. This reflected their view of themselves as political prisoners. The gangsters cleaned only when the humour took them. A certain high-ranking prison officer (who I'll refer to as 'Chicken Thief') would lead us over to E-Block after dinner to go over everything the IRA and the INLA had already done.

The Provos had history with Officer Chicken Thief. When Angelo

Fusco, Tommy McMahon, Martin Ferris, James Pius Clarke, John Crawley, Peter Rogers, Peter Lynch and Robert Russell tried to escape from Portlaoise in 1985, they had two loaded handguns, Semtex explosives, two prison officers' uniforms and a copy of an internal master key. During the escape attempt, Peter Rogers came across Chicken Thief. He threw the officer to the ground, shoved his gun into his mouth and pulled the trigger three times. The gun misfired each time before Rogers was dragged away by his comrades. (Rogers was subsequently beaten up by the other IRA men, because if the gun hadn't misfired, Officer Chicken Thief would have been dead and every one of the IRA guys would have been sentenced to forty years.) Tommy McMahon was in charge of placing the explosives and blowing open the three main prison gates. Unbeknownst to Tommy, the middle gate was hollow, and the force of the explosion welded the lock into it.

I was put in charge as cleaner on E2, which housed the INLA and breakaway republicans, and I got on well with a few of them. I would have to be very careful when talking to these guys, because if the screws caught me at it, I would have been either sent to join them on E-Block or shifted to another prison. Luckily, the screws were usually off drinking tea and paying no attention. I was friendliest of all with INLA leader Dominic McGlinchy. Every day, he and I would talk in his cell. The alleged Saor Éire member Peter Pringle was doing forty years for killing two police officers. (In 1995, after serving fourteen years, his conviction would be overturned.) He was a happy-go-lucky type of guy and a talented painter – I saw some of his work in his cell. Peter Lynch was a down-to-earth guy. Any time I chatted with him, he would take me away from myself and I would forget I was actually in prison. It was like we were standing on a street corner having a yap.

Then there was little Tommy McMahon, who blew up Lord Mountbatten and who had broken away from the Provos. Tommy wasn't the greatest conversationalist – I think he was somewhat shy – and only began to acknowledge me after he twigged that Angelo Fusco and I were friends. Angelo was on E3, and I would sneak up the flight of steel stairs from E2 to E3 to meet him nearly every morning before he went out for his jog.

Martin Ferris was the OC, and he ran the show on the Provo wing. None of the IRA inmates did what the prison officers said. For example, when it was time for the Provos to 'fall in' to get their dinner, the screw would just tell Ferris. Then, speaking in Irish and positioned at the top of the landing, Ferris would issue his orders. Every one of the IRA prisoners would stand hidden from view behind their cell doors. Ferris would command them to 'céim ar aghaidh' (step forward), and in unison they would all step into his view. Then, on his instruction 'iompaig thart' (about turn), the Provos would all turn and stamp their feet. Ferris would say 'luí isteach' (fall in), and the Provos would then march up for their dinner. The same procedure was done at breakfast, dinner and tea, and it was amazing to witness. I used to watch from E2, looking up through the wire mesh to E3.

In Portlaoise

I went to school at Portlaoise and continued working on my writing. One of the teachers and also the governor informed me that Fr Brian D'Arcy, who had a radio show at the time, was looking to interview a prisoner. The governor asked if I would be willing to give a frank interview about my crimes and life in prison. I was honoured to have been asked. Fr Brian came in, and the two of us sat down and chatted away. I was very open and honest, and the interview went down very well with the governor.

The following day I was told that, because of my performance, the drug incident in Wheatfield prison would be forgotten about. Like all the other inmates in D-Block, my sentence would be cut in half.

As I had done in St Patrick's, I was forever brewing my own hooch. It may be a consequence of all the hooch I was drinking and all the Valium I was swallowing, but I have no recollection of the lead-up to my release from Portlaoise. Nor of going home – nothing.

Upon my release from prison, I went heavy on the drink. And I hooked back up with Frank Sinclair, who was still on the run following our bank robbery.

About two weeks after my release, I was out drinking with Frank. He told me that his house had been robbed two nights previously. He said he knew who had done it. Of course, I straight away insisted that the two of us go over to the guy's house, kick in his front door and break him up. I flagged down a cab and jumped in the front passenger seat, while Frank got in the back. When we had driven out of my area, I asked the driver to pull over to the side of the road, as I wanted to take a leak. When the driver pulled into the kerb, I took out a mountain knife and stuck it to his throat.

The driver pleaded with me not to hurt him.

I replied, 'I'm not going to hurt you, mate. I just want you to get into the boot.'

Fearing for his life, the man panicked and leaped from the car. He ran up to the front door of a stranger's house and began banging the door down, screaming for help. I jumped into the driver's seat, and myself and Frank headed for the south side, where the guy we were looking for lived.

Halfway across the city I decided to stop off at a twenty-four-hour shop, to buy cigarettes and a bottle of orange. As I walked out of the shop, I saw that the whole street was surrounded by police. I was taken to Store Street Garda station and thrown into a cell.

I was brought before the courts the following morning and charged with hijacking the taxi at knifepoint and with robbery. The police objected to bail, and so I was remanded in custody. Once again I found myself back in Mountjoy. I was gutted. But at least this time there was no question of me going on to protection. All the inmates welcomed me, and that was a massive psychological relief. I was able to mingle with the general prison population without fear.

On the last day of my trial, I got into the witness box and pleaded personally to Judge Michael Moriarty for leniency. He sentenced me to three years, with a review after eighteen months.

Back at my second home, Mountjoy, I befriended a black guy who was doing eight years for importing what was at that time the largest amount of cocaine ever seized – not only in Ireland, but in Europe. His name was Danny Gwira, and he was a brilliant chess player. As I'd learned from Mr Brohan in St Patrick's, when you play someone better than yourself, you learn more. Danny was unbeatable at chess, but I loved playing him and learning from him.

Flyers were handed around Mountjoy by an RTÉ film crew who would be in the prison filming a documentary on prison life. Gemma McCrohan would be interviewing the governor, John Lonergan, as well as prison officers, welfare officers, the chaplain and some specially selected inmates. I was disgusted that I had not been asked to be interviewed – I wanted to be a part of it! I wrote up a four-page thesis on Mountjoy and life in prison. Mr Lonergan's secretary typed it out for me, and then gave copies to Ms McCrohan and the RTÉ producer, Ms Stephanie Fitzpatrick.

I was later called into a meeting with the producer and interviewer, and they gave me a good grilling. I was told that I would be interviewed later that evening in my cell. I was delighted – I hadn't been hand-picked by the prison authorities, I'd done it off my own bat (with the kind assistance of the governor's secretary). The interview went well, and I featured twice in the programme. I was then asked by Governor Lonergan if I wanted a transfer over to the Training Unit. I jumped at the chance to serve out the remainder of my sentence in comfortable surroundings.

I again threw myself into drama and my creative writing. I completed a script that was a piss-take of the programme *Crimeline*. Using equipment from the TV production class in the Training Unit, and cobbling together a costume with help from a screw, I dressed up as a police superintendent and produced my own version of the programme. It was great crack, pulling the piss out of the Ol' Bill. I managed to get a copy of the recording and had it smuggled out from the prison and delivered to a family member. I still have it to this day.

For eighteen months, I maintained an excellent prison record. Before I went back before Judge Moriarty, in February 1994, I had compiled many character references to further my chances of early release. When the judge released me, I told myself that I was finished with my life of crime. I had spent just under nine of the past ten years behind bars.

9

Trying to Go Straight

After my release, I was hoping the police would leave me alone. But it wasn't to be. Whenever they drove past me, they'd get out, search me, ask where I was going and what was I doing. They used to love ruining my night. If they saw I was dressed up to the nines and heading out, they'd nick me on suspicion of one thing or another and take me down to the station. Hours later, as the bars and clubs were closing, I'd be released without charge. The home raids were just as bad. Every couple of weeks, rest assured, I'd receive that early-morning bang on the front door. They'd say they were looking for guns and ammunition, explosives or stolen goods, but most of the time it was just harassment. The raids upset my mother, and that really bothered me.

I saw an advertisement in the paper for the position of a fitter's mate with a company that installed and repaired steel shutters. I typed up a fake CV, applied for the job and, to my surprise, I got it. I now had my first ever PAYE job, and I was determined to make it work. My job description was going around Dublin as a helper in a van, fitting and repairing shutters, and I got my training on the job.

Late one night, I was sitting at home – not drinking, because I was on call – when my phone rang. It was the van driver that I worked with, Noel. He told me that we had to go out on a call to repair an 'up and over' door that had been rammed during a robbery. Noel picked me up and, as we made our way to the job, he told me that the Brinks Allied depot in Clonshaugh had been robbed, with millions of pounds taken. When we got to the depot, we had to be passed and cleared by Brinks Allied security personnel, and Special Branch detectives were all over the place.

The following day, myself and the driver went back to the depot to replace the door with a new one. When we arrived, the two of us were told not to mind the man going around taking photographs, as he was an officer with Interpol. While I was up on the ladder, fitting the new door, there were hordes of detectives and forensic guys in white jumpsuits walking around the loading bay, all looking for evidence. I couldn't believe that I, with a list of criminal convictions the length of my arm – including one for armed robbery – was in the loading bay of one of the most secure buildings in the country. And I was later to learn that at least one of the guys who allegedly took part in the Brinks Allied raid was an acquaintance of mine!

Now that I was out of prison and had a job, I tried to disassociate myself from all known criminals. While locked up I had been writing to a girl called Tara (not her real name). She had initiated the correspondence, intending at first only to be a prisoner's pen pal, but then she started visiting me frequently. Tara came from a very wealthy family and she was studying at a major college. Now that I was free, I very much wanted to be a normal person and to do what ordinary people did. And dating Tara fitted nicely into that. All I had ever known was chaos, disruption, abnormality, drinking, acid trips and crime – but I knew what love was, because I had always got it from my mother.

Making the break from criminal circles wasn't easy. Sometimes guys I'd robbed with, or had done jail with, would knock up to my door or bump into me in a pub. One night I was out with two guys who were still involved in criminal activity. I told them I was going straight. One of the two was pissing me off, so I whispered to the other that, if he kept it up, I was going to give him a belt of a blade across the face – despite my intention to change my life, I still had that violent instinct in me.

Sometime later, and totally unawares, I was grabbed from behind and dragged to the ground. The two guys jumped on me and kicked me unconscious. I remember waking up and trying to walk up to a woman's front door, then collapsing. I don't recall my stay in the hospital, but I do remember sitting at home afterwards, with my head literally the size of a basketball. I heard from people who saw the beating that the two guys just continuously kicked me in the head for about ten minutes non-stop. Even after I was unconscious, they still continued to kick me.

That beating changed me. Afterwards, I was terrified of everybody. The father of one of the guys involved in the attack came over to my house and asked me not to retaliate, explaining that his son was addicted to drugs and didn't know what he was doing. I told the guy's father not to worry, that I would let it go. Secretly, I was just hoping that I didn't bump into either of the guys who'd given me the hiding – I couldn't be sure how I'd react.

It was only a short time after that beating that myself and Tara were walking through a housing estate after leaving a pub. I had taken an Ecstasy tablet earlier that night, and I still had another two in my pocket that I planned to take later. We walked past a large crowd of guys who were congregating on a street corner.

One of them shouted out to me, 'Hey! Do you want to buy any E?'

I told the guy, 'No, thanks.' I had my own, and we continued walking on.

He shouted after me, 'Is there something wrong with our E?'

I totally ignored him, and walked on.

Then, out of the blue, I got an awful bang on the back of the head. I turned around and there were five or six guys with masks over their faces, all carrying poles and bars. I told Tara to run, and the group of guys just lashed into me. Whenever I ran to grab one guy, another would attack me from behind. Then I'd turn to try to grab him, and another would again attack me from behind. I was knocked to the ground, where they bombarded my head and body with bars, poles and cavity blocks. They eventually ran off. I went to the hospital and received eight stitches to the back of my head. The most insane part of the night was that, while I was waiting to be seen to in the A & E department, I decided to take the two Ecstasy tablets that I still had. I soon found myself outside, dancing to no music in the middle of the hospital car park. Unsurprisingly, my relationship with Tara ended shortly thereafter.

It seemed like it was open season on Alan, because Alan had decided to go straight. I think the younger generation in my area felt a need to kick the shit out of people who, like myself, had a reputation. That would give them some sort of standing within the criminal fraternity. I did my best to put the beatings behind me, but it was hard. I knew that if I retaliated, I would be right back to square one. But a lot of people were beginning to form the opinion that I was some sort of a pushover. My head was really messed up. I didn't want to hurt anyone, and I didn't want anyone to hurt me.

Around this time, I was asked to do a parachute jump for the blind. I got plenty of people to put up money, because they knew I was afraid of heights. I raised £670, and then the day of reckoning came. Along with a couple of students who were also doing the jump, I was trained by a good-looking lady parachutist for more than six hours. The main focus was on what to do in the event of a malfunction. By the time I was due to get into the small aircraft, my nerves were completely shattered. I was fully convinced I was going to have a malfunction. But I hid it well, and was full of false bravado. I knew I was bottling it, but when I looked over my shoulder and saw all my family and my new girlfriend, Gill, all taking pictures, I knew I had to go through with it.

I got into the light plane. As the little piece of junk rattled, coughed and spat its way along the airfield, I became more and more nervous. The college lad was to jump first, then myself, and last was the female student. When the plane had climbed to 5,000 feet, the college guy took the plunge. Now it was my turn to sit out on the edge of the little side door as the plane circled into position. With clouds right in front of my face, I heard a big scream.

'Go! Go! Go!'

I nearly shit myself. I looked to the beautiful instructor and said to her, 'Are you insane? I'm not jumping to my death.'

Before I had a chance to say anything else, the young female student behind me was practically climbing over my shoulder to jump out of the plane. I was as sick as a pig.

When the plane landed, I looked to my right and there were all my family and girlfriend, all in a single line together, flapping their arms and singing, 'I feel like chicken tonight, like chicken tonight!'

At least the blind got their money.

One day, I drove to Limerick with a friend of mine (who I'll call 'Carl'), to catch the Circuit of Ireland Rally when it hit the city. When we got to Limerick, we hooked up with two girls who worked at a hairdresser's. After a pub crawl, we went back to their house in O'Malley Park. I envied Carl for the way he always managed to hit it off with the ladies, especially the good-looking ones. To me, he already had the perfect girlfriend, 'Claudia', who had a beautiful face with lovely brown eyes, long black hair, a gorgeous figure, and a down-to-earth personality. She was sound, and I fancied her like mad. I thought Carl was insane to even look at another woman.

Upon our return to Dublin, Carl had to travel up North. I saw this as an opportunity, so I rang Claudia and arranged to meet up with her. We met in a pub car park, and I said I had something important to tell her. I told Claudia I would give her this information in confidence, because I cared about her as a person and as a friend. It was true that I cared for her and wouldn't have done anything to hurt her – but I had another motive. I was, for some insane reason, thinking she was likely to jump into bed with me if I confided in her that Carl had met a bird in Limerick.

After Claudia promised me that she wouldn't relay anything I said to her back to Carl, I told her everything. Claudia reassured me she would not involve me but would catch Carl out in her own way. I believed her, and we sat in her car yapping. Then, stupidly, I made a move on her. She made it clear she didn't like me in that way. Later, as I got into my own car and watched Claudia drive away, I realised I had betrayed my best friend and I hated myself for it.

Two days later, I got a phone call from Carl. He said Claudia had told him everything, and he wanted nothing to do with me again. A few weeks later, he arrived at my home and came up to my bedroom to speak with me. He was totally calm; he obviously knew why I'd done what I'd done.

I confessed, and apologised for betraying him.

Carl said he could live with that, but he reiterated that he'd never speak to me again.

He and I do acknowledge each other with a simple nod of the head on the street. But our friendship is well and truly over, and I have no one to blame but myself.

Soon after this, my life took another devastating turn for the worse. I was at a house party with two former mates of mine (who I'll call 'Bob' and 'Anto') and a group of other lads. There was alcohol everywhere, kegs on tap, trays of cans and a big bag of cocaine on the table. We were all milling the gargle and shoving the coke up our noses. Whenever I had a piss in the back garden, this guy called 'Simon' (not his real name) always seemed to be having a piss as well. Simon was really attractive, and I was drawn to him. At this stage of the house party, the beer was running low. So I suggested that myself and Simon should nip to my place and pick up a few more trays.

Back at my house, I made a pass at him. He pushed me away and stormed out of the house. I panicked and went after him, apologising and asking him to stop and listen to me. But it was to no avail. Eventually, I gave up. My mind was racing a million miles an hour, and I didn't know what was going to come of this – all I knew was that I was fucked. Having feelings or wanting sex and/ or a relationship with someone of the same sex was totally taboo in that time and place. The general consensus of most red-blooded males I knew was that being into guys was worse than being a rap-ist, and just as bad as being a child molester. I knew I would have to get offside.

As I made my way towards my house, I bumped into Bob and Anto. They asked where Simon was, so I told them that he had gone home. Now I was lying to my mates. But I knew I couldn't tell them what had really happened. We made our way up the road, and then this car came skidding to a halt beside us.

Simon's elder brother jumped from the car, roaring, 'What the fuck did you do?'

I surreptitiously took out my blade, then asked him what he was on about. I would have said anything but the truth. Anto then talked Simon's brother back into the car, and he went off with them. Myself and Bob sat on a corner railing. I told Bob that Simon had begun getting smart with me and that when I put it up to him, he legged it.

About fifteen minutes later, Anto came walking back up the street. He told Bob he wanted nothing to do with me ever again. I knew Anto was dead right in everything he was doing and saying.

I said to Bob, 'You head off with him.' Bob asked what was going on, and I said, 'Listen, mate, you're better off just going with him. I'm bolloxed tired, and I'm going home.'

I turned and walked away. I didn't want Bob to make a stupid decision.

Word of what happened spread around my area like wildfire. The people who knew me wanted nothing to do with me. And the people who knew of me thought I was nothing short of scum. My life as I knew it was over.

I decided to leave Ireland.

10

On the Run

I told my family that I was going to the States to begin a new life. After a tearful farewell, I jumped in a taxi to the airport. I flew to Boston via Heathrow – I knew no one in the States, and chose Boston simply because of its large Irish community.

On the flight I sat beside an American gentleman by the name of Tom Gooding. He had his own business in Lowell, just outside Boston. Tom and a business partner of his owned some properties, and he offered me a place to stay in one of them. I jumped at the chance. After we landed, Tom gave me a lift to a motel and told me that he and his friend would pick me up the following morning and take me to my new accommodation. That night in the motel I ordered a pizza and sat in front of the TV, watching porn films all night. The following morning, I was hit with a massive bill for watching them. I'd thought you could watch the bloody things for free!

Tom and his friend collected me from the motel in his Dodge van. They brought me to a massive house that looked like something from *The Amityville Horror*. It was situated in a nice quiet neighbourhood, and Tom charged me $280 for a month's rent (which also included gas and electricity). Tom offered me a job in his business, making plastic bins for $5 an hour, cash in hand. This wasn't very appealing, so I kindly turned down his offer.

It was coming up to St Patrick's Day, and I decided I would try to get a job in a bar. I was told that South Boston was the place to be if you were Irish, but I didn't have a clue where it was. Pretending to be a lost tourist, I walked into a police station in Lowell to ask for directions, and it was there I met Officer Paul G. Goyette. The minute I opened my mouth and he heard the Irish accent, we hit it off. Officer Goyette put me into his squad car and drove me around to five different police stations to meet his colleagues.

When I went into a captain's office, he handed me a few police-uniform badges and said to me, 'Don't tell the inspector I gave you them.' And when I went into the inspector's office, he'd do and say exactly the same.

I had photographs taken of me sitting in cells, police cars and vans, as well as posing with the officers – and, of course, I had to give the impression that I'd never seen the inside of a cell or a squad car. Later that day, when Paul dropped me back to my apartment, he invited me to a policeman's dinner and ball that was happening the following evening. Tickets cost $130, but I was invited for free.

Boston's finest, with me in the middle

'Alan,' I thought to myself, 'you're stone mad, mate. What the fuck are you up to?' But I was loving the attention, and really looking forward to the ball.

The following night, I was collected by Paul and Sergeant Angus MacDonald and taken to the function. There I met dozens of police officers of all ranks. Many of them gave me their home, mobile and work numbers. They said that if I ever needed anything, I was to just ring them and they'd sort it. They also offered to help fast-track a Green Card for me. It was clear that their amazing hospitality was based solely on my nationality. At the function I got up on stage and sang Irish rebel songs – 'Sean South of Garryowen', 'The Gibraltar Three' and 'The Sniper's Promise' – and they loved it. For that night, I forgot about all my troubles back home.

In South Boston I met an Irish-American bar manager who invited me to a rooftop party he was throwing in his apartment on St Patrick's Day. I spent a very warm Paddy's Day dressed in boxer shorts and sandals, drinking beer and nibbling from the barbecue, looking out at the parade and the city from the comfort of a perfectly placed sunlounger.

The following evening, I ventured into a small Irish bar where I met a Northern Irish girl called Kathleen who had been living in Boston for a number of years. After many drinks and a couple of Irish ballads from me, I told her I'd come over looking for work and that I planned to stay on as an illegal. Kathleen told me she would meet me in another Irish bar later, and she gave me directions.

When I went to the bar later that night, it was dimly lit and full of smoke and there was a two-man band playing rebel songs in the corner. It was obviously an IRA shop. When I walked in, I naturally got the cold suspicious looks. There were a few Irish guys there, and I knew by the look of them they were hard cases. One of them walked over and asked me what was I doing in the pub. I felt very uncomfortable, but Kathleen had a quiet word with the big guy. Eventually, he came over to me, shook my hand and introduced himself as Martin. Then I got the Q&A. Who did I know in Ireland that could vouch for me? What made me come to the USA? And so on.

I felt I had no choice, so I told Martin about my life of crime, and did some name-dropping. Martin told me to come back into the bar the following night, and he would see what he could do for me. That night, Kathleen let me stay at her place. She told me that Martin would have me 'checked out', and if everything was as I said it was, there'd be no problem.

The following night, I met up with Martin. He shook my hand and said, 'You know how it is, Alan, I have to check everyone out. I didn't mean to be blunt with you yesterday, but you're on my turf now. If you want to work for me, you'll do as I say. I won't take any shit.'

I didn't like the guy, but I needed work. Martin told me that I could start the following week, cleaning the windows on high-rise buildings for $120 a day, cash in hand. Despite the fact I was terrified of heights, I accepted the job.

I was missing my mother and my family terribly. The first time I talked to my Ma on the phone, I broke down in tears. I couldn't control myself; I felt like a baby. I told her that I was missing her, and I didn't really want to be in America. I didn't want the phone call to end, but I ran out of change.

I thought about going home and what my situation would be like if I returned. I then formed the conclusion that, whatever happened to me – and whatever people thought about me – I wasn't going to let it keep me away from my mother and family. That same week, I bought a ticket and flew back home.

As soon as the wheels of the plane hit the tarmac at Dublin Airport, I immediately regretted coming back. All the reasons why I'd left Ireland in the first place came flooding back to me.

Once I got to my house, I went into hibernation. I wouldn't leave my room, and I was frozen with fear.

After a few weeks of sitting at home, bored and depressed, I knew I needed something to do, something to get me away from myself. I didn't care what it was. I felt completely alone, I had alienated everyone, no one wanted anything to do with me. And I thought, 'Who can blame them?' I didn't value myself any more.

This was my mindset when I found what I thought was a great little job in the back pages of *In Dublin* magazine. An 'escort agency' required a 'male escort'. I called the mobile number that was listed with the advertisement and got through to an Alan Costello, who arranged to meet me outside the Burlington Hotel. I asked how would I know him, and he said I'd recognise his sports car.

Shortly after I arrived, Costello pulled up in a tiny yellow sports car. We went for a drink, and he asked me a number of questions, including whether I was straight, gay or bisexual. I told him I was bi. After an hour of chatting, he gave me the job. It entailed going out with lonely women – 'Happy days!' I thought. The agency also advertised 'coffee & cream' for punters who might require a male and a female together. 'Hey, better again!' I thought. And I would have to entertain gay male clients – this was not so great, but I wanted the job, and I didn't think there'd be much demand for my services from men.

The agency was housed in a luxury apartment on Appian Way, in a plush part of Dublin 4. The first time I visited, there were six sexy girls sitting on a sofa and chairs, all dressed in revealing lingerie. I straight away got looks from the girls, and this made me feel attractive. Costello seemed to feel a need to show off his superiority, and he ordered one of the girls to get up and make the two of us a cup of coffee. I didn't like what I saw of how he treated them.

Costello took a 50 per cent cut of everything the girls brought in. On top of that, he demanded £70 from each of the girls every week towards the rent, phone bills and laundry. The girls also had to supply their own condoms, towels, tea bags, milk, sugar, coffee and food.

I suggested to Costello that it would make sense if I drove the girls on call-outs to clients and waited for them to finish. If they weren't out within the allocated time, I could knock on the client's door. Costello liked the idea. He said I could also watch the girls for him, to make sure they didn't rip him off. But as far as I was concerned, the more the girls ripped him off the better. He also insisted that I must not have sex with any of the girls – he maintained that if I did, I'd end up wrapped around their finger – but I would break that rule a number of times. None of the girls liked Costello. The only thing they were glad of was that he never had sex with any of them, because he was gay.

Costello invited me to his apartment one night, saying he wanted to discuss 'business'. When I got to his place, he showed me an old front-page story from the *Sunday World*, exposing him as a pimp. There were pictures of him on crutches, living it up in sunny Spain with his gay lover. He was really proud of the article!

Then he made a pass at me. I didn't fancy him, but I felt if I wanted to hang on to my job, which I really liked, I wasn't in a position to refuse. I let him perform oral sex on me. It took ages for me to ejaculate – I had to close my eyes and pretend I was getting a blow job from one of his girls.

A couple of nights later, Costello rang me and said one of his clients wanted a 'guy & girl' show. I would be paid £100 for the hour. When the client arrived at the agency, he picked out a girl he fancied – she used the name 'Sade' – and all he wanted to do was sit in a chair masturbating while watching myself and Sade having sex. It was the handiest hundred quid I ever earned. On another occasion, a male client rang in. He was looking for a guy, and I had to go out to the client's house. I could tell from the car in the drive and the furnishings inside that he had a lot of money. There was a panic alarm beside his bed. After an hour there, I got paid and left.

At the end of every shift, about seven in the morning, I would drive most of the girls home. A few of them preferred to hit the early houses, and would ask me to join them. Who was I to say no? By midday, we would be pissed. No matter how hard I tried to get rounds in, they wouldn't let me. They'd say I had a car to run, and that I was very good to them. That made me feel all the more embarrassed, but we would have great crack together. To my way of thinking, they were the best bunch of girls ever – they loved their alcohol, and they loved sex. Sometimes we would visit sex shops for toys, creams and videos. Then we'd head to a public park, chill out in the sun, drink cans of beer, snap photos of the girls topless and of us all kissing each other, and then nip into the bushes and have sex. I never had it so good.

Sade was a really good-looking girl with a fun personality, and I liked her a lot. We began to have a relationship. Sade was delighted that she had finally met a guy who knew what she did for a living and was OK with it. But as our relationship progressed, it wasn't long before Sade began getting jealous of me working at the brothel. She talked me into leaving the job, insisting that she was earning more than enough money for the two of us to live on, which was true. She was the type of girl you'd live on a mountain with, so I left the job and moved in with her. Every morning, I would collect her from work.

We had many a wild time in the bedroom, especially when we were both coked out of our heads and full of alcohol. Sade was big into threesomes, and one night she got me to call a girl from another escort agency to come out to our apartment. Sade said she would hide underneath a quilt on the spare single bed in the corner of our bedroom, so that she could watch me having sex. When the other girl arrived and we were both naked on the bed, Sade stuck her head out and, with a big smile on her face, asked to join in.

Sade also loved to have sex in open and risky places. One summer's day, while I was driving, she suddenly bent down, opened my jeans and began to give me a blow job. On another occasion, at a street parade, we walked down a flight of steps to someone's front door and Sade proceeded to perform oral sex on me. Once, we had sex in her mother's kitchen, over the cooker. The kitchen door was wide open, as was the door to the sitting room where Sade's mother and sister sat watching daytime TV. All either of them had to do was walk out into the hallway and they would have caught us at it. We loved the danger. Eventually, we were caught when Sade's mother walked right in on us. Even more embarrassingly, I was wearing Sade's black fishnet tights.

Sex with Sade was always spontaneous. Whenever she wanted it – no matter where we were – she had to have it, and I was game ball. Once, in the apartment, she asked me if I'd ever been tied up. I told her I hadn't, and she told me to strip. I stripped naked on the bed, and Sade tied my hands behind my back. Then she tied my ankles together, tied my hands to my ankles, put a blindfold on me and told me not to move. I could hear Sade walking around the apartment, whistling to herself. Then I heard the front door open and close. After about five minutes of complete silence, I began calling out for Sade, but there was no reply. As time went on, and I was left in complete darkness with just my thoughts, I began to really panic. About three hours later, which felt like a lifetime, Sade returned with bags of shopping.

She coolly lifted up my blindfold and, with a big smile on her face, she cheerfully said, 'Hiya!'

I thought, 'She's a fucking nut-job.'

We had a massive argument, and I ended the relationship. Sade went to her mother's house. Later that evening, I got a phone call from her sister to say that Sade had taken a drug overdose and was in Beaumont. I went straight to the hospital, and I stayed by her bedside for the whole night.

The following morning, Sade was fine. The doctors said she had never been in any real danger of losing her life. She was delighted to see me – and to be honest, I was happy to see her. As I sat by her bedside in the A & E, she asked me to pull the bed curtain closed. And when I did, she asked me to lie beside her. One thing led to another, and we ended up having sex in her hospital bed, with her glucose drip still attached to her arm.

When Sade got out of hospital, she took me into a designer clothes shop and bought me a Kenzo suit for £900, a Versace shirt for £125 and a pair of Bruno Magli shoes for £140. She apologised for tying me up and leaving me like that. Dressed in my new suit, myself and Sade went out for a meal and a few drinks to celebrate. While we sat in the pub, I bumped into my old friend, Anne Doyle, who joined Sade and me. We talked about my days in prison, when myself and Anne first met. Anne asked Sade what she did for a living.

She replied, 'Oh, I'm a stewardess with Virgin Atlantic.'

I nearly choked on my drink! While I was chatting to Anne, Sade got up and said she'd be back in five minutes. When she returned, she handed me a gift-wrapped present. It was a solid-gold bracelet that she had decided to buy on the spur of the moment for £480.

Sade was making lots of money, but the money was becoming a problem. She began to form the opinion that I was only with her because of the money she made, and we had many arguments because of it. I told her she could keep her money and everything else she had bought me. In a fit of anger I grabbed the Kenzo suit and Versace shirt, ripped them to shreds with a blade and threw them in her face. Sade apologised, and the following day we went back to the shop, where she splashed out another £1,000 to replace the suit and shirt.

By this time I was getting jealous about Sade's sex work, and I wanted her to give it all up. Our relationship had made me realise that I was a very possessive individual. I wanted the two of us to go to England to begin a new life together. It took a lot of persuasion. But in the end, Sade reluctantly agreed to leave the job and come with me.

We moved to Harrow, in north-west London, where Sade's sister, who I'll call 'Laura', owned a flat. She lived elsewhere in the UK, with her wealthy boyfriend, and we became her tenants. I got myself a job in a factory that made plastic casings for mobile phones. It was not a great job, and my take-home pay was only around £260 a week. With me making so little and Sade not working at all, our standard of living dropped considerably. Sade began dropping hints about going back to work as a prostitute. I was totally opposed to this, but she was very insistent. She painted a very rosy picture – she told me she would only work two or three nights a week, and I wouldn't have to work. We would be able to eat in nice restaurants, buy nice clothes. Under protest I agreed, but I told Sade that I would not leave my little job making the mobile-phone casings.

She began working for a lady by the name of Kirsten who ran an escort agency with her husband on Regent Street. Of course, as soon as Sade began working, our financial circumstances changed for the better. The money I made in the phone factory went towards the bills, and the money Sade earned was used for fun.

Sade started working five and six nights a week, contrary to our agreement. Then she told me that Kirsten had introduced her to a guy who produced pornographic movies, and that she was now doing porn. I wasn't into this at all – my head was wrecked with jealousy – but Sade was adamant she was not going to stop. She began to tell me about gang-bang scenes she was filming. The more she told me, the more upset and jealous I became. Then she went quiet about what she was doing at work, which was worse.

One night, as I sat up watching the TV and waiting for Sade to come home, I heard a car pull in below. I knocked off the sitting-room light and peeked out through the second-floor window. Sade was sitting in the passenger seat of a blue sports car. She leaned out of my view, obviously to kiss the driver, and then leaned back into my view when she had finished. The driver opened his glove compartment, took out a card and wrote something on the back of it. Sade placed the card inside her Walkman. The driver then leaned into my view and kissed Sade full on the mouth.

As Sade got out of the car, I switched off the TV, ran into the bedroom, jumped into bed and pretended to be asleep. When Sade came into the flat and turned on the bedroom light, I pretended she had woken me up.

I asked how her night had been and how she'd got home.

She replied, 'Oh, I just got a black cab.'

I got up out of the bed, took the Walkman from her bag, opened it, took out the business card and said, 'You're a fuckin' liar!' I threw the card at her, and I slept on the sofa that night.

The following morning, Sade told me that she didn't love me any more and wanted us to break up. I was devastated. I even found myself apologising and telling her that I wouldn't interfere in her life any more. But I was wasting my breath. That same day, I got a flight back home to Dublin.

I was only home an hour when my phone rang; it was Sade. She said she'd never realised how much she loved me until I was gone, and she asked me to come back so that we could try again. I was over the moon. I had a return ticket, but it was not valid until the following week. I went to a friend of mine, Kathleen, and asked her could she help me out. Kathleen rang up the airline and pretended to be my mother. She broke down in tears on the phone and said that my father had just been admitted to hospital in London and wasn't expected to make it through the night. It was an Oscar-winning performance: the airline told my 'mother' that they would put me on a flight later that evening. That evening, I was back up in Dublin Airport. Now it was my turn to play the heartbroken son. I wet my eyes and rubbed them hard to make them bloodshot. As I boarded my flight, I received condolences from check-in and cabin crew.

That night, I landed in London with about thirty quid to my name. Hungry and tired from hauling my bags, I arrived at the outer security door of the apartment block and rang the buzzer. Sade stuck her head out of the bedroom window and said she'd changed her mind. She was sorry for dragging me back over to London. She then closed the bedroom window and disappeared back inside. I was left standing there – cold, hungry, alone, with hardly any money and with nowhere to stay. I shouted up at the window, pleading with Sade to reconsider. I told her I was starving and tired, and I begged her to just let me stay the one night. The window opened again. She threatened to call the police, then slammed the window shut. I continued to press the buzzer, but I got no reply.

Eventually, a police van pulled up with about six officers inside. I explained everything, and they said there was nothing they could do. I was told if I continued to bother the 'lady' and didn't move along, I would be arrested. They asked would I like to be dropped off anywhere. I asked them to drop me near Kilburn High Road – I knew a couple of guys who drank in a pub there, and I hoped that I would find them there that night. The police dropped me at the underground station, and I took the tube to Kilburn High Road.

When I went into the pub, I spotted my two old mates – they were drinking and playing pool. I told the lads everything that had happened. They bought me gargle for the rest of the evening, got me some fish and chips, took me back to their place and put me up for the night.

The following morning, they bought me an airline ticket. And off I went home again.

I found it very hard to come to terms with the break-up. I was still very much in love with Sade, and I didn't leave the house for about three weeks. I felt very much alone. I knew everyone in my area still hated me, and now I had also lost the girl I loved.

After about three weeks of sitting in my bedroom, just watching TV, I thought to myself, 'Hey, fuck that! I'm off to Amsterdam.' I didn't know anybody there, but I knew it was the place to be for sex and drugs.

After booking myself into my bed and breakfast for the weekend, I set out and scored a couple of grams of cocaine. Then I was off 'window-shopping'. On the second night, slightly drunk and with a few lines of good coke inside me to keep me balanced, I could hear loud music coming from somewhere. But for the life of me I couldn't suss out where it was coming from. Eventually, I looked down over a railing and, at the bottom of two steep flights of steps, I could see blue neon lights.

When I entered the club, it looked like the inside of a cave, all lit blue. It was a very cool place – busy, but not too packed – just perfect. I found myself a seat at the bar that gave me a good view of the place. I was drinking beer like a fish, and every so often I'd nip into the Gents and snort a few more lines of coke.

I could see lots of sex play – guys with girls, girls with girls, guys with guys. A German girl sitting next to me at the bar looked at me and smiled. She then reached across and unzipped my fly and began to masturbate me. I was dumbfounded, but it was great. The bar girls and men casually continued to serve me my drinks, while the German bird masturbated me at the bar. Half an hour later, I found myself on my knees outside the Gents toilets, performing oral sex on another girl who had lifted up her very small miniskirt to reveal she was wearing nothing underneath. As I went down on her, three of her mates just stood there looking at me.

The next day, I bought a few pairs of clogs and three windmills for presents. After spending £1,700 on drugs, drink and sex in the space of three days, I returned home.

Of course, when I got back home nothing had changed, and I knew that I had to get away again. I applied for a job as a barman in a pub/ nightclub in north London. After a telephone interview, I secured myself a position.

Like other members of the staff, I lived in a room above the pub. It was a great little job: I loved the customers and the people I worked with, and I was making new friends who knew nothing about my past. The manager could see straight away how well I got on with the customers. He advised me not to get too friendly with a certain individual who I'll call 'Mick H'. He was an 'English Paddy' and a devious-looking character. He was aged about forty, with straight shoulder-length hair which covered his eyes – a dead ringer for Gérard Depardieu. Whenever he and his right-hand man – an Irish guy who I'll call 'Joe C' – came into the pub, they went out of their way to talk to me, and they always tipped me well.

On one such occasion, Mick H gave me a £20 tip. The following day, I went to buy cigarettes in the shop across the road, and it turned out the banknote was a dud. I didn't say anything about it, and my relationship with Mick H grew even friendlier as the weeks went on. But I made sure it was on a barman–customer basis.

Some weeks later, I was using the toilets when I realised that Mick H was standing behind me, breathing down my neck. Joe C was blocking off the exit door, holding it slightly ajar and watching for anyone who might come in on top of us. Mick H's jacket was open and he made sure I could see the automatic handgun that was stuffed down his waistband.

He took out a small bag of cocaine and said, 'I know you're not a copper, Alan. But Joe here thinks different. I know you said you done a bit of coke before, so I have a little surprise for you.'

I remembered a very strange conversation I'd had with them during which Joe C had accused me of being an undercover policeman. I'd shown them my seven tattoos and asked, 'Would a copper have all these tattoos on his body?' And I'd confided in them about my life of crime.

Mick H had turned to Joe C and said, 'He's not Ol' Bill.'

Now, in the loo, Mick H was putting lines of coke on the window sill. He snorted one through a rolled-up banknote and then handed it to me to do the other one. I snorted up the line.

Mick H then said he had a little business proposition for me. He explained that he had two keys: one for the back door of the pub, and one for the safe in the manager's office. He said he wasn't sure if the locks had been changed, so he wanted me to try the key in the back door. If it fitted, he would give me the key to the safe to try. If that fitted, too, I'd get £5,000 for my trouble.

My heart was racing, and beads of sweat started rolling down my forehead. I was in a toilet with two serious criminals, one of whom was armed. I did not feel I could say no to their little business proposition. I'd be finishing work at seven that evening. Mick H told me he would meet me outside the pub at seven thirty.

My nerves were completely shattered, and the coke didn't help. Every time I walked into the manager's office to try the key in the back door, someone would walk into the office. After about four failed attempts, I did a quick check of the lounge and bar: all of the staff were in the middle of serving customers. I quickly opened the back door and walked out with a bag of rubbish to dump in the skip. I turned around, fumbled, then finally put the key into the door lock and got a full turn on it. As I took the key out of the lock, the door was suddenly pushed open on top of me.

The manager barged out, saying, 'What are you doing out here?'

I could feel the blood drain from my face as I told him I was putting out some rubbish. Trying to act completely normal, I casually brushed past him and walked back into the bar.

That evening, I met up with Mick H and Joe C and told them the key fitted the back door to the office. They were pleased to hear it. As a thank you for a job well done, they brought me to a 'massage' parlour where they paid for me to spend an hour with a girl of my choice. Mick H then took me to a little pub somewhere in north London, full of rough-looking guys in leather jackets and with shaved heads. As they all sat around drinking and smoking, I could feel their eyes piercing through me. When Mick H made his way to the end of the bar, everyone in the pub made a point of shaking his hand. For some reason I felt flattered to be in his company. This guy commanded respect. I didn't have to put my hand into my pocket for the entire night; Mick H paid for all my drinks. I was introduced to the manager of the bar. He told me that if I ever wanted to find him, I need only come to that bar.

At the end of the night, Mick H handed me the key to try on the safe the following morning. He said, 'Alan, I don't need to tell you what will happen to you if anything happens to that key.'

I had a good idea what he meant.

The plan was that if the key fitted the safe, they would 'hit' the pub on the night of the coming Bank Holiday Monday, after closing time. I was to put in a call to Mick H on the Monday night, after the manager had put the takings away. All I was to say on the phone was, 'Come over for the video,' then hang up and destroy the mobile phone Mick H had supplied me with for the purpose. Mick H and Joe C would come and help themselves to the takings from the safe and make good their escape. The plan seemed foolproof – and for my troubles I'd be making five grand.

Through the grapevine I heard that the takings from the pub had been stolen in similar circumstances a few years earlier, and the barman who was believed to have been involved was never seen again. This got me thinking: there was nothing to stop Mick H from stiffing me. He might take the view that I had served my purpose and that as long as I was on the scene, I was a living link between the burglary and him. I couldn't confide in anyone, and I didn't know what to do. I had come over to England to start a new life and to get away not only from the people who hated me but also from a life of crime. Now I found myself in the middle of a crime I wanted no part of.

I walked up to the manager in the lounge and told him the truth: that Mick H had asked me to try this key in the safe. I handed the key to the manager, who took it and tried it in the safe. It fitted.

Before I knew it, the landlord's head of security, Jim Dorman – a large and intimidating man – was called in. Everything after that seemed to happen very quickly. I recall being ushered upstairs into the closed nightclub area, so that we could talk privately. Mr Dorman sat me down, and I explained everything to him. He thanked me for doing the right thing, and then asked if I would go down to the police station to make a statement. I refused point blank to do that. I wanted nothing more to do with it. Then Mr Dorman's attitude changed, and he began to pile on the pressure to go to the police. Panicking a bit, I got up from the table. Mr Dorman got up and followed me. I then literally found myself dodging between the tables of the empty nightclub to try to get away from him.

He finally got me to sit down, and ordered the manager to bring over a large glass of brandy. The manager placed the drink in front of me, and I was told to 'drink it back in one'. As I drank the brandy, I looked up and saw two detectives walking in. They sat down beside me. They were Detective Sergeant Alan Barr and Detective Constable Dai Roberts from New Scotland Yard's CID. The minute they walked in, they assumed control and instructed Mr Dorman to leave the club.

Detective Sergeant Barr asked me would I just tell them 'in my own words' what had happened to me. He reassured me, saying, 'Just tell us exactly what happened. And as you do, we'll just take notes and scribble it down. We are only here for you. To protect you and to keep you safe. We have nothing but your best interests at heart.'

After I had recounted what happened, I was asked to sign the notes the detectives had taken. I did so, and asked what was going to happen now.

Barr said casually, 'Oh, at some stage in the future, uniformed police will probably just pick them up off the street. I don't think you'll even have to attend court. They're not big time, so you've nothing to worry about.'

I was relieved to hear this.

Barr then said that if Mick H denied he had anything to do with it, I might have to make a court appearance. To eliminate this possibility, he suggested a different approach. I could hand the key back to Mick, tell him that it fitted the safe, and make the phone call on the Monday night as instructed. The police would be there, waiting for them.

I recoiled with fear and said, 'I'm not setting anybody up. No way! I done what was required of me. I handed up the key and I have no problem going to court as a witness. But I'm not setting anyone up.'

Later that day, as I worked the bar, Mick H and Joe C were drinking in the pub, sitting in their usual seats. The manager came in and brought me up to his apartment above the pub. Jim Dorman was also there, and he told me to join him at the window overlooking the street and watch what was about to go down. As I peered out through the curtain, I could see a battered yellow Ford Escort van pull up across the road. The van had ladders on the roof, and two painters in white overalls got out. As soon as the two men stepped from the Ford van, one of them spoke into a walkie-talkie. Then, out of nowhere, marked and unmarked police cars and vans came screeching up to the front door of the pub. Black-clad figures jumped from the cars, armed with Heckler & Koch MP5 submachine guns and automatic pistols, and they stormed the pub from the back and front.

As I watched Mick H and Joe C being led away by the police, I realised they must be far from the petty criminals the police had earlier made them out to be. I also knew that the two lads would soon be aware that I had handed up the key and had told the Ol' Bill everything. I was fucked.

A short time later, Detective Sergeant Barr and Detective Constable Roberts walked into the manager's apartment. Barr turned to me and casually said they had just picked up Mick H and his buddy. I told him I had seen them do it. The detective sergeant shot the pub manager and security boss such a look that, if looks could kill, they'd have dropped dead there and then.

After that, Detective Sergeant Barr started questioning me. Did I know any members of organised crime gangs? Had I any links with paramilitary organisations? How much information about myself had I shared with Mick H? I asked the detective sergeant why he was asking me these questions. Then he dropped the biggest bombshell of my life.

'Alan, did you ever hear of the Witness Protection Programme?'

I nearly choked! After a lot of hysteria, I was eventually calmed down.

Barr decided to level with me. He said, 'Alan, I won't lie to you. Mick H is an extremely vicious and dangerous criminal. Over the years, he has been the chief suspect in many serious crimes, including a number of murders. But we have always been unable to catch him, or pin anything on him. Up until now! We can get him sent down for at least ten years on this charge. But we need your help.'

I was then offered a fully furnished apartment anywhere in England, Scotland or Wales. I would be given a new identity with passport, driver's licence, birth certificate and bank account. I would also be given some starting-off money and would set up in a new job of my choice.

The detective sergeant went on to say, 'The only downside to this deal, Alan, is that you will never be able to see any member of your family again. You'll have to sever all connections with them – not only for your own well-being, but for your family's sake, too. If your mother needs to send you a message, she will have to contact your police handler, who'll then convey the message to you. And the only way for you to make contact with your mother will also be via your police handler.'

Was I really hearing all this? The police wanted me never to see my family again, to live a lie for the rest of my life as a different person. For what? For doing what was required of me as an individual and as an employee to prevent a crime? My head was in a spin.

I told the police that I would go into the Witness Protection Programme. But I would need to go home first, to see my family and to let them know what was happening. The police asked me how my mother would feel about me going into the programme and giving Crown's evidence. I told them my mother would support me in anything I decided to do. I was also reminded that if I failed to come back over, Mick H would be released. And he would make it his business to track me down and pay me back for grassing him up. The detective sergeant informed me that the police would buy me a return airline ticket, and I would be collected later that evening and driven to the airport. I was then left alone in the manager's apartment.

After some deep thought, I decided I'd run away and buy my own ticket home. But when I went to let myself out of the manager's apartment, I found the door was locked. I was a prisoner with no way out – even the keys from the window locks were missing. There was plenty of alcohol in the apartment, and I helped myself to it. I needed it!

That night, I was collected and brought to Gatwick Airport, where I boarded my flight home. When I got home, I told my mother everything that had happened. I then went to my local police station and asked to speak to a detective.

I was brought in to see my old friend Detective Sergeant Cathal Cryan, and I explained the whole situation to him. I told Cryan that I wished to withdraw the statement I had made to the UK police, and that I most certainly did not want to go on any Witness Protection Programme. I wanted nothing more to do with the Mick H case.

Cryan said that once I had made a statement to that effect, he would then contact Detective Sergeant Barr and fax him over a copy. I made my statement, and then left the station.

Over the next couple of weeks, I was to receive daily phone calls from Detective Sergeant Barr, asking me to come back over to give evidence. Each time, I simply told him I wanted nothing more to do with the case. Barr finally told me he could no longer protect me: I was now on my own.

Although some fifteen years have elapsed, I still fear ever meeting Mick H again. I don't think that fear will ever leave me.

12

Access All Areas

I saw an advert, placed by a company called Servisair, who were looking to recruit ground handlers at Dublin Airport. I applied for the position and secured myself an interview, which took place in the office of Mr Gerry O'Reilly, the general manager. I was shown to a seat by his second in command, Mr Danny Fitzpatrick. Mr Fitzpatrick was impeccably turned out in a spotless white shirt with three gold stripes on his shoulders. He was clean-shaven and dosed in aftershave, and his hair was carefully gelled. Throughout the interview he stood as though he was Mr O'Reilly's bodyguard.

I was nervous that they'd cop on to my criminal record. But they never asked about that, and I never mentioned it. Still, it was a daunting interview. I tried not to show I was bluffing and lying through my teeth about my employment history, inventing jobs to fill in the years I'd been locked up. It came as a surprise when Mr O'Reilly told me I had the job and I would be starting my training that same week. I hadn't even been asked to fill in an application form.

Along with five other new recruits I was brought to visit the airport police, who would issue us with our airside access IDs. At this stage I was convinced my criminal past would be rumbled. I was third in the queue, sweating like a pig and contemplating legging it, but I decided I had to take the chance. When my turn came to go into the security office, I found myself standing before an aged airport policeman with unkempt hair and no tie. His shirtsleeves were rolled up over his hairy arms, and he had a fag hanging from the side of his mouth. He looked as though he had been locked away in that office for the past thirty years. Without even glancing at me, he told me to stand with my back to the wall. My photo was taken and then, after a number of minutes spent in cold and uncomfortable silence, I was handed the ID that allowed me access to any part of the airport.

I lived about four miles from the airport and needed my own transport, because I was doing shift work. I bought a little gold-coloured Renault 11 for £60; it was about twenty years old, and it was in bits. The driver's seat kept falling backwards, so I got the spare wheel and wedged it between the front and back seats to hold the driver's seat in place. The starting motor was also banjaxed, so I had to push-start the car every time.

Servisair looked after British Airways, Czech Airlines, Spanair, Air 2000, Eurocypria, Monarch, Britannia, CityJet/Air France, Crossair, Continental and Delta. My job entailed offloading baggage from aircraft, marshalling the planes in after they had landed, liaising with the pilot on headsets while the plane was in the process of being pushed back, as well as doing checks on the fuel and toilet-flap doors, the baggage doors and the blocks that prevent the aircraft from moving when it's parked.

I had always wanted to visit Los Angeles. So after I'd saved up some money from my new job, I took the opportunity to go there for a two-week break.

From LAX I got a taxi to the Village Motel on Santa Monica Boulevard, where I had a room booked. I did all the things tourists do. At Universal Studios I volunteered to dress up as Marty McFly from the film *Back to the Future III* and re-enacted a scene from the movie. I visited the sets of *Psycho*, *The Best Little Whorehouse in Texas*, *Jurassic Park*, *Batman*, *Jaws* and others – it was amazing. I also sat in the studio audience of Donny and Marie Osmond's chat show.

After the show, I brazenly walked up to the stage, extended my hand to Marie and said, 'How are you, Marie? I'm Alan, from Ireland.'

As we chatted about 'little old Ireland', I grabbed a chap from the floor and asked him to take a picture of the two of us.

On the flight I had made friends with a sexy German girl – we got quite close to joining the mile-high club before someone knocked on the door of the toilet, wishing to use it for its intended purpose.

But a week into my holiday, I wasn't having much luck with the ladies. I was flicking through a magazine in my room when I spotted an ad for escorts. I rang one of the agencies listed, and the girl went through a list of the escorts they had available. I opted for the Halle Berry lookalike; an hour later, I got a knock at my motel bedroom door.

Marie Osmond and me, in LA

The girl that came in was very pretty, although she was no Halle Berry. She took off her top and bra, and then she asked me had I ever been tied up. I told her I had been once, but it wasn't a great experience. 'Halle' assured me that she'd make up for it and would show me the time of my life. Using my shoelaces, she tied my hands to the steel headboard, and then strapped my feet together with my belt. Once again I found myself lying naked, tied up and helpless. But this time I was excited, and the little general was raring to go.

Then the girl got up from the bed, put her flimsy black top back on and picked up my jeans from the floor.

'What the fuck . . .?' I enquired.

But she ignored me – it was as if I wasn't even in the room. She took my wallet from my jeans and relieved me of $750, my holiday savings, all in brand-new crisp fifty-dollar bills. I began screaming and spitting at her, but she simply carried on with what she was doing and then very calmly walked out of my room, even closing the door behind her. I was fuming!

I eventually bit through the laces, and freed myself. But by then Halle had disappeared into the night. Determined not to let her get away with it, I rang the police and said that I had been robbed by a prostitute. I knew I had broken the law myself by enlisting the services of a hooker, but I didn't care – I wanted my money back.

Two policemen came to the motel. One of them happened to be an Irish-American copper called Murphy. I told them everything that had happened. They looked at each other and smiled. I told them that I wanted her tracked down and caught. Trying to conceal their laughter, the cops informed me there was nothing they could do.

After the police left, all I had in my bedside locker was $32. The following morning, I got a cab to LAX to see if I could get a flight home. I told the cab driver what had happened, and he kindly charged me only $10 for what should have been a $25 trip. I had the intention of repeating the full story at the British Airways ticket desk. But when I walked up to the desk, there was this young and beautiful sexy-looking blonde girl behind the counter, and I wasn't sure I'd be able to tell her I'd been tied up and robbed by a prostitute.

But I knew I had to do it. I explained everything that had happened to me, and the girl was OK about the whole thing.

The ticket was non-transferable, though – if I wanted to get home I'd have to purchase a new ticket. I was devastated; how on earth was I going to buy a new ticket when I only had about $20 dollars to my name? I then told her I worked at Dublin Airport and I looked after British Airways flights, and I showed her my ID. Suddenly, everything changed, and she issued a new ticket for me there and then.

When I got back home, I confided in my colleague John 'Rasher' Bacon about what had happened. He assured me he'd keep it to himself. The next day, when I went into work, there was a torn-out A3 picture from a magazine posted on the noticeboard. It showed a guy handcuffed to a bed, and someone had scribbled 'Alan in LA'. I turned around, and there were about fifteen of my fellow workers all standing there.

They were pissing themselves laughing; Rasher had told the lot of them.

I had my eye on a good-looking pilot, who I'll call 'Alexis'. She flew into Dublin twice a day. I made sure that I was always detailed to her flight, and I'd flirt with her while the aircraft was being pushed back. Doing the headset on an aircraft is meant to be a very serious and technical job, because you're the pilot's eyes: you tell him or her when to release the brakes, when to set them, when to start engines 4, 3, 2 and 1; then you disconnect the tug and bar, complete your external security checks and release the flight for take-off. However, myself and Alexis still found time to flirt and chat with each other.

The more I got to know Alexis, the more I wanted to ask her out. My mates thought I was insane. The way they saw it, she was loaded. She had a great job, a beautiful cottage beside a lake in England, and a seaplane. So why on earth would she be interested in me? I saw the logic of this – but I thought perhaps opposites really did attract.

One day, as her aircraft was in the process of being pushed back,

I blurted out, 'Alexis, do you fancy coming out for a drink with me when you fly back in tonight?'

I couldn't believe it when she looked down from the cockpit at me, smiled and said, 'Alan, I'd love to.'

We arranged to meet in the Great Southern Hotel at the airport later that night. After the push-back, I bragged to my mates that I was meeting Alexis later on. They were gutted that I had actually scored a date with a pilot. But underneath it all I was beginning to panic. What would we talk about? Would we be compatible? Then I began to visualise myself sitting beside the log fire in her cottage on a misty night, looking out at the picturesque lake with her sea-plane tied up, while Alexis poured some fine wine. That's how my mind worked when it came to women – if I was attracted to some-one, I'd be designing wedding invitations in my head.

As I sat in the lounge of the Great Southern, waiting for Alexis to make her appearance, my mind was racing. Did I look OK? Was I sitting right? I was checking my teeth with my tongue to make sure they were clean of debris, blowing my breath into my cupped hands and smelling for bad breath. When Alexis arrived, I insisted on get-ting the drinks in, despite her objections. The conversation flowed, and we were very easy with each other.

I asked her did she want to head into town to a club.

She said she had an early flight, but added, 'I have another over-night in two weeks. And we'll be able to head out dancing then, as I'll be due out on the late flight.'

I saw Alexis each week for nearly two months. One night, I went out clubbing with her and some of her wealthy friends – a Ryanair captain and his girlfriend, and another pilot who was shagging a stewardess. I felt like a fish out of water. Foolishly I had told my mates where we were going. Unbeknownst to me, they all followed us there. Now, in the corner of the club, I could see them laughing at me. I was on a budget and watching the few quid I had. But cash was not a problem for the pilots, and I felt very uncomfortable when they began to buy rounds with their credit cards. When it came to me, I was fumbling around with fivers, tenners and loose change. I was usually comfortable mixing with people – no matter who they were, or what they did for a living – but that night, I felt embarrassed.

It wasn't long after that night that I began asking my ramp controller to allocate me to any flight, provided he didn't detail me to work on Alexis's aircraft. For a while, Alexis asked my mates where I was. But eventually, she stopped asking.

By this time I had saved a few bob, and I decided it was time I invested in a new car to replace the ancient Renault. I went to a garage and got a Rover 214 Si on hire purchase.

Shortly after I had purchased the Rover, I drove it into the city centre to go clubbing. I fully intended getting a taxi home that night and collecting the Rover the following morning. But when I left the club, I decided to take a chance and drive home. As I drove through the city centre, I saw a police car pull out behind me; the lights and sirens went on. The copper informed me that I was drunk. He placed me under arrest, then brought me to the Bridewell. I denied I was drunk. A doctor was called in, and a blood sample was taken and sent off for analysis. I was later released and told to collect my car the following morning from the police station.

I hadn't felt drunk, but I knew it was possible that I'd been over the limit. I couldn't believe how stupid I'd been. I knew if I was served with a summons for drink-driving, I risked losing everything I had.

Another work colleague of mine, Denis, often came out drinking with myself and a few other lads from the airport. But more importantly, Denis also palled around with a police officer. I can't recall his name, so I'll just call him 'Steve'. (If he stood in front of me now, I don't think I'd recognise him.) I knew Steve was stationed in the same district as the copper who'd arrested me. When I'd been out clubbing with Denis, we occasionally met up with Steve – and we hit it off.

I finally got a summons to appear in the District Court to answer the charge of drink-driving. According to the document, I had been seven times over the legal limit. I began to really panic: I knew that once I went up to court on that summons, I would be going back to jail. The night before I was due to appear in court, I was out in a club with my mate Denis and his mate Steve, the copper. I was hesitant about asking Steve could he do anything for me. But after downing a number of pints, I finally got the courage up and told him about my court appearance the following morning.

Steve asked the name of the officer who had me up. When I told him, Steve replied that the officer was one of his best friends – and that he would not be up in court, because he'd been injured at work and would be out sick for a number of months. Steve assumed a colleague would appear in court in the arresting officer's place. He said he'd see what he could do, but he couldn't promise anything. He also said that if I'd confided in him immediately after the arrest, he would have been able to wipe it from the system before the case went through.

The next morning, I went to court. As I walked into the courtyard, I could see Steve dressed in his Garda uniform.

He walked over to me and said, 'Jesus, Alan, am I glad that you told me about this case last night. When I went into work this morning, there was a note in my drop file from my mate. He has asked me to get this case remanded for four months. I wouldn't have known where to look if you hadn't said anything to me, and then you walked into this court!'

When the case was called, Steve got into the witness box and said, 'Your Honour, my colleague was seriously injured on duty and will be away from work for at least another six months. I have no objections to a strike-out.'

My solicitor, not having a clue what was going on, jumped to his feet and blurted, 'And that would be my application also, Your Honour.'

The judge turned and said, 'Strike out.'

And that was the end of the case. Happy as a pig in shit, I walked out of the courtroom.

Steve came out behind me, and I said, 'I owe you a pint, mate.'

I shook his hand, and we arranged to meet up later that night. I bought him more than a pint – he had saved me from a certain jail term, and losing my job.

Suddenly, and impulsively, I got bored with the job and decided to resign from my position in the airport and move to Spain.

One reason, perhaps, was that I had a major hang-up about my past coming back to haunt me. It seemed it would inevitably do so, if I stayed for too long in any one job. Also, I used to see people going off happily on planes every day, and then see their disappointed faces when they returned to gloomy Ireland. I felt I was missing out on something better.

I was drinking heavily, including at work, but I had no awareness that I had a problem. I wanted to drink whenever I liked, I wanted to have money all the time, I wanted the easy life, and I didn't want to work too hard to obtain it. My mad head thought that a job in a bar in sunny Spain was the solution.

13

2,800 *Pesetas and an Envelope of Cocaine*

I didn't have the courage to tell my bosses face to face that I was leaving. So I booked two weeks' holiday leave, and then wrote out a very nice letter of resignation. After my plane took off from Dublin Airport, my mate Rasher was to put the letter into the in-tray, from where it would then make its way to management.

My first-class return ticket from Dublin to Malaga with CityJet only cost me a fiver, because I'd booked it as Servisair staff. I also booked and paid for my accommodation on a half-board basis at the Hotel Balmoral in Benalmadena. With my accommodation, breakfast and evening meal all paid for, the only worry on my mind was that I had two weeks to find myself a new job.

As I'd bought my ticket on a 'staff travel' basis, I had to fly out when a seat was available – a day earlier than expected. I owed the hotel manager 6,000 pesetas for the extra night in my room. Although I offered to pay him there and then, he insisted I pay at the end of my stay – a mistake, as things worked out.

Before I tackled the employment end of things, I went out partying on the Saturday and Sunday nights. My reasoning was that if I wanted to work in a bar, I'd be better off getting to know the people who worked in the local bars first. On the Sunday night I went to an all-night bar called Stringfella's, where I recognised Peter Mitchell, otherwise known as 'Fatso', who I'd been locked up with in St Patrick's Institution many years ago.

Peter, who was suspected of being one of John Gilligan's henchmen and is still wanted by the Irish police, invited me over to his table. I joined him and two blonde Irish girls who were living with him. As the night progressed, Peter asked me to follow him into the toilet. When I went in, he took out a hunting knife and a very large bag of cocaine. He slid the knife into the coke and brought out the blade with a mountain of coke on it, which he then put into an envelope and gave to me. Then from his own bag he put out four lines, and we snorted two each. The coke was rocket fuel, and we partied away for the rest of the night.

I remember walking back to my hotel, totally out of my head, and meeting some Spanish guy and his girlfriend. For some reason they began to walk along on each side of me, talking nonsense.

I got so fed up with their ramblings that I turned to them and said, 'Listen, will you two just ever go and fuck off away from me!'

When I got back to my hotel, I did another couple of lines of cocaine and began playing some Irish rebel songs on my stereo. I heard a loud banging on my door, which I opened to find the manager telling me to knock off the music. I refused. He walked into the room and switched off the stereo. I told him to get the fuck out of my room, and I switched the cassette back on. The manager stormed off, saying he'd get the police.

'Get who the fuck you like!' I replied, and kicked the door shut as he left my room.

Sometime later, still totally out of my head on coke and alcohol, I heard a loud banging on my door. I swung the door open and found myself face-to-face with four policemen, all dressed in black baseball caps, black combat attire and boots, and bearing side arms. The manager, hiding behind the policemen, began shouting for me to turn off the music. I told the manager that I could play my music if I wanted to.

The manager replied, 'Yes, yes you can. But it four thirty –'

'Yeah, it's only bleedin' four thirty!' I said.

Then I walked over to the window, and pulled back the curtains – to see it was pitch dark outside. Suddenly I was brought back in touch with reality: it was four thirty in the morning. I switched the stereo off straight away and couldn't apologise enough to the manager.

I got straight into bed, and tried to sleep. As I lay in the darkened room, I opened my eyes and I looked over at my glass of water, watch and cigarettes sitting on top of a small locker by the window. The small locker then slid quickly across the tiled floor. I began to laugh at this: I believed that there was someone underneath the bed, pulling the locker across the floor using a bit of string.

I looked down under the bed, still laughing, and said, 'Ah, give it over, will ya?'

Then I got out from the bed and pushed the locker back over to the window. But when I returned to my bed, the same thing happened again. I now began to get really scared. At the foot of my bed, sitting on a stool beside my writing table, was a big dark human figure. He had his right foot resting on his left knee, and he was puffing away on a cigarette. He was a well-built black guy with a doll-sized head and a mass of bushy black hair.

I jumped out of bed, saying over and over, 'It's only the DTs! It's only the DTs!'

I banged on all the lights, put on some music (low), threw loads of water on my face, and sat down and had a smoke. It was some time before I was actually able to get to sleep.

The following morning, dying with a massive hangover, I picked up my jeans to see how much money I had spent. After searching all my pockets, I could only find 2,800 pesetas (about £17). In a panic, I jumped up out of the bed and began searching the room for the other 95,000 pesetas that I had brought over with me. I upended the bed, emptied out my suitcase, searched the drawers – everywhere. I must have searched everything in the room at least four times. I was shell-shocked. On the second day of my move to Malaga, I had managed to lose all my money; all I had left to my name were a measly 2,800 pesetas and an envelope of cocaine.

Then it clicked with me. It must have been that Spanish couple who I'd met the night before and were talking shite – they must have dipped me. I didn't know what I was going to do. So, like I always did, I ran away. I got a taxi to Malaga Airport to try to get back home. But, first things first: I had to try to stop that letter of resignation being handed into the Servisair management.

I tried to call my mate Rasher, but his mobile phone was switched off. Frustrated and feeling I was in a race against time, I rang my mother and reversed the charges. I asked her to get in touch with my mate asap, and to tell him not to hand in that letter of resignation. The taxi to the airport cost me 1,900 pesetas (about £10), leaving me with 900 pesetas to my name. (I had no savings in the bank: I'd brought all of my money with me to Spain.) I went to the Servisair ticket desk, as they handled CityJet in Spain, and I flashed my airport ID to the Spanish girl at the desk. After spending an age trying to explain everything that had happened to me, I was told that because my ticket was a staff/stand-by ticket, she could not endorse it for me to travel on another flight. Then I learned that CityJet only flew in and out of Malaga on Saturdays and Sundays: I would have to come back in five days' time and hope I could get out on one of their flights then.

My state of mind at that time was one of contemplating doing bad things to myself. I thought I was cursed, and I started dwelling on other bad things that had happened to me. I had a litre bottle of vodka in my bag. I found myself a seat in the airport and began drinking the vodka straight. At 5 a.m., having drunk three-quarters of the bottle, I dragged my three heavy bags a quarter of a mile to the train station. I rode ticketless on the train back to the resort.

When I arrived in Benalmadena, I hadn't got a clue where the hotel was. And I just hadn't got the energy to carry my three big bags. I asked a cab driver how much would it cost to take me to the Hotel Balmoral, and he said 600 pesetas. That was two-thirds of my remaining cash. But I didn't care any more: I just wanted to get back to the hotel, where I was guaranteed a bed, breakfast and an evening meal. I didn't even want to think about how I was going to get back to the airport, or survive the intervening five days.

I explained everything to the hotel manager, but the only thing the man was concerned about was how was I going to pay him the 6,000 pesetas I owed him for the night I arrived early. I told the manager that I could not pay him, and he said he'd bill my travel agent.

I walked away, thinking, 'You can bill whoever you like, mate. That's the least of my worries!'

I'd no money, and I felt like a prisoner. I couldn't go anywhere, couldn't buy anything, eat out or buy gifts – I didn't even have a book to read. I ended up just sitting in the hotel, day after day, surrounded by Spanish old folk. There was no point in ringing my mother and asking her to wire over some cash, as my Ma was in the same boat as myself. I found the management and employees of the hotel the most unsympathetic individuals I have ever come across. In all the days I sat in that hotel lobby, twiddling my thumbs, not once did any of them approach me and offer a word of comfort, or ask did I want a cup of tea or coffee.

Each day, I'd check all the Irish bars in the hope that I would bump into Peter Mitchell, but I couldn't locate him. As I passed a couple of builders working on the side of a road, I asked them would they be interested in buying my camera. I had bought it a couple of weeks before I went away for £110. After examining the camera, they offered me 2,000 pesetas – about a tenth of what I'd paid. I felt I had no choice but to accept.

The night before I was due to go back to the airport, the hotel was having a 'variety night'. I really needed cheering up and desperately wanted to go. I sat down to do my calculations. It would cost me 600 pesetas in a taxi from the hotel to the train station, then 400 pesetas on the train to the airport, and a further 100 pesetas for a trolley to carry my bags on. That came to 1,100 pesetas, which would leave me with 900. A bottle of beer in the hotel cost 165 pesetas. That meant I would be able to buy five bottles of beer. I almost shouted aloud.

I went to the variety night, and I had a ball. I got up and sang Rolf Harris's 'Two Little Boys'. At the end of the night, I got a certificate and a glass of champagne. After a grim week, that night was just what I needed.

I got to the airport nice and early on the Saturday morning. I'd made a decision: if I didn't get out on the next flight, I was just going to walk into a police station, tell them I'd no money, nowhere to stay, no way to support myself, and I intended to live rough and commit all sorts of crimes. When I got to the Servisair ticket desk, there was a different Spanish girl working there, so I went through the whole rigmarole of retelling my story. The girl told me that the flight departed at 1 p.m., and I should come back to her at noon. She also mentioned that the flight was overbooked, and customers paying the full fare would be given preference.

As I wandered around the airport, I met an elderly man who had been visiting his daughter in a villa he owned. I found myself telling him my story; he bought me a cup of coffee, and gave me 2,000 pesetas. Then, as I stood in the check-in line, I met two middle-aged couples who were also on their way home to Dublin. Again, I found myself pouring my heart out to them. As they walked through to the departure gates, one of the men came running back and shoved something into my hand. When I opened my hand, it was 5,000 pesetas. I then met Ray, a guy who I knew to see from Dublin Airport. He was with his girlfriend, Deirdre, and they were also just coming home after a week's break. Once again, I told my story; Ray gave me 5,000 pesetas.

Despite my good fortune in meeting these extremely generous people, I still did not know if I was going to get out on the flight. At twenty minutes to one, there were fourteen stand-by passengers waiting to see if they could get a seat on the already overbooked flight – and each of them was a full-paying customer. Before I knew it, I was the last person standing at the check-in desk: the others had all got on the flight.

Eventually, I was told I could be checked in. I ran through the boarding gate to catch the flight – to be told the plane had missed its slot and would be delayed. I didn't care; I knew I was going home, and my Spanish nightmare was over. I met all the people who had given me the money in the departure lounge, thanked them again for their kindness, and offered them the money back. Every one of them refused to take it, so I went up to the bar and bought everyone a drink. We sat down and had a good yarn, and for the first time in two weeks I felt really happy. I will be forever grateful to them all.

I knew all the members of the CityJet crew. As a result, I was upgraded to first class. I filled the stewardesses in on what had happened to me, and I sat back in the luxurious surroundings of the first-class section as the flight took off. The sexy flight attendants handed me a nice bottle of chilled champagne and as much beer as I could drink. For that brief moment in time I was in heaven.

When I got back to Dublin, I was hoping and praying I still had a job. It turned out Rasher had put my resignation letter into the in-tray for it to go to senior management, as instructed. But before it had a chance to go anywhere, the rest of my mates, including three of my duty managers, all had a good read of it. The duty managers had notified the general manager by phone that I had resigned. But when one of the duty managers was sent to retrieve the letter, it had mysteriously disappeared. So I reported for work as usual at the end of my two-week break.

When I walked into the manager's office to clock in, the manager looked baffled. 'Alan, what the hell are you doing here? You resigned, and your position has been filled.'

I replied, 'Resigned? Me? Who told you that? Well, you can just go and unfill it, mate – I never resigned.'

The manager said he'd read my resignation letter. I asked him to show it to me, which he couldn't. I again denied I had ever written such a letter, and suggested that maybe one of my work-mates had written it to wind the company up. I think they knew full well that I had resigned. But legally there was nothing they could do, because they had no evidence. My job was safe, and I was back on track.

One of my tasks at the airport was transporting passengers to and from their planes on a 58-seater coach. I didn't even have a driver's licence – I was using a forged one. Late one wet night, I had to collect passengers from an incoming flight and bring them to the arrivals hall. After the passengers had boarded, I decided to take a short cut across the apron. I could see no oncoming traffic. But as I drove across the front of the air-bridges, the inside of the coach suddenly lit up. I looked to my left and saw the nose of a British Midland airbus that was taxiing up right on top of me. The power beam from the plane's halogen spotlight was blinding, and I swerved the coach sharply to the right, nearly running over the British Midland worker who was marshalling the plane.

I drove the frightened and shaken passengers to the arrivals hall. As they all nervously stepped off the coach, I was shaking. The minute the passengers were gone, I lit up a smoke. The flight dispatcher came over to me and said the captain had only spotted me at the last minute; I was to consider myself very lucky that he wasn't going to make a report on the incident. In future, I was to stick to the road. I never heard anything back from Servisair, so I presume that none of the passengers reported it either.

That incident apart, I loved driving the coaches. I was one of a relatively small number of trained coach drivers in the company, and this meant I never had to load or unload baggage from the flights. That left me with a lot of time on my hands. I spent much of it on the departure floor, chatting to the good-looking girls at the check-in desks. For some reason I always found myself in the dreaded 'friend zone': the girls would pour their hearts out to me and tell me their most intimate and personal problems. But it never went any further than that. I loved listening to them and going out drinking and partying with them. But I did quite often think about sleeping with them, too.

In May of 1999, a chartered Concorde flew into Dublin Airport. Servisair was handling the aircraft, which was waiting to fly ninety-three consultants to Heathrow. A couple of hours before the flight was due to depart, I decided to take a walk up to the departure floor for my usual chat with the girls. As I walked past a little check-in office, I could see the door was slightly ajar and I overheard people whispering. I heard one of them say something about 'a free seat on Concorde'. I pushed open the door, to find a room full of check-in staff.

'What's the story about Concorde and free seats?' I asked.

'Sorry, Alan,' said one of the guys. 'All the seats are gone.'

It turned out that the captain had told one of the check-in staff there were seven free seats available. Because Servisair had looked after his flight so well, he was prepared to give them to any member of staff that wanted them. There were twelve check-in staff who wanted to go, so they'd decided to secretly raffle off the tickets among themselves, without letting anybody else know, and they'd booked accommodation at Heathrow and flights back to Dublin the next day for the lucky seven. I reminded them that check-in staff were not the only people working for Servisair, and I said that the ground-handling guys should have been included in the raffle. They insisted the tickets were gone, and that was the end of it.

There was no way I was going to let this go: I wanted a chance to fly on Concorde. I stormed off to the general manager's office, where I explained everything. He knew nothing about it, and immediately contacted the manageress in charge of check-in to find out what was going on. I then rallied up three other ground handlers who also fancied a flight on Concorde. The general manager decided that there would be a new raffle, involving the twelve from check-in and the four ground handlers. The first seven names pulled out would get the seats.

Word of the raffle spread quickly, and employees gathered to see what the outcome was going to be. The first three names pulled out of the hat were from check-in. They were pissing themselves with excitement, and slagging the ground handlers off. I was fuming. But the next four names wiped the smiles from their faces: myself and the three other ground handlers were all pulled out in succession. The check-in staff were glaring at me with anger and disdain, but that didn't bother me. I felt I had achieved something.

I rang my Ma and told her I wouldn't be home that evening: instead, I was flying to London on Concorde. I was still in my work overalls, and I didn't even have a change of clothes – none of the ground handlers did. So the four of us had to go on board the fastest and most glamorous commercial aircraft in the world dressed in our dirty working clobber. The check-in staff who'd won seats on the flight wouldn't even look at me. And when they began taking photographs of themselves walking up the steps of Concorde, they refused to let any of the ground handlers in on the photos. But I had more pressing things to worry about. I was skint – I didn't even have the price of a packet of smokes. I didn't know how I was going to get back home from the UK, or where I was going to sleep when I got to Heathrow.

Then the general manager, who must have got an inkling of the situation, called me and stuck £150 into my hand. He said, 'Here the fuck, go and enjoy yourself! Pay it back in instalments. No rush with it.'

The cabin of the supersonic jet was tiny, but very luxurious; the leather bucket seats were massive. As we powered down the runway, my body, neck and head were physically pinned to the seat. The captain told us that the front wheels had left the ground at a speed of 275 mph, and he gave us regular updates as to our speed. As we climbed, the captain announced that we'd be making a detour via the South of France, where we'd fly supersonically over the coast. We climbed at a remarkably steep angle: it was like sitting in a La-Z-Boy tilted all the way back, looking up at the ceiling.

When we reached 58,000 feet, the captain said, 'Ladies and gentlemen, in the next minute or so I'm going to do something. I don't want any of you to be alarmed. I am going to kill the thrusts for a couple of seconds, and you will feel a slight heave.' With that, the pilot killed the thrusts.

The engines fell deathly silent, the nose of Concorde suddenly dropped and then the aircraft seemed to sway up and down. It felt a bit like floating in a swimming pool on your back. Everyone's stomach heaved; then, out of nowhere, the thrusts kicked back into life and the aircraft just took off. All of this was completed within seconds, but it felt a lot longer. There was a digital screen in front of us which told us in red lettering that we'd hit Mach 2. We were travelling at 1,350 mph for a full two minutes. The manoeuvre the pilot did before we accelerated is known, I believe, as a tailspin or a wave drag. We were flying on the edge of space.

After we landed at Heathrow and taxied in, we had to wait for about twenty minutes for a set of steps to be brought over to the aircraft. While everyone was waiting in their seats, I got up and began chatting to the cabin crew, telling them what had happened back at Dublin Airport. As everyone began to disembark, the stewardesses called me aside. They had got me a signed certificate from the captain, stating I'd flown supersonically on Concorde. They also gave me two Concorde bags full of souvenirs and memorabilia, along with five large bottles of Krug champagne. They said they really admired me for the stand I'd taken back in Dublin.

Because of all the yapping I was doing, I was the last passenger to disembark from the aircraft. As I came down the steps with my hands full of champagne and souvenirs, the look on the check-in girls' faces was priceless – it was definitely a Kodak moment.

The other ground handlers and I knew that the check-in crew had pre-booked hotel rooms, so we followed them to their hotel and, much to their disappointment, ended up getting rooms at the same rate. I gave each of the three lads a bottle of champagne. As the check-in staff walked past us in the hotel lobby, totally ignoring us, we all cheered and I popped open the fifth bottle.

I turned to the lads and said aloud, 'Good enough for the Queen, good enough for me!'

After flying back to Dublin on my day off post-Concorde, I went into work as usual. A few minutes after clocking in, I was called into the manager's office and introduced to Sergeant Vinnie McGrath from the airport police. Sergeant McGrath told me that he had a letter from the Gardaí, informing him of my criminal past. I was told that I would have to hand over my airside access ID. I felt as if someone had just hit me with a lump hammer across the face. In front of all my workmates I was escorted from the airport.

The airport authorities made no fuss, and it didn't take long for me to work out why: they'd allowed me to work within restricted areas of Dublin Airport for fourteen months, despite my criminal record. If that got into the public domain, a lot of serious questions would have been asked. I had never lied about my record – I'd never had to. They never asked me to fill in an application form. I was interviewed on spec and given the job in haste, simply because it was at the height of the summer season and the company was very busy.

My mother was distraught; she had finally seen me in a decent job and away from crime, and that made her happy. Now my past had come back to haunt me, and her world had been turned upside down. My family and friends all suspected that this setback would send me off the rails and back into a life of crime. But that did not even cross my mind: there was no way I was ever going back to that life.

One day, sitting at home and talking with my mother about what my next move should be, I got a call on my mobile from the company I'd bought my Rover from on hire purchase. I had fallen behind in my monthly repayments on the car, and they wanted to know why I was missing the payments. As I chatted to the guy, I glanced up. Outside the gate, I saw two repo men jumping into the Rover and driving it away. As soon as they'd got the car, the phone line went dead.

Although I was depressed by this turn of events, I was determined to get back into work. I got an excellent letter of reference from Servisair, and I applied for a job as an overseas holiday representative with Panorama Holidays. They called me in for one of their open days. This consisted of drama improvisations, singing and various team tasks. I loved it, but it was nerve-racking. At various points throughout the day, Panorama management would split us up into two different rooms. Each time they did this, one group of people was told to go home. You never knew if it was going to be your group or the other group that was going to be given the bad news. If you were still there at the end of the day, you had the job. By the end of the day, I was still there – I couldn't believe it.

In Tunisia

I was sent to Tunisia. I would spend my days looking after my guests, organising bingo, crazy golf, quiz nights, sing-songs and parties. I loved it: I thrived on looking after people. Even on my days off, I still found myself going around my hotels and making sure my guests were OK.

On one of my days off, I came across a young couple. I could see that the girl was quite distressed, and I asked were they all right. It turned out that the couple, who were travelling with another tour operator, had had the time of their welcome meeting changed at the last minute, and they hadn't been notified by their rep. As the couple had never been to Tunisia before, and their rep was nowhere to be seen, the couple didn't know where to go or what to do. I got a Panorama holiday welcome pack, sat them down and gave them their own personalised welcome meeting. I didn't do it to make Panorama look good; I did it because these were two people in a foreign country for the first time. The young couple were delighted with all the information I gave them. Throughout the remainder of their holiday, they came to me any time they needed to know anything. A couple of weeks later, I got a letter from the human resources director of Panorama Holidays in the UK, congratulating me on my performance. Unbeknownst to me, the couple had written to the company when they got back home.

After six months working in Tunisia, the novelty of the job began to wear off. I made the decision to pack it all in and go home. When I handed in my letter of resignation, my bosses tried to convince me to stay. Nearly every week, guests were writing letters of praise to the company about me. But I just wanted to get on to that plane. I wanted to be at home.

But as soon as I had settled in at home, I began to get itchy feet again. All I wanted to do was get away: I wanted to see as much of the world as I possibly could. But I think it went deeper than that, too. It was like I just couldn't settle anywhere – I just wanted to keep on running, moving, meeting new people who didn't know me. I loved having a clean slate. I was haunted by my past; I had no rest from it, no peace.

I wrote out an apologetic letter to Panorama, asking could I come back. They said they'd love to have me back, and this time I was sent to Ibiza.

I'd had good luck with sex-hungry guests in Tunisia, but Ibiza was a whole other level. It was amazing: women who wouldn't have looked at me twice back home would throw themselves at me in Ibiza. Groups of girls staying in the hotel sometimes held a 'shag-a-rep' competition. The idea was to see which one of the girls could get me into the sack first. Who was I to object? I'd hate to be a spoilsport.

In Ibiza

I had a great time in Ibiza. But after three summer months of insane drinking, partying and sex, I burned out and hit a brick wall. I had had enough. I resigned and returned home.

I had no idea what was coming next.

14

The Homeless Journalist

I will always be a writer. I won't ever be a plumber, an electrician, a carpenter, a stockbroker or a solicitor. All I can do is write.

I started to get serious about my writing around the turn of the millennium, although I had no real understanding at the time of how important it already was for me. My eldest brother, Declan, was by that time a successful TV scriptwriter. His childhood had been less chaotic than mine – he'd gone to school, and he'd never been involved in crime. But he was my brother, and in lots of ways we were alike. When he began getting plays staged in Dublin, I went along to see them when I could, and that must have influenced me. By 2000, he had written episodes for *Ballykissangel* and *Where the Heart Is*, and he was making inroads into writing for *The Bill*. When he encouraged me to write a full-length play, it seemed like the most natural thing in the world for me to do.

I studied Kathleen E. George's *Playwriting: The First Workshop*, and then I got stuck into writing the play. It told three different stories, set in three flats; by the end, the three stories came together. After many months of writing and rewriting, I sent the script to a number of theatres in Ireland and the UK. I received enough rejection letters to wallpaper my bedroom, but I got some very positive feedback from professional theatre people, and that really boosted my confidence.

I was unemployed after leaving the Ibiza job, and I suspected the local employment exchange was about to send me out on menial work experience in order to get me off the dole. All I really wanted to do was write, so I decided to enrol at Ballyfermot College of Further Education as a mature student and get a Higher National Diploma in print journalism. This would keep the employment exchange off my back, and I figured I could make good use of the facilities of a college. After two years, I would walk away with a diploma in print journalism – although, at that stage, becoming a journalist was the furthest thing from my mind.

On the first day at Ballyfermot, I felt a bit weird walking into a classroom full of people who were mostly a fair bit younger than me – and mostly middle class. But I was determined to stick with it and, as I got to know the other students, I got on very well with my classmates. One was a gorgeous dark-skinned girl who turned out to be Emir-Maria Holohan-Doyle, a former Miss Ireland. As the days turned into weeks, myself and Emir became really good friends. One evening, after college, the two of us went out drinking, and we ended up back at her apartment. Emir grabbed two cans of beer from the fridge, then sat down right next to me on the sofa. I fancied her like mad, and a part of me wondered if I might be in with a chance. She was talking to me, but nothing she said was registering. My mind was logged into a completely different network: she was on Google Chat, whereas I was on a dating website. But I snapped out of it. She could have any guy she wanted, so why would she be interested in me? I didn't make a move on her, and we remained good mates.

As part of an assignment for college, each of us had to interview someone who we thought was newsworthy. I proceeded to chase down an interview with my former landlord, Mr John Lonergan – the top prison governor in the country. Mr Lonergan was more than happy to give me an interview. He was delighted to see that I was now bettering myself by pursuing a journalistic career (although, by the time you finish this chapter, you might conclude I was going from bad to worse). Mr Lonergan allowed me complete access to the prison. The best part for me was being allowed access to the 'Hang-House', where Kevin Barry had been executed in November 1920.

John Lonergan spoke very frankly to me, and I was impressed by his humanitarian spirit. I was so pleased with the interview that I rang the *Sunday World* to see if I could sell a story to them. I got through to Joanne McElgunn, a staff reporter, who asked me to come into their offices to speak with the news editor, John Donlon. The newsroom was like a scene from *All the President's Men* – hacks typing away at their desks or rushing around and talking on the phone. There was a real buzz about the place.

I must have looked like a gobshite when I sat down to face John Donlon, hugging my school bag tight to my chest. But as soon as John opened his mouth, I felt at ease. He read my copy and liked it. The following Sunday, after less than a month in college, I had my first story printed in a national newspaper with a readership of more than half a million. The students and lecturers at college began to treat me differently. I tried to be cool, but my ego was sky high and I loved the attention.

My next big story idea arose from my old job at the airport. On a number of occasions, I had walked through security without my air-side access ID being checked. I decided to head up to the airport at 6 a.m., when I knew it would be in the middle of a really busy shift changeover. As it was still dark, I threw on a high-vis vest and fell into line with all the workers. The works entrance was at the back of the airport, and the workers went through a gate in single file. The air-port police officer manning the entrance was supposed to inspect everyone's airside access ID. But as I stood back and watched the first ten or so workers enter, I saw that the officer remained inside his security hut. He was reading his paper, and simply waved the work-ers through. As I walked up to the window and casually flashed my college ID, the officer didn't even look up at me; he just waved his hand, and I was in. Dublin Airport was now my oyster.

I wandered around, taking photographs of the belly-holds of the aircraft parked on stands. I ventured into the baggage hall and casu-ally asked an airport employee would he swipe me through with his security card, allowing me access into the arrivals hall – I told him I had forgotten my own ID. The worker walked over and, without questioning me, swiped me through. I then walked through the red 'goods to declare' section of Customs and Excise – again, without challenge – and into the main terminal of the airport.

I approached the *Sunday World* with the evidence of how I'd breached security at the airport. I had also subsequently interviewed my old friend Anne Doyle, and she'd told me some good yarns. So I had the two stories with me when I met with John Donlon. He took the Anne Doyle interview, but decided against running with the airport story. I think he and his colleagues might have been a bit sceptical about the authenticity of the story: perhaps they couldn't believe that a student journalist had blagged his way through airport security.

I took the airport story to Paddy Murray, the editor of the *Sunday Tribune*. Paddy and the news editor, Martin Wall, fired question after question at me. I'd never felt as nervous under questioning in my entire life – it was far worse than any police interrogation. In my nervousness I let the folder of papers that I was holding slip out of my grasp, and they fell all over the office floor. I scrambled to my knees and nervously gathered them up; then, as I went to sit back down in my chair, I missed the seat and ended up on my arse with the folder of papers, again, going all over the floor. But despite my jittery performance, they decided to run with the story.

In the interest of fairness I had to ring up Aer Rianta's press office to give them the opportunity to comment. I made the phone call late on the Saturday afternoon – too late for Aer Rianta to lodge a High Court injunction to halt the story. I told them who I was and what I had done, and I asked them would they like to make a comment. There was a long silence on the other end of the phone. Eventually, the Aer Rianta spokesperson stuttered, 'No . . . no comment,' and hung up.

These photographs were taken during a 20 minute stroll around a restricted area of Dublin Airport. Only when Alan Croghan took a photograph from a civilian area was he approached by Airport Police

Questions asked of airport security

Donning a visibility vest and flashing college ID **Alan Croghan** was able to gain access to and take photographs of restricted areas of Dublin Airport

The appearance of the airport story in the *Sunday Tribune* and the Anne Doyle interview in the *Sunday World* brought me lots more recognition, and that meant everything to me. Journalism was now my addiction. It was like cocaine or heroin: each time I completed a story, I was getting my fix. I had lined up two weeks' work experience with the news editor of the *Star*, Danny Smyth. But after the airport story ran in the *Tribune*, John Donlon told me that the *Sunday World*'s deputy editor, John Sheils, wanted me to stay with them for the summer. For the first time in a long while, I was genuinely happy. Although I wouldn't be paid for any shifts – I was just being paid per story – I jumped at the chance to work in the newsroom of the *Sunday World*.

When I attended my first editorial meeting, I didn't know what to say or where to look. The editors believed a certain lap-dancing club was a front for a brothel. They wanted me to go in undercover, wired up with a hidden microphone, and get the girls on tape selling sex. It was the general consensus within the newsroom that, because I had had the bottle to breach security at Dublin Airport, I would be perfect for this job.

That night, I met up with Damian Lane, a senior reporter, who strapped a tape recorder and wire to my body. He then handed me £500, to cover lap dances and drinks. As I approached the doors of the venue, feeling a mixture of nervousness and excitement, I avoided eye contact with the shady-looking doormen.

I only needed to record one of the girls offering sex for cash. But after spending half the money on private dances, drinks and asking for 'extras', I left the club with nothing but an erection. When I sat in my car and checked the recording, I found that the lead of the microphone had somehow popped out of the cassette – there was nothing recorded. Luckily I hadn't lost anything of value!

The following night, I went back in. And this time I gave the microphone lead plenty of slack so that it wouldn't pop out.

As I was getting a lap dance from a girl I had met the night before, I said to her, 'What's up, honey? Come on, there must be extras going. You know I'm cool.'

She looked me in the eye and just smiled. Then, in a whisper, she asked did I want a private dance.

Just then, another stripper began a topless dance with a guy sitting next to me. I looked at the other stripper and realised I knew her – in fact, I knew her whole family. And she knew me – not only as a friend but also, I was pretty sure, as a journalist. (The news had spread around Coolock like wildfire: that headcase Alan Croghan was now a journalist with the *Sunday World*.)

She leaned over and whispered into the ear of my dancer, who then abruptly insisted that none of the girls did any 'extras'. I'd been rumbled. I left the club and removed the tape – at which point I realised that instead of rewinding the tape to the start for recording, I had fast-forwarded it to the end. Again, I'd recorded nothing. 'Alan,' I thought to myself, 'you're a fucking gobshite.' Rather than tell the *Sunday World* the whole truth, I just said that I had been rumbled. (Sorry, John . . .)

I hadn't told anyone at the paper about my criminal past. I assumed that, if I did, I would be shown the door so quickly my feet wouldn't hit the ground. I loved the work and was becoming friendly with my colleagues, and I didn't want it to stop. The only thing that has never sat easy with me was not confiding in Joanne McElgunn, who was a good friend and an inspiration to me.

Through my long-standing friendship with many members of the Travelling community, I got hold of a gruesome video tape that showed Travellers bare-knuckle fighting. The tape was filmed on a country road in Co. Monaghan. The footage was not big news to me – I grew up with Travellers, I robbed with them, and I collected scrap with them – but when I told John Donlon about it, he was very interested.

The following day, when I brought the tape into work, there were five people waiting for me in the office of Neil Leslie, the assistant news editor. There was one guy present who I had not met before. He seemed to know a lot about the Travelling community, so I figured that he'd been brought in to ID some of the faces on the tape. As we made our way to a larger office so we could all sit in comfort to watch the video, the guy who I didn't know went into the canteen to grab a mug of coffee.

In order to suss out what his role was, I said, 'Yeah, I'll grab one with ya, mate,' and I introduced myself.

He said his name was Colm, and we shook hands. We made the coffee, talked briefly and then headed down to the office together. As the video played, the room filled. Before long, every reporter from the newsroom was glued to the screen.

We then broke for lunch. The five of us went to an Italian restaurant, and I made a point of ordering the cheapest thing on the menu, with a glass of water to drink. I was asked did I want a proper drink, and my completely untruthful reply was, 'God, no, thanks. I don't drink during the day.'

At the end of the meal, the guy I didn't know took out his credit card and paid for everybody's grub.

I thought, 'Who the fuck is he?' As we all walked back to the office, I asked Neil, 'Who's the tall guy called Colm?'

Neil replied, 'You mean you don't know who Colm is? That's Colm McGinty, the editor of the paper.'

After we got back to the office, Colm turned to me and said, 'Go write it up. Give me a thousand words on it. I want to splash it this week.'

The assignment and the deadline scared the shit out of me. Up to that point I was always able to work at my leisure; now I had to write fast. I went to my desk and sat in front of my computer for about thirty minutes, not knowing how to start. After rewriting the intro about ten times, I finally got into it. There wasn't much of a story – it was mostly to do with how vicious and bloody the scenes were.

It was my first front-page story – in fact, it ran on pages 1 through 5. On the Saturday night, I went to my local pub before the first edition of the paper came out. When the paper guy entered the pub and started selling the *Sunday World*, I sat there on my own and watched the customers reading my story.

Sales of the *Sunday World* were up, according to the JNLR figures just released, so the editor threw a party to congratulate the staff. It was held in the back room of Brady's, the pub across the road. The deputy editor, John Sheils, invited me along, and I was really chuffed to be asked.

Half jarred, I was making my way from the bar back to where I was sitting with Joanne McElgunn, Colm McGinty and John Donlon, when I bumped into a guy and spilled my pint of Guinness all over him. I had never seen him around in the newsroom, and so I figured he must have been one of the printers who worked on the lower ground floor. The guy's beard and suit were covered in Guinness, and I couldn't apologise enough.

Neil Leslie turned to me and said, 'Alan, I'd like to introduce you to the managing director of the *Sunday World*, Michael Brophy.'

Well, I nearly melted on the spot! But Mr Brophy was cool about the whole thing.

As Colm McGinty said to me, 'At least now, Alan, the MD will know who you are.'

My Ma was delighted at how well I was doing – every morning that I got up from bed and went to work was like a tonic to her – and she loved telling people about my new job. As a devoted *Coronation Street* and *Emmerdale* fan, she was elated when I came home and told her I had got an invite to Granada Television and TV3's birthday party in the Shelbourne Hotel. The party was great, and I met loads of stars. The highlight for me was meeting Leah Bracknell, who played Zoe Tate in *Emmerdale*. She was even more beautiful in person than she was on screen – a real head-turner. Later that night, the actor Simon Gregson, who played (and still plays) Steve McDonald on *Coronation Street*, turned up in the VIP bar in Renards, where I had a few drinks with him and beat him in a game of pool. Unbeknownst to Simon, myself and the character he played actually had a lot in common.

On my way home, I stopped off to grab a bite to eat in Supermac's. As I drunkenly sat down to eat my burger and chips, I got chatting to a highly intoxicated girl who was giving me the eye. We ended up in a laneway behind Supermac's where she proceeded to perform oral sex on me. I was standing with my back to the wall, and she was down on her knees, when I saw the headlights of a car driving into the laneway – a police car. The girl, undeterred by the beaming lights, continued to give me head. The police car slowed down to a stop about four feet from us both. I could see the copper in the passenger seat, trying to look past the laughing driver in order to get a better look at the girl. The police car then accelerated away. After the girl was finished, and I was in the process of doing up my jeans, a police van with three coppers in the front came speeding into the lane. When they saw we were finished, they disappointedly continued on their way. Dirty voyeuristic buggers!

When I wasn't out socialising with reporters from the *Sunday World*, I would often head to the Beaumont House, where I drank with a friend from the airport. At the weekends, it would be a starting-off point for me before I headed into the city centre. The Beaumont House was also frequented by Bertie Ahern: every Friday or Saturday, the Taoiseach would be there drinking with some of his 'Drumcondra Mafia' buddies. I had found Bertie to be very approachable on a few occasions in the past. Now that I was a journalist, I decided to ask him for an interview. I was nervous, but I took the bull by the horns.

Bertie was totally cool about it, and said to me, 'Ahh, sure, that would be no problem, I'll give you an auld interview. Just contact Ben Dunne in my office. Tell him I said it was OK, and to arrange it.'

I was delighted to have scored an interview with the Taoiseach at such an early stage in my journalistic career.

The following day, I contacted Ben Dunne, and he told me to send in a list of questions. I sent in thirty-six questions on a number of issues, including Northern Ireland, homelessness, the fight against crime, health, drug-treatment programmes, education and much more. Ben Dunne asked me to narrow down my questions to six, which I did. Sometime later, he told me he had set up an interview for me – with Bertie's PA. I declined the offer on the basis that I wanted to interview the Taoiseach himself. Again, I approached Bertie Ahern in the Beaumont House and told him what had happened.

He said, 'That is disgraceful. I told Ben that I would do the interview personally. Leave it with me, and I'll get back to you.'

I had a feeling he was spinning a yarn. In any case, I never got the interview.

Although my byline was appearing in the *Sunday World* every week, I wasn't making a great living – in fact, I was struggling. Realising I needed another source of income, and wanting to go to New York on holiday, I jumped at the chance of doing three weeks' work in a burger catering unit for Santa's Lapland, down in Goffs in Co. Kildare, in the run-up to Christmas. As I was off from college, I worked fourteen hours a day, six days a week at Goffs, where I was clearing up to a grand a week. While I was working in the catering unit making my burgers, I met a few reporters who came to Lapland with their children. They seemed amazed to see me working there, and I did feel a bit embarrassed. But I simply told them I needed the extra few bob. By the end of the three weeks, I had more than enough money for my holiday.

I flew to New York and booked into a cheap hotel in the theatre district of Manhattan. I loved everything about the city, and I partied hard. One night, while drinking, I decided I would love a bit of coke – just to sort my head out. So off I went, not knowing where I was going or how I was going to get any. I just wanted coke, and that was it – that was the way my mind worked back then.

I noticed three black guys hanging about on a street corner; they looked dodgy enough to me, so I figured they might be dealers.

I approached them and asked, 'Any coke, lads?'

One of them said, 'Sure, just walk around here with us.'

I followed them down a semi-lit back alley where one of them said, 'We have to search you, just to make sure you're not a cop.'

They then proceeded to search me. After they were finished, I was told to walk with them. We ventured down through some alleys and walked a few more blocks. Then one of them said he needed two dollars as an 'entrance fee' into the drug den. I gave the guy the two dollars, he crossed the street and then disappeared around the corner. The other two lads stayed with me. Upon his return, he produced a wrap of cocaine and asked for a hundred dollars. I asked to test it first. When he opened it, I stuck my finger into it and rubbed it on my gums. After about thirty seconds, my gums were numb; I knew it was good coke. I handed over the hundred dollars, and he slipped me the wrap.

When I got back to my hotel, I cut the coke finely with my blade. I still carried a knife every day of my life, and at that time I would have been afraid to do otherwise. I rolled up my note and snorted a line – which burned the fucking nose off me. Another line had the same effect. I tasted it and got no numbness. Then the penny dropped, and I realised it was baking soda, probably purchased with the two dollars. They had made the switch while they were chatting to me during the sale. The only thing I could do was laugh. Fair play to them, I'd been suckered.

Back in Dublin, I mentioned to John Sheils that I knew a guy who was part of a big forgery ring that supplied fake Irish passports, driving licences, car insurance certificates, tax discs and birth certificates. This person was, in fact, a good friend. And he was quite elderly now. Why was I willing to betray him? It was definitely an ego thing with me, and I was desperate for acceptance. I knew that what I was about to do was very, very wrong. But I did it anyway. Staying in with the *Sunday World*, showing them what I could do, having editors and reporters sing my praises – all of that took precedence over anything else. I wanted the picture byline, I wanted the recognition, the clap on the back. So I set out to do the story and expose my old friend, the forger.

I contacted him and asked him would he be able to get me a passport. I guess he hadn't heard that I was a journalist now – or perhaps he just couldn't believe that I'd betray him.

He said, 'No problem, Alan.'

I gave him £1,500 cash, as well as photos of myself and the false name to go on the passport.

I rang Neil Leslie with the news that a deal had been done and money exchanged. He told me to make my way straight into the office. When I got there, the editors and their staff lawyer were all in a meeting. As I sat and waited, realising that this story was really going to happen. I was overcome with panic and terror. I got up, left the office and headed towards the bus stop.

I thought to myself, 'The *Sunday World* will never work with me again. And I'll find myself out of a job, if I don't go through with this story.' Not knowing what to do, I walked back into the office and sat down to wait.

The editorial staff were all still in their meeting, and now I thought about my mother – sitting at home alone, riddled with fear of reprisals from criminals I'd betrayed, and unable to protect herself. Would the house be smashed up with my mother and two young nephews there? With my head in a terrible place, I once again got up and walked quickly out of the office, ran to the bus stop, got on a bus and switched off my mobile phone.

When I got home, my mother told me that the *Sunday World* had rung the house four times looking for me. I explained everything about the passport and the forger. My mother said that I was not to worry about her, and that she would always be there for me – no matter what. Job or no job, the decision was mine. I rang the paper and I got through to Neil Leslie, who told me that he had taken a lot of flak over me doing a runner; if I wanted to be a journalist, I should start acting like one. I told him how I felt, and he assured me that they would run with any ideas that I had in order to put my mind at rest. But they wanted the story.

I decided to give them the story, but on my terms. I said that I would not give evidence to the police against the forger, I would not hand over any information I had obtained, and I would withhold all the taped conversations. Neil agreed to my terms, and the story ran the following day. I got my picture byline and front-page splash. The forger was not named, and his face was blurred out in the paper.

Despite these precautions, and despite being told by Colm McGinty and the *Sunday World*'s staff lawyer that criminals would not bother me as a result of the story, I was panic-stricken. I felt I couldn't go back home, where I'd easily be located. I was broke after the New York holiday, so the paper gave me an advance of £500 to keep me going. The deputy editor told me to book into a hotel or a B&B and to keep receipts so I could claim it back on expenses. I began hiding out in the city. The only thing I could think of to do with my time was go drinking, all day and night.

On the Tuesday morning, I got a call from Neil Leslie, who asked me to meet him in Brady's. When Neil came into the pub, he told me that John Sheils wanted to see me. Neil drove me to the *Sunday World*, where we walked in the back way, through the printing press area, and up a tight stairway I'd never seen before; it was real cloak-and-dagger stuff. Neil told me to wait in the newsroom: the editors would call me when they were ready.

Then John Donlon came out and said John Sheils was ready to see me. I followed him into the office; John Sheils was sitting at his desk, with Neil standing beside him. As I closed the door, John Sheils turned to me and told me to sit down.

He said, 'Alan, I've received a phone call from the police, and they told me about your criminal record. You must understand, we have a lot of friends within the police force, and they wouldn't take too kindly to us having an ex-con working for the paper.'

The deputy editor then dropped the bombshell. 'Alan, I can't give you a desk job. I'm really sorry, mate.'

John Sheils then handed me a further £500. Again, he apologised to me.

I made my own apology for not telling them at the start about my criminal record. I felt badly, because John Donlon was – and still is – one of nicest men I have ever met. Then I walked down to my desk to get my bits and pieces.

Joanne, seeing that I was nearly in tears, asked me what was wrong. At this point I broke down. I told her what had happened, and apologised to her for not confiding in her about my past.

It was only after I left the *Sunday World* offices and walked down the road that the reality of what was happening actually hit me. I was on my own, with no job, and I didn't feel safe going to my own home. What on earth was I going to do?

The first thing I did was head to the nearest pub and get pissed.

I assumed that the passport story had spread like wildfire through-out the criminal fraternity. Due to my paranoia, I was afraid to enter various parts of Dublin where I might encounter criminals who would know me: I assumed that such criminals would gladly see their way to administering their own brand of justice. I found myself just wandering around the streets of Dublin, and drinking heavily. As a result, I fell behind in my studies at college; after nine months of getting merits and distinctions on my assignments, I dropped out. I wasn't properly aware of it at the time, but I was sinking into despair and hopelessness.

Once again, I decided to just get away from Dublin. I got the boat to Liverpool, where I stayed in a 'down and outs' YMCA hostel: it was the only place I could afford. The building was a run-down shack: there were vagabonds scattered all over the place, drinking cans of cheap beer and two-litre bottles of cider; others walked aimlessly around, picking up cigarette butts from the floor. I found myself in a completely new and different world of poverty, depression, homelessness, drug abuse and alcoholism. The only thing that took my mind off my situation was the alcohol. When I was intoxicated, I was in my own world – and nothing mattered.

While under the influence, I met up with another homeless guy who said he'd be able to get me some nice heroin. Not caring about my life any more, I gave him £40 to get it for me. And surprise, surprise – that was the last I saw of him. By this point I hated my life, and I hated myself.

After six days, I was just about out of money, so I had to leave the hostel. I ended up sleeping on the streets of Liverpool and begging for money. Each night, I drunkenly cried myself to sleep. One morning, having slept outside a shopfront, I woke up to find my Walkman and bottle of vodka had been stolen. I remember sitting outside that shop, wrapped in a blanket and holding a paper cup in my hand, and thinking, 'Alan, what the fuck are you doing? Look at yourself.'

Although my mind was in a mess, and I had a great fear of meeting anyone I knew, I made the decision to return to Dublin. There, at least, I wouldn't starve. And I'd have my mother, who loved me and would help me. After three days and nights of sleeping rough, I got the boat back home on my return ticket.

When I got back to Dublin, I was still afraid to go home. So I ended up sleeping rough outside the Custom House, beside the River Liffey. I couldn't think clearly, and I was living in constant fear.

I had a little 'begging patch' beside a bank machine on Grafton Street. One day, I looked up from where I was begging and noticed a gentleman in a nice suit, carrying an attaché case; as we made eye contact, I realised he was a former journalist colleague of mine. I felt as small as my fingernail.

At night, I'd climb over the steel railings of the Custom House and go to sleep. I drank myself into a very dark place, and I needed money for more drink. Before long, I was to find myself walking the streets around the red-light district near the Grand Canal, prostituting myself. For some reason it felt different than when I prostituted myself in the escort agency: this time, I felt like a piece of dirt. I recall a stout man pulling up in a big Jaguar, and I got into the passenger seat. His stomach was huge, and he had a massive double chin. He was very well dressed and spoke with a refined South Dublin accent.

He asked me, 'How much for oral?'

I said, 'Eighty quid.'

The man said, 'Without a condom.'

And I replied, 'A hundred and twenty.'

Then I directed him down Herbert Street and into the secluded Herbert Lane.

After a number of weeks sleeping rough, I went to the Eastern Health Board in Charles Street to register myself as homeless. They couldn't believe they had a homeless journalist in front of them. One of them joked, 'We'll give you ten out of ten for imagination.' It was only after I produced a copy of one of my stories that they realised I was actually telling the truth, and they put me up in a B&B.

As the days and weeks went by, I steadily became more confident in myself. I went back to my mother's house. I then rang the bureau chief of the *News of the World*, John Moore, and explained to him that I was a journalist and that I had a criminal record. He asked what my convictions were for, and I told him. John said he would not have a problem working with me; if I came up with good stories, he'd be more than happy to buy them. He said it was people such as myself, with 'guts and bottle', who made the best journalists. It was just the boost of confidence I needed.

Around this time, I received a visit at home from Danny Gwira, the guy who had been arrested and sentenced to eight years for importing the largest amount of cocaine ever seized in Europe, and who had regularly beaten me at chess in Mountjoy. He had been released about a year earlier, and now he was back in business. He asked me to try to bribe my contacts at Dublin Airport to carry in suitcases full of his cocaine.

It would have been very easy for me to arrange such a set-up: I'd recruit a baggage handler, who would get himself detailed to look after the flight carrying Danny's suitcase, and who would know which case to look for. He'd take Danny's bag, throw it into a works vehicle, then drive through the employees exit gate, up to the public car park, where he'd pass the bag on to another contact, thus bypassing airport police, customs and sniffer dogs. But I wasn't prepared to throw away everything I had worked so hard for. It got to the stage where I began to feel under constant pressure from him, and I didn't know how to say no.

Finally, I thought to myself, 'The only way I can get rid of him once and for all is to expose him.' Also, in truth, I wanted another story published: my ego was at me again.

This could be my first big scoop for the *News of the World*, and it didn't matter to me who I sacrificed in the process. I had no morals, no empathy – and the fear that had gripped me after the passport story had passed. It was as if I had a stone where I once had a heart. I had become empty, careless, self-centred, unfeeling, emotionless, cruel. I was living entirely in the here and now, and the Gwira gig was a new game of chess.

I went to work on exposing Gwira. This consisted of me going out socialising with him in nightclubs, where he'd give me free lumps of 'uncut' cocaine and I'd snort line after line. I would often meet him during the day, too, and each time I had a hidden Dictaphone running. Our final meeting took place in a restaurant, where I led him to believe that I had some baggage handlers at Dublin Airport who were onside. I said I needed a sample bag of coke to keep the airport guys sweet. The *News of the World* photographer, Tony, secretly photographed Gwira walking down the street with me. And the news editor, Chris, sat across from myself and Gwira, posing as a customer.

While talking to Gwira, I was aware that I was overusing key words for the benefit of my hidden Dictaphone – for example, 'cocaine' as opposed to 'cola' or 'candyfloss' – and I noticed he was becoming increasingly paranoid. By that stage I knew I had enough. So with the taped evidence, along with the sample gram of cocaine he had given me, I went into the newsroom and wrote up the story.

That Sunday, my story ran on the front page of the *News of the World*, where Danny Gwira was named and pictured. The police did not get involved, and I believed I had done Gwira a favour, because the story boosted his status within the drug world.

A couple of weeks later, I had another front-page story – this time with *Ireland on Sunday* – and I also published stories in the *Star*, the *Daily Mirror* and the *Sunday Mirror*. I was emailing showbiz stories over to London, to the girls in the *Mirror*'s '3am' column, and I was building up a lot of contacts in the media – not only in Ireland but in the UK, too.

Things were going well for me again. Then one day, I got a phone call from a Detective Sergeant Michael J. O'Leary from the National Bureau of Criminal Investigation. He wanted to see me, but he wouldn't tell me what it was in connection with over the phone. He asked did I want to meet him in my local police station or at my home. Thinking I would be safer in my home, I suggested the latter.

As I waited in my bedroom for Detective Sergeant O'Leary's arrival, I hid my Dictaphone underneath a folder on my locker. When I saw O'Leary and another detective pull up outside the gate, I turned on the Dictaphone. They came upstairs to my bedroom. The other detective was called Leo Clayton. O'Leary told me that they were investigating the recent rape and murder of a young German woman – a journalist, in Drogheda – and they wanted to question me about it.

I was shocked – I didn't know anything about any such case. I told the detectives that I had never met the German girl, whose name was Bettina Poeschel, and I couldn't remember when I'd last been in Drogheda. They asked me if I had any objections to the police tracing my bank account, to see if I had used my card in a bank machine in Drogheda; I had no objections whatsoever. I was then asked did I consent to the taking of a DNA sample, and again I had no objections.

During the interview, Detective Clayton put his briefcase on the locker, on top of my folder. This caused the folder to slip down on to the floor, along with the Dictaphone. The three of us stared at the Dictaphone for a moment.

I picked it up and said to Detective Sergeant O'Leary, 'I didn't know what you wanted me for, so for my own protection I felt I had to secretly record our interview.'

They looked at each other, and then told me to switch it off – which I did.

After the detectives left, my head was in a mess. I had been questioned in connection with the rape and murder of a person I'd never met in my life. I can only guess that the detectives, knowing about the false rape allegation from 1990, and knowing that the German woman who had been raped and murdered also happened to be a journalist, put two and two together and came up with five.

To make matters worse, the following week I received a call from detectives who wished to question me in relation to a car-bomb explosion in Kilbarrack. I was asked to account for my movements and to provide an alibi for the night in question, when a pipe bomb had been placed under a car. I didn't know what they were talking about, and I told them as much.

Between my heavy drinking and the stress of the police enquiries, I went back into a very dark place. I wanted to forget that Alan Croghan had ever existed. Once again, it seemed to me that the best way to do this was to get out of Dublin. I packed myself a bag and took the boat and the bus to London, with about £200 sterling in my pocket. I'll always recall the loneliness I felt, sitting at the back of the coach. As far as I was concerned, my life was over – I'd no future, and nothing to look forward to except hurt, fear, loneliness and depression. I removed the bottle of vodka from my hand luggage, and opened it.

In London, I began sleeping rough in the West End. I remember one night, sitting wrapped in a sleeping bag, drinking vodka with rain falling on me, and thinking, 'Yes. This is the life. Now, at long last, I am completely free. No enemies, no bills, no stress, no danger. I am free. I have pure peace of mind. Thank you, God, I love you.' But the feeling did not last long.

As the following morning dawned, I aimlessly wandered the streets, drinking my vodka, shivering with the cold and tapping people for money. I hated my life and the situation I now found myself in. I tried reasoning with myself. Should I go back home and fight my corner? Or should I spend the rest of my days living and sleeping rough on the streets of London?

One night, as I sat begging on a busy side street, two police officers walked up and arrested me. I was put into the back of a police van and taken to Charing Cross police station, where I was charged with begging. I was to appear at Bow Street Magistrates' Court five days later, and was meanwhile released on my own bail. The arresting officers were genuinely nice people, very concerned about my welfare, and curious as to how I'd ended up living on the streets. Sergeant McMillan directed me to a shelter for the homeless, and told me to make sure I appeared in court. He said that I would more than likely get the benefit of the Probation Act.

As soon as I left the police station, I decided to go back home. There was no way I was going to spend the rest of my days living in the gutter, riddled with fear. I would go home and fight everything and anything that was thrown at me. I made my way to the bus depot, and slept there for the night.

The following morning, with my open return ticket, I got the bus back on to the boat, and sailed home.

15

In the Control Tower

I turned up at home with a bag of cans, cold, hungry and tired. My Ma was delighted to see me, and I was dead chuffed to see her and to be home, safe and secure.

She said to me, 'Why don't you have a bath, son? While I do you something to eat.'

I had a shower and a shave, and when I went downstairs my Ma had fish and chips and a mug of tea on the table waiting for me. I just picked at the food, as the only thing on my mind was the beer in cans beside my feet, waiting to be drunk. My Ma sat up chatting to me, and I was wishing she'd ever go to bed so I could open a beer and watch the TV in peace. Eventually, I couldn't bear it any longer. I reached down, picked up a can and cracked it open.

My mother said, 'Would you not try and cut down, son?'

In a frustrated tone, I replied, 'Ah, Ma, leave it out, will ya? Jesus, it's the only bleeding thing I have, me few cans. I've nothing else.'

Standing up, my Ma said, 'Do you know what? I give up. I'm going to my bed.'

I was delighted: now I could sit back and enjoy my beers in peace.

I was relieved to read in the newspapers that a Co. Louth man, Michael Murphy, had been arrested and charged with the rape and murder of the German journalist – the police wouldn't be bothering me any more about that. (Murphy was later convicted, and sentenced to life imprisonment.)

One day, as I stood at a bus stop, I happened to look to my right. There was Danny Gwira, walking past. I expected some reaction from him. But he just increased his walking speed, and hurried on up the street. Gwira had not got into trouble with the police as a result of my article. (Later, in April 2002, he would be arrested at

Dublin Airport for trying to import €400,000 worth of cocaine, and was eventually sentenced to ten years.)

I got a call from Chris McCashin, the editor of the Irish edition of the *Sunday Mirror*. We arranged to meet in a pub, where Chris told me that he'd like me to work for him. He added that he would be able to throw a couple of shifts and other bits of work my way. I wasn't going to hold back on anything any more: if I was working for anyone within the newspaper industry, I was going to have no secrets. I told Chris everything about my criminal past. Having heard this, he was still happy to work with me.

I often scoured the job sections of newspapers and magazines, searching for ideas for stories. A company called Top Security was having an 'open day' in a Dublin hotel, looking to recruit security guards. So I went along to see if I could get myself a position without my criminal history being checked. Twenty minutes after I walked into the hotel, I had a job; nothing had been checked.

I knew Top Security handled security for the air traffic control tower at Dublin Airport, and that was where I wanted to be. But my first placement was in a hut at a large industrial estate in Blanchardstown. I was very efficient in my work – I filed reports, made sure all incidents were logged and reported, offered suggestions to management about how security could be improved upon – and the bosses were very impressed with me. I began to drop hints about leaving the job, while also showing a keen interest in the air traffic control tower. The manager eventually offered me a job at the tower, and assured me that it was a 'cushy number'.

I was brought up to the tower, expecting to be put through security clearance by the Dublin Airport Authority (which had succeeded Aer Rianta). Instead, I waltzed straight in with no security check. I was left in control of the outer electronic security gates, the internal magnetic doors, all the CCTV cameras, every key (including master keys) and the hidden sensor alarm beams that ringed the tower. I was the person who verified and checked visitors and air traffic controllers' identification – in other words, it was up to me who was allowed into or out of the building.

The control room was like my idea of the interior of a submarine: it was full of big round screens, all bleeping. I asked the controllers I had befriended to take photographs of me up in the tower, down in the control room and at my security desk. After two weeks of working at the tower, I knew I had enough evidence to expose the security company and the DAA.

My story ran on the front page of the *Sunday Mirror*, under the headline: HIJACKER ... AND HE'S IN CHARGE OF SECURITY AT DUBLIN'S AIR TRAFFIC CONTROL. I wasn't prepared for the amount of publicity that was to follow: I was interviewed by RTÉ's Marian Finucane, 98FM's late-night radio talk show, Cork FM radio and TV3 News. The daily newspapers all followed up on the story, too. The editors of the *Sunday Mirror* and *Daily Mirror* both told me that I came across very well on radio and TV.

I had mentioned in the article and in subsequent radio interviews that I had another airport scoop running the following week. I had found an air traffic control security manual in a skip outside the control tower. The airport authorities, who must have heard one or more of my interviews, called in the police, who wanted to question me. Chris McCashin assured me nothing would come of it. But he said that if I was in any way worried, I should contact a solicitor. I'd be entitled to free legal aid, as I was a freelance journalist.

My immediate thought was that I was on my own, facing possible prosecution on a charge of 'theft-by-finding'. This was an offence that was originally introduced in the USA to prevent the paparazzi from rooting through celebrities' bins for stories. In the end, we returned the airport manual to the DAA – and the story never ran.

As a journalist, you're never off duty: you're always looking out for a story. Around May of 2003, drinking in the Beaumont House, I started noticing that Bertie seemed to be paying particular attention to one lady among his group of friends. I contacted a source of mine close to the Taoiseach's camp for some information on this woman. Her name was Anna Bogle.

I began following the Taoiseach. I observed that on its way to the Beaumont House, Bertie's chauffeur-driven state car would make a detour to Anna Bogle's house to pick her up and then take her to the pub. When the car arrived at the Beaumont House, Bertie would let Anna step out from the state car and walk in alone; he would then follow, some thirty steps behind. Inside the pub he would not even allow her to put her hand in her pocket. The state car would drop Anna home at the end of the night, and Bertie would sometimes go into her house for a period – on some occasions, as long as an hour and a half.

It turned out that Anna Bogle's husband, who was a close friend of Bertie's, had passed away in January 2003. Bertie was comforting his pal's widow. In September of that year, I ran the story on the front page of the *Sunday Mirror*. On Monday, most of the daily papers followed up on my scoop.

*

In February 2004, I was asked to appear on *The Late Late Show*, along with a children's solicitor, a retired Garda sergeant and a child psychologist, to discuss the topic of juvenile crime. Pat Kenny told me that I would be sitting next to him, as I was the primary interviewee.

Before the interview, I took advantage of the free bar in the green room. But I made sure I didn't get drunk; I didn't want to fuck this up. What amazed me was how relaxed I felt during the interview: it was as if I was in my sitting-room, having a one-on-one chat with Pat Kenny, and nobody else existed. I got to meet Carrie Fisher, aka Princess Leia, who was also on the programme that night.

Pat Kenny came over to me at the end of the show, and said, 'Alan, you stole the whole show tonight.'

I was over the moon.

Because I was freelancing and had a lot of spare time on my hands, I started working on a film script. I got hold of a book by Cole and Haag entitled *The Complete Guide to Standard Script Formats*, and read the whole thing twice. I already had plenty of storylines, but the book helped me understand how to format a script. Eventually, I finished a script for a four-part TV drama, with the title *X-RAY 7*. I sent copies to a number of production companies. None of them bit, but I received many encouraging letters of reply.

I was having fun with journalism. But one of the stories I worked on around this time led me into a very dark place. A member of the public rang the *Sunday Mirror* and claimed he knew a GP who was falsifying medical reports for non-existent accidents in order to get a compensation pay-out claim. Wired up with a hidden Dictaphone, I met up with the informant, and he introduced me to the GP, a Dr Maharaj. I told him that I'd had an accident about a year ago, but I'd never gone to hospital or seen a doctor, and now I wanted to make a claim. Dr Maharaj said that was no problem. Over the next two weeks, he compiled an extensive file.

Then I decided to push the GP further. I went to his surgery, wired up, and informed him – falsely – that I was dating a sixteen-year-old girl and that she was now eleven weeks pregnant. I told the GP that if her family found out she was pregnant, I was looking at going to jail for statutory rape. I was just chancing my arm – I had no specific reason to believe that Dr Maharaj performed abortions on underage girls at the behest of men who were committing statutory rape. Dr Maharaj suggested a D and C.

When I asked what that was, he replied, 'It is where I scrape the walls of the womb out of her. I scrape the foetus out.'

The following Saturday afternoon, I went to Dr Maharaj's home in the company of a photographer and identified myself as a journalist for the *Sunday Mirror*. I said we'd be running a front-page story the following morning in relation to his illegal abortions. Would he like to comment? The photographer stuck the camera in the doctor's face and began snapping pictures of him. The doctor staggered backwards, stumbled and fell into his hallway, where he frantically kicked his front door shut.

The next morning, his picture was plastered across the front page of the *Sunday Mirror*. On the basis of the evidence I had obtained, the Irish Medical Council issued High Court proceedings against the doctor to have him struck off for professional misconduct. Five days before Dr Maharaj was due to appear in the High Court, he was found dead at his family home; I was informed that he had died of a heart attack. I also heard from two sources that the doctor had deliberately taken tablets to induce a massive heart attack.

I'll never know what killed Dr Maharaj, who was a middle-aged man. But either way, I often ask myself whether I was responsible for that man's death. To be perfectly honest with you, I believe I was. I had invented a story about a fictitious girl with a fictitious pregnancy. And now, it seemed to me, a man had died on the basis of a lie. My only agenda had been to get the doctor on tape, so that I could get the juicy story. And all because I wanted to be popular and successful.

That is something I will have to live with for the rest of my life.

I interviewed a 'lady of doubtful virtue' who told me about a place she had worked in – a five-bedroom house on the outskirts of Dublin, where young foreign girls were brought via Dublin Airport. Once there, they would have their passports taken from them and be allocated to brothels throughout Ireland. I was given the name and home address of the pimp who ran the network; I was also given the name of the company he used to launder his ill-gotten gains. Armed with all this information, I felt the story warranted a full investigation involving human surveillance and cameras.

I went to RTÉ's investigative programme *Prime Time Investigates*, where I had a meeting with a commissioning editor. After I explained the situation to him, the editor got up from the table and said he'd be back. A short time later, he returned with a producer. In conversation I happened to mention another story I was looking at. I knew a guy who had worked in a nursing home for nine years and often witnessed abusive treatment of the residents. I told the RTÉ guys how much this disturbed me.

The editor said to me, 'Alan, I'm going to trust you. And what I'm about to tell you is strictly confidential. We are looking at trying to get into a nursing home where this abuse is taking place. Would you have a chat with your friend to see if he would apply for a position with one of these nursing homes to uncover the truth?'

I told him I would have a chat with my mate, and I would get back to him. The illegal trafficking of the prostitutes into Ireland was temporarily shelved while I worked on the nursing-home piece.

I met my friend, Cathal, a day or so later and ran the proposition by him. He was very nervous at first. He didn't want anything to do with it: his wife was currently employed as a nurse, and he feared for her job. I assured him that his identity would be kept secret, and that he'd be well paid by RTÉ. And I asked him how could he stand by, knowing that this abuse was taking place, when he could do something to end it. I eventually convinced my friend to meet with two RTÉ reporters. After the meeting took place, the reporters said they'd be in touch with me soon.

As the days turned into weeks, I hadn't heard a thing from anyone at *Prime Time Investigates*, or from my mate Cathal. One evening, I tuned in to watch. The programme was based on hidden-camera footage of OAPs being verbally and physically abused and neglected at a nursing home called Leas Cross. The moment I heard the voice of the guy who was wired up with the hidden camera, I knew it was Cathal.

I rang Cathal the next day. He told me that RTÉ had told him not to talk to anyone about the investigation – not even me, the guy who had introduced him to RTÉ. He was apologetic, but he was also keen to continue doing that sort of investigative work.

I said, 'Don't worry about it. You did what you had to do, and fair play to you. But listen, mate. You'll never hear from those people again. You were a means to an end for them, the same way I was. They used me to get to you, and they used you to get into Leas Cross. Don't delude yourself by thinking you're going to get a job from them.'

It was the run-up to Christmas of 2005. I made the decision that in the New Year of 2006, I would start afresh. I would be the new Alan. I'd sort my head out and forget all the people who hated me, who wanted to hurt me, who despised me. I would make an effort to put all the bad things I had done behind me, and try to get on with my life in a more positive and constructive manner.

Looking back, I realise that I had no clear idea of what this might mean in practice. Certainly, it did not mean giving up drink. As far as I was concerned, drinking was not the problem; it was part of the solution.

Throughout the Christmas period, I drank from morning to night. I had stocked up on beer as though prohibition was imminent. I stopped eating, didn't wash myself, shaved my head bald so I didn't have to wash it – I lived, you could say, just for drink. Drinking, for me, was like breathing. Alcohol was like oxygen: I felt I couldn't function without it, and I believed it made me better.

As the New Year of 2006 dawned, I was convinced in my madness that through my alcohol intake I had at last found comfort in my own thoughts. In my own mind, I felt safe in my home – alone and drinking. I knew if I stayed away from the rest of the world, and remained indoors, I could do no harm to anyone. And no one could harm me. If a problem entered my mind, I'd 'channel-hop' to something different – something positive – such as all the beer I had left to drink.

I was living in my own hell. But I thought it was 'peace of mind'. Little did I know that 2006 and 2007 were to be the two worst years of my life.

16

Isolation and Madness

For two years, my life followed a strict pattern. Every week, on the Wednesday, I would collect my unemployment benefit, buy eight trays of the cheapest and strongest lager – roughly a week's supply – and get a taxi home. On the Sunday, I would mark out my TV guide for the next seven days. Every day, I sat in my armchair in front of the box with my tins of beer within reach, my tobacco by my side and the remote controls on my lap.

How my family felt about this didn't even enter my mind. I recall sitting across from my two pre-teen nephews, dressed in their school uniforms and eating their breakfast, while I drank a can of Dutch Gold. No child should ever have to witness anything like that. Not ever. Even today, as I write this, I still feel shame and guilt around it. I love those two kids more than anything in the whole world.

I didn't want anyone in my life; I just wanted to be left on my own. They say isolation is the darkroom for developing negativity, and as a sociable person I ought to have understood that it would be so for me. But at the time, I did not see it that way. I just wanted to be alone with my alcohol. In my head, my heart and my skin, I felt contented, joyful, happy, free and at peace within myself. I lived for alcohol, and I loved drinking. I loved what alcohol did for me; I enjoyed where my thinking went during my bouts of drinking.

I worked on plays, film scripts and short stories. And always, I would be drinking when I wrote. My insane reasoning was, 'Good enough for Brendan Behan, good enough for me!' It got to the stage where I felt I couldn't write unless I was drinking: alcohol, I thought, was the source of my inspiration.

I became obsessive-compulsive. Before I would open up the first can of beer, I had to have my ashtray clean; I had to have exactly forty hand-rolled cigs prepared; the television guide had to be marked out for the week ahead, my washing done, a full mug of coffee in front of me; my bladder had to be empty, my teeth brushed. I had to say my prayers early in the day, in case I forgot to say them later on when I was drunk; at night, I kept a pint of water beside the bed in case I woke up thirsty. All of this seemed completely normal to me.

During 2006, my brother Declan decided to buy my mother's house; she would continue to live there, rent free, until the day we celebrated her life and all she had given us. For the first time in her life, my Ma was financially OK. She spent €42,000 on a new extension, and she paid my father his share of the value of the house.

My mother also gave me €6,000 from the proceeds of the sale. Everyone was expecting me to drink myself to death with the money, but I mostly blew it on other things: I went out and spent about €4,500 on a new wardrobe, locker, a wall-mounted stereo, a PlayStation, a flat-screen TV, a beautiful stained-glass TV table, games and DVDs, a petrol-running remote-controlled car, new jeans and shirts, a digital camera, curtains and other bits and bobs. After that, I had about €1,500 left – which I spent on binge drinking, cocaine, lap dances and prostitutes.

A few days after my money was gone, I hadn't a penny for a can of beer, let alone the price of a pint. I needed alcohol like I'd never needed it before. As I sat in my bedroom, pondering where I was going to get drink, I convinced myself that I didn't really need all the gear I had just purchased, and decided to sell it. I offered the TV, the stereo, the PlayStation, the table and the games for a mere €500. A guy offered me €300, which I turned down. After about five minutes, the need and want for drink was so powerful that I contacted the guy again and accepted the €300. As soon as I had the cash in my hand, I felt in control and secure. With my pocket full of notes I grabbed a taxi to my local supermarket and bought a few trays of beer. A week or so later, I was to sell the €700 mini racing car for €100. Again, just for drink.

As summer was approaching, I would often venture out to my front driveway and sit on the garden bench drinking. Although I would not go outside my gate, I still carried a blade in my pocket – just in case anyone walked past the house and 'started' on me.

Nobody was ever going to hurt me, no matter what. All I wanted was to be left alone. But my mind would give me no peace.

By this stage I had put on a lot of weight: I weighed 21st 4lbs. I was now a 48-inch waist, where I used to be a 32-inch or a 34-inch. Declan gave me €1,000 to buy myself a new wardrobe of clothes. Strange as it may sound, that is exactly what I did. I then bagged all the clothing that didn't fit me and gave it to the St Vincent de Paul. My feet were like elephant's feet, and my ankles and legs were badly swollen. When I pressed my fingertips against my legs or feet, the impression would leave a dent in the skin. As for my man-tits, they were so big I could have got away with wearing a bra.

As my physical decline intensified, I began to sweat profusely. I'd very often wake up in the middle of the night and find that my sheets and quilt were saturated. I began to get panic attacks: I was fully convinced that I was going to take a heart attack and die right there and then. When my panic attacks would kick in, I'd get up from my bed in the middle of the night, switch on the TV, read a newspaper, make some tea – anything to divert my thinking. But the visual change of my environment and the psychological diversion did nothing. I would still feel suffocated, trapped, unable to breathe or think. My internal organs and stomach would jump all over the place, my hands would shake terribly. I would often get light-headed and feel close to the point of collapse.

One night, convinced I was having a cardiac arrest, I found myself pacing up and down my street in the middle of the night, barefoot, dressed only in pyjamas. I was begging God not to let me die. I got headaches that seemed to subside only after I had five or six cans of alcohol in my system. My memory stopped working, and it got to the stage where I would carry a notepad and pen with me. If I thought of anything that I had to do, I immediately wrote it down so that I wouldn't forget. Every night, before I hit the hay, I would write out my 'to do' list for the following day.

I eventually ended up in hospital over my legs. My GP said the swelling was due to varicose veins, which would need to be treated surgically. When I was admitted to hospital for the operation, I brought with me a large bottle of Coke mixed with vodka. On the day of my operation, I was supposed to fast. Although I had nothing to eat the night before my operation, I recall drinking my vodka and Coke right up to being taken down for surgery the following morning. As soon as I came round from the operation, I reached again for the vodka and Coke. After my discharge from hospital, I still had the severe swelling. When I went to the toilet, there was blood in my stools and a vile odour.

Not only was I physically isolating myself from the world by never going out, but even more damagingly, I was psychologically alienating myself from my family. I had built a wall around myself, and I just shut everyone out. I couldn't recognise that what was happening to me was a direct result of my drinking. Despite what I was going through, and how I was feeling – the psychological torture, hurt and pain I put myself through daily – I never even looked at my drinking. I was completely deluded.

My poor mother had always tried to get me to stop drinking, and I had become very skilled at switching off when she did. Now I was blocking her out completely, no matter what she said – it went in one ear and out the other, as though she was a priest reading the mass.

As far as I was concerned, she was the one with the problem, not me.

At the beginning of 2007, I fell down the stairs, busting my forehead open, bruising my eye and fracturing my wrist. The doctors told me that I was an alcoholic and that I needed to do something about my drinking. (I was also diagnosed as having yellow jaundice, though I didn't find out about that until later.) I left the hospital without being discharged. For the life of me, I can't recall how I ended up in an alcohol rehabilitation centre in Co. Limerick. I do remember the place itself. It was a kip – full of teenagers in tracksuits and runners, hoping to get a good letter from the centre for their next court appearance. I knew exactly where those kids were coming from, but I wanted nothing to do with that place. On my first night there, I caught the last bus home to Dublin.

It wasn't to be very long before I found myself back in hospital again. I was light-headed, I was getting sick all the time, and there was blood in my vomit and stools. The doctor in the A & E asked me would I mind if he did a complete 'MOT' on me. At this stage I would have done anything to feel well again. I hated everything about my life and about myself. Why did I even exist? I was a useless specimen of a human being.

I was kept in hospital and put on a seven-day alcohol detox programme. I had two bags of pure vitamin K drip-fed into me. I sweated, I got sick, I hallucinated, I was paranoid. I cried, because I hated myself.

At the end of the detox, I was discharged from hospital. I was detoxed, I had a clear head and I felt OK – so I went drinking.

At my appointment to receive the results of my blood tests, the doctor sat me down and told me that I had chronic hepatitis C, genotype I, subtype A, along with cirrhosis of the liver. He said I had a maximum of eighteen months to live.

I couldn't believe what I was hearing. Even after relaying the news to my mother, I didn't really feel anything. It was as though I had been told that a man in Yemen had died: that's how distant the reality of my illness was to me. Absurdly, I felt almost boastful when I told people the news.

Eventually, the fear kicked in: underneath the false bravado, I was a quivering wreck. The thought of never seeing my family in the flesh again, of leaving them forever – for all eternity – scared the living daylights out of me. I hadn't a friend in the world, because I had either turned them against me, driven them away or shut myself off from them. One day, as I sat at home drinking myself into oblivion, I picked up a knife, stuck it into my stomach and ripped the blade across my belly. I was taken to hospital, where I received twenty-eight stitches.

While I was in Beaumont Hospital, recovering from my self-inflicted knife wound, there were no beds available up on the wards. I was put into a single room within the A & E department. My door was left wide open, with a nurse stationed just outside. If I went outside for a smoke, or went to the toilet, the nurse would shadow me. I didn't mind; I felt protected and at ease. I met strangers who liked me, and all I could see was pure goodness in the staff. They were kind, considerate, tolerant and compassionate.

I can't say enough good things about the staff at Beaumont. The doctors, nurses, students in training and catering staff were the loveliest bunch of people I have ever come across. These people talked with me, they listened to me, they put up with my madness and my sickness. There are four doctors that stand out in my memory. Dr Stephen Patchett is one of the kindest men I have ever come across. I didn't really see eye to eye with Dr Conor O'Brien, who told me I had eighteen months to live, but I admire the man for his honesty. Dr Deirdre Mahony really went out of her way to help me – well above and beyond the call of duty. And last, but not least, was my liver specialist, Dr Tariq Tajuddin (we will come back to Tariq later).

One night, there was a commotion: police officers and doctors were rushing about. From behind the closed door of the resuscitation room I heard a young male voice cry out.

'Please don't let me die! Please don't let me die! Please don't let me die!'

No more than thirty seconds had elapsed when a doctor emerged from the room, pulling down the mask from his face. In the corridor he met another nurse, who was rushing to meet him.

The nurse asked, 'How's he doing?'

And the doctor replied, 'He just died.'

What occurred on that terrible night will forever be imprinted on my mind. Those words the young man spoke before he died will always stay with me. That poor guy wanted desperately to live; he pleaded for his life and then, within thirty seconds, he was gone from this world. It turned out that the young man who passed away had been parked up with his girlfriend at a lovers' area at the back of Dublin Airport when car thieves tried to hijack his VW Golf. As he tried to prevent the thieves from taking his car, he was badly beaten.

At the end of my week's detox, I was transferred to St Ita's psychiatric hospital in Portrane, north Co. Dublin, to be evaluated. Before I left Beaumont, I went to the hospital shop and bought a thank-you card. I wrote out the names of all the doctors, nurses, student nurses and catering staff that I could remember, and I described the ones whose names I did not know. I basically wrote how much I cared about each and every one of them.

They are marvellous people who put up with all sorts of abuse from drunks, addicts and argumentative people from all walks of life. They work extremely long hours and, with the exception of the doctors, they are grossly underpaid.

I placed the card in the nurses' empty canteen, and then left.

St Ita's was a horrible place. I was given Valium and Librium tablets during the day, and sleepers at night. There was nothing constructive to do there; you were kept behind locked doors. There was a corridor of about sixty yards in length, with green floor tiling, which I nicknamed the 'green mile'. All I did – day after day, night after night – was walk up and down it.

As soon as I was discharged from St Ita's, I headed straight to the pub to get drunk. I had two weeks of drying out behind me, and I was fit and ready to go again. Considering that I was going to die anyway, why not drink? I never thought about what my family might be going through. But I did feel that everyone ought to feel sorry for me – I was the one who was dying, not them. I thought, 'Sure, there will be many people who'll be delighted to see me dead.' I even began to visualise who'd be at my funeral.

One night, as I sat alone in a pub, I met a middle-aged man who told me he was selling DF 118 tablets – codeine-based painkillers. I asked him would he sell me forty of them. I got the tablets, and he gave me his mobile number in case I ever needed any more. But I didn't expect to see that man again. My plan was to drink a right few pints and then overdose on the DFs. I swallowed the tablets in handfuls of ten at a time, on top of about eight pints.

The next thing I remember is waking up in the Mater Hospital with a doctor at my bedside.

He said, 'We didn't think you were going to pull through. You're a very lucky man.'

Still groggy, I didn't know what day it was or how long I'd been there. I ripped the drip from my hand and arm, got dressed and walked out of the hospital without saying a word to anyone. I went straight down to the pub where I had started drinking prior to my overdose, and resumed my drinking.

As the night progressed, I became really down. This time I didn't want to harm myself. I knew I needed help. I had no clue what sort of help I needed, but I wanted my life to change. I walked back to the Mater. I told the receptionist that I was feeling very depressed and suicidal, and that I needed help. I informed her that I had been admitted after a suicide attempt but had discharged myself. The lady told me to take a seat.

Six hours later, I was still sitting in the waiting room outside the A & E. I was at the end of my tether, so I pulled out a small Bohemian blade and walked into the toilet. I ran the blade across the top of my right hand, knowing I would sever my tendons. I walked back up to the receptionist and showed her the wound on my hand.

'Will you see to me now?' I said.

I was immediately admitted to the A & E, and underwent an emergency microsurgery operation to reattach my tendons. After the operation, I was seen by a psychiatrist and was transferred back to St Ita's. Once again, I was put through a detox, which just about brought me back to myself. My mother visited, and she pleaded with me to stop harming myself.

When I was released from Portrane, I got the train into town and rang the guy who'd sold me the DF 118s. We met again in the same pub. This time I bought forty-five tablets. I downed at least ten pints, and I swallowed the forty-five DFs. I remember waking up in the Mater again and realising I still wasn't dead. In a sudden burst of energy I got dressed, and literally ran from the hospital. I didn't know where I was going, or what I was going to do. I ended up going back to where I felt safe. Half drunk and carrying two trays of beer, I turned up at my Ma's doorstep. I was now back in my comfort zone; I had my TV and my computer, and I had my family around me.

For a time I felt safe, but my physical illness was only getting worse. Eventually, it made it impossible for me to drink: each time

I put beer into my mouth, I would immediately throw it back up. My body was now rejecting the alcohol. I resorted to sticking my fingers down the back of my throat, forcing myself to be sick. I would then press my hand against my stomach, and I would have a little bit of leverage. I'd say to myself, 'Yeah, Alan, you'll get another mouthful of beer in there.' My body was telling me it couldn't take any more abuse, but the need to have alcohol inside of me far exceeded any logic.

At one stage I had only three cans of beer to my name, and I thought to myself, 'I'm not going to get drunk on that.' I then remembered that my brother William, who used to do rubbish removals from people's homes, had once shown me an old bottle of Riga Black Balsam spirit that he had thrown into the shed in the back garden. At about 2 a.m., wearing my pyjamas, I found myself down on all fours, rooting through heaps of garden tools, old toys and other bits and bobs in search of the bottle. Eventually, I found it. Bingo! I went back into the house, and I mixed it with the cheap lager I had. The spirit was black, and it poured from the bottle to the glass like Bovril. It was revolting, but I forced it into me anyway.

The taking of my own life became an obsession with me. I got a knife and stuck it deep into my leg, ran it down about seven inches, pulled the knife out, then repeated the procedure. Blood began spurting everywhere from the two deep wounds. There was a lot of blood but, oddly, I wasn't feeling weak or unwell – in fact, I was completely aware of what was going on. I said to myself, 'Fuck this! I'm going to the hospital.'

After A & E had stitched up the wounds, I was seen by a psychiatrist, Dr Diane Mullins, who diagnosed me as having an 'antisocial personality disorder and alcohol dependence syndrome'. The doctor asked me was I going to harm myself while in the hospital. I took a small blade from my pocket, handed it to her and assured her that I wouldn't. I was again shadowed by a nurse everywhere I went, and kept under watch twenty-four hours a day. After a week detoxing, I was sent to St Ita's psychiatric hospital. Back to hell on earth!

I detested that madhouse, and obviously my previous stays there had not done much for me. People were taken from society, placed into that kip, written off as another statistic and completely forgotten about. The hospital had nothing to offer a patient – except handfuls of sedatives.

Again, I was released from St Ita's. And again, I got the train into town. I went straight to the bar in Connolly Station and ordered a pint.

My mother rang me and asked where I was; I told her that I was window-shopping. Then she heard the noise of glasses, and she knew the truth.

17

Rock Bottom

By late 2007, I hated the person I had become. I was lost, alone and riddled with fear. I believed other people would be far better off if I did not exist.

I made the decision that I was going to take my life, and to do it right this time: I would cut my throat. I left a suicide note for my mother.

Ma, I'd like to say how much I love you – my loving mother and my two little boys (Robbie + Lee) and I can never forget my favourite brother Declan – the four most important people in my entire life. I love and adore each and every one of you, more than you'll ever know. Please, please FORGIVE me. Please, I am sorry – really sorry – I love you, Ma. I love you to bits – I love you more than Heaven and Earth . . . (Robbie + Lee will finish the sentence off, just ask them). I am sorry, Ma. I'm sorry, Declan. I am sorry, Robert and Lee – my two great kids.

I'll always be looking down on you from Heaven, guiding + protecting you. Don't be sad – just because you kids won't see me again – I'll be watching, loving and guiding you for the rest of your lives. I LOVE THE FOUR OF YOU XXXXX.

Ma – goodnight – you're my Angel. I pass all my love on to you xxxxxx.

Your son,

Alan x

The events that followed are very sketchy for me, but it seems that I ran a small Bohemian blade across my neck. I have no recollection of how I got to Beaumont Hospital. When I came round, I was sitting on a hard plastic chair in the A & E department. I had a blood drip going into my left arm and another drip going into my right arm, and I had received eight stitches to my throat.

The first person I met was a nurse who said to me, 'You're the chap who gave us a thank-you card, aren't you?'

I replied, 'Yeah. But I'm sorry, I don't remember you.'

And the nurse said, 'No, you wouldn't. We never met, as I was away on holidays the last time you were in the hospital. But I saw your card in the nurses' canteen, and it was the nicest card I've ever read. It was lovely.'

She put me in a comfortable armchair, handed me a blanket and got me some tea and toast – I felt as though I'd been bumped up to first class on a flight.

I also recall a doctor coming up to me and saying, 'Alan, we get a lot of people who cut their wrists, and basically we look upon that as just a cry for help. But when we get someone who cuts their throat, especially in the manner in which you did, we know that's a real attempt to take one's own life. And you were just a few millimetres from your jugular vein. You're lucky to be alive.'

I was transferred to a ward that had eight beds in it. The only other patient in the ward was a Traveller woman in her seventies. The main lights were off, and the ward was in semi-darkness. I got chatting to the lady, whose name was Jinny, and I poured my heart out to her. I told her everything about my drinking, my criminal career, my jobs, my suicide attempts, my hepatitis C, and the fifteen months or so I had left to live. Jinny listened; without saying a word to me she made it clear that she was interested in me as a person. I will never forget her.

I was evaluated by two hospital psychiatrists and then, once again, sent to St Ita's. After a few days in that awful place, I began to get some clarity in my mind. It was very strange. I started to write down my feelings and my thoughts.

I feel like taking my own life. I want to walk into a police station with a gallon of petrol & set it on fire. I hate my life but I love my family & hate the thought of leaving them. I need help. I am an alcoholic & very depressive. I don't want to hurt myself or anyone else – I just want to live. I love my family to bits & it kills me to let

Jinny and me

them see me this way – but my mind is messed up. I also feel like committing a serious offence just to get into prison so I can't drink, that's how bad it is. I'm afraid – very afraid – I hate Portrane but I need help – I need to stop drinking – my life is a mess. I also feel I want to be famous/infamous – to go down in history & to be remembered. Each day & night I cry and feel sad – I love my family but hate my life.

I want to kill myself. I hate myself. I hate my life. I hate me.

I began to look at the other patients in the mental hospital with empathy. For the first time in a long while, I was able to think outside of myself and look at where others were.

I met a patient who, I was told, was a great chess player. He looked very sophisticated, wearing gold half-rimmed reading glasses, a smart shirt and a tie with a British Army tiepin. He and I played a game. We were just beginning, when another patient called my name. As I looked over my shoulder, I could see in my peripheral vision that the chess guy was moving pieces. When I turned to face him, a number of my pieces were missing from the board, and the top of a bishop was protruding from his mouth. He stared at me and slowly brought his hand up to cover his mouth. Then he brought his hand down with the chess piece in it and slipped it behind his back, dropping it to the floor. I had to laugh. There were many such characters at St Ita's – completely gone in the head, but lovable guys who wouldn't harm a fly. My heart went out to them.

I decided to go along to the Christmas party. A tiny CD player was playing 'Mr Punch and Judy Man', and there were pointed paper hats, balloons and paper whistles, crisps, sweets, cakes and lemonade and, of course, the 'outside visitor' who spent the guts of an hour tuning his guitar until someone took notice of him. I eventually got used to the setting, and had a ball. By the time I had sung two or three rebel songs, all the mental patients in the room were convinced they were red-blooded fightin' Irishmen, reliving the Easter Rising.

At this stage I had gone three or four weeks without a drink. A few days before Christmas, I was informed by an orderly that a team of psychiatrists wanted to see me that morning. When I walked into the office before the panel of five doctors, I began to feel very nervous. The four men and one woman, of various nationalities, sat facing me from behind a long desk.

The only psychiatrist I had ever trusted was Dr McCormack, who I used to see when I was locked up in St Patrick's Institution. He was genuinely concerned about me and my weekly use of LSD from the age of thirteen into my early twenties. (Apart from Dr McCormack, I've always found it hard to trust psychiatrists. They have the power to keep you under lock and key in a madhouse for life, merely on their say-so, and that terrifies the shit out of me. At least in prison you have a release date on your cell door – or if doing a 'life' term, you're eligible for parole after seven years.) Thus, I was unnerved to come before an entire panel of psychiatrists; my insides were jumping all over the place.

Through the window behind the panel of doctors, I happened to see a small-framed man – aged in his seventies, and stark naked –

marching military style around an enclosed garden. It was a bitterly cold morning in December. I said to the psychiatrists, 'You know, there's a guy marching naked outside the window.'

The doctors looked, and one casually remarked, 'Ah, that's just old Joe. He's always at that.'

One of the other doctors picked up the phone, and said, 'Joe's at it again.'

After asking me a number of questions, one of the doctors said, 'Alan, we're letting you go home today.'

I was still very nervous, but for some reason I had complete clarity about the implications of this. I said to the psychiatrist, 'Doctor, I need to go somewhere that is totally alcohol free, like a rehabilitation centre of some kind. It's Christmas, and I know I won't make it down the road without hitting a pub.'

The doctor replied, 'Alan, we'll deal with that in January – we're all going home now for Christmas. But we'll see you in January, and we'll arrange something for you then.'

I walked out of the office, totally bewildered. I went into the security guard's office and asked him could I use his phone. The guy told me to 'work away'. I rang directory enquiries and asked them for the number of Sister Consilio's drink rehabilitation centre, Cuan Mhuire, in Athy, Co. Kildare. I had heard about the place from other alcoholics and from family friends. I then rang Cuan Mhuire, and got through to a member of staff there. I explained who I was, where I was and the situation I was in, and asked could they help me.

The guy said, 'We were due to have a guy arrive last night. But he was a no-show, so we have a bed available. Can you get down to us this evening?'

I told him I'd be there in three hours, and hung up the phone. I then rang my niece Gemma and asked her would she collect me from Portrane and drive me to Athy. She said she'd be down to me within the hour.

I walked over to the doctors' office, and knocked. When I went in, I told the team of psychiatrists I was going down to Sister Consilio's within the next hour.

One of them asked, 'How'd you do that?'

I replied simply, 'I made a phone call.'

They all just looked at each other, as I left the office and closed the door.

My first impression of Cuan Mhuire was that it was very well kept, very upmarket. My mother and my sister Frieda had travelled along with Gemma and myself, and they all raved about how good the place looked.

And yet, my sixth sense was telling me different: I didn't like the place. But I knew I had to go in, because I didn't want to drink. After I checked in, I said my goodbyes to my family. I was told I had to wear my pyjamas for the first two weeks of what was to be a twelve-week alcohol treatment course, and I was placed in a detox ward with five other guys. I had a feeling Cuan Mhuire wasn't going to work for me, but I was there for only one reason – to keep sober over Christmas and the New Year.

The regime was tough, with lots of rules and regulations, some of which were ridiculous. Once I heard an announcement over the tannoy that I was to report to the nurses' station at once. When I got there, I was escorted into my dormitory, where a nun pointed at my bed and spoke to me sternly in her deep Cork accent.

'What do you see wrong here?'

I had years of experience of making my bed 'military style' while in prison, and I could see nothing wrong with my bed. I told the nun as much.

She said, 'Look at the design of the trees on the bed-throw. The top of the trees are pointing downwards, and they should be facing upwards.'

I couldn't believe what I was hearing. She then proceeded to pull apart my neatly made bed, and threw the blankets on the floor.

She said, 'Now, make it properly.'

I had two options: snap and wreck the place, or laugh and just make the bed. I opted for the latter. Anything to shut her up!

For some reason, despite the regime at Cuan Mhuire, I began while there to have faith in the power of prayer. I don't know why I suddenly became aware of God's presence in my life, but I did. The rehabilitation programme was centred around the Blessed Virgin and the rosary. I suppose I had always had a belief in Jesus, Mother Mary and St Francis Xavier – even as far back as when I was in St Patrick's Institution. Now, I found myself talking to God every night, speaking aloud to him about what was going on inside my head. I just knew that God was listening to me. In that place, God was the only person I could trust.

At times, it all got a bit too much for me: it felt like I was being force-fed religion, and I didn't like anything being forced upon me. The nuns who ran Cuan Mhuire saw me as a negative influence – an argumentative and non-compliant individual. As a result, I had many an office door slammed in my face. But I never stopped praying, even if it was just an Our Father or a little conversation with the man above. In times of self-doubt, even if I was sitting on the toilet, I would turn to God. I don't know where this faith came from; I just had an overwhelming feeling within me that God is real and that He exists. (It's very easy to understand God – as long as I don't try to explain him!)

I was still very far from well – I still had that mind-bending obsessional desire to drink. I was very argumentative and snappy, and unable to think straight. But after two weeks in Cuan Mhuire, with Christmas and the New Year just about behind me, I felt I no longer needed the treatment centre. So, on the night of 31 December 2007, I left – very much aware that I was doing so on the most dangerous night of the year for an alcoholic.

But I was sick of Cuan Mhuire, and I wanted to be with my mother to ring in the New Year. I knew in my heart that I'd rather die than go back to the hell of my drinking life. Having God to speak to was the best deterrent of all.

As I left, the Cork nun's parting words were, 'You'll drink again.'

18

Trying to Stop

When I got home from Cuan Mhuire, I still had the insane urge to drink. I was feeling very unwell – due to my hepatitis C and my liver cirrhosis – I weighed more than twenty stone, and I assumed that my death was imminent. And yet, I was very happy to be home with my mother and two little nephews, and I wanted nothing to take me away from that. I didn't want to die.

After a few hours at home, I went upstairs to my bedroom to think. I came to the conclusion that I wanted to die a sober man, regardless of how long I had left to live. I threw on my jacket, and I went to an AA meeting. I had gone to meetings in prison, but only to take the piss. This time I really wanted to go – not for my mother, not for my little nephews, but for me.

At first I was really paranoid about bumping into an enemy at a meeting, or on my way to one. I was scared about how the AA members might feel if they heard about my past. I put this fear to an old-timer, who advised me to be prudent when sharing in the meetings. In any case, he said, it didn't matter what anyone heard about me, as there would be people in the room who would have done things I couldn't even imagine. Although that advice made me feel a bit better, I was still very paranoid. I carried my small blade – just in case anyone I met tried to administer their own brand of justice.

Arriving at my first meeting, I was welcomed with a friendly handshake that was genuine – not the fake shake of people who just wanted me to get them a drink or sub them a few quid. The AA members made me feel very welcome. But I was convinced that when they got to know and hear about the real me, their opinion of me would change and, like everyone else, they wouldn't want to know me.

At that first meeting I heard about the 'Big Book' and the twelve steps. I was introduced to such simple mantras as 'keep it in the day', 'easy does it', 'keep it simple', 'don't walk past pubs', 'don't carry cash', 'don't read newspapers'. I wasn't sure what to think. But there was one thing that stuck with me, a sign above the doorway that read: 'Keep Coming Back'. I did. Come hail, rain, wind or snow, I made sure I got my ass to at least two meetings every day. If I didn't have the bus fare, I walked.

I still very much wanted to drink – and that desire scared the daylights out of me. I was seeing a psychiatrist, Dr Robert Daly, who diagnosed me as having a 'long-standing personality disorder with antisocial personality traits and a clear history of alcohol dependence syndrome'. The shorthand for this was 'ASPD'. I couldn't argue with 'antisocial': I was a car thief, a bank robber, I'd stabbed people, hijacked a taxi at knife-point, and so on. But 'personality disorder' didn't feel right: I felt I had a good personality, and I knew I got on well with most people I came into contact with.

I researched ASPD on the internet. The disorder involves a pervasive pattern of disregard for and violation of the rights of others that begins in childhood or early adolescence and continues into adulthood. Other elements are: impulsiveness or failure to plan ahead; irritability and aggressiveness; reckless disregard for the safety of self or others; consistent irresponsibility; a repeated failure to sustain consistent work behaviour or to honour financial obligations; and, finally, a lack of remorse. At the time, I didn't recognise myself in that diagnosis. Today, I can see the justice of it.

Dr Daly told me that when I was under the influence of alcohol, I'd get a 'flash' of an idea in my mind, and once that idea sat easy – whether it be murder or stealing a pint of milk – I would proceed to carry it out, regardless of the consequences. Now that I was not drinking, the doctor concluded, I would no longer suffer from these sudden impulses.

At AA meetings I was guilty of what they call the 'three Cs': I 'criticised', I 'compared' and I 'condemned' others. I thought people were judging me and talking about me; I believed they hated me, and wanted something from me. And yet, I kept going to the meetings: I knew I had to. AA was my last port of call.

My elder brother, William, who was delighted that I was staying off the drink, offered to give me a little car he owned, a Seat Ibiza, if I got my full driver's licence. I applied to sit a test for my full licence, and began taking lessons. Within two months, I had passed the test. William was delighted that I had completed my part of the deal, and handed me the keys to the car. I will always be eternally grateful to my brother for his trust and generosity. I taxed the car and took out an insurance policy; for the first time in my entire life, I was completely legit on the road. No amount of cocaine could have given me the natural high I was on that day when my brother gave me that car. Now I could drive to my meetings in comfort, and give other members lifts.

One night, as I sat in a meeting, I listened to this guy sharing the causes of alcoholism and describing his own experiences. He was not only intelligent but also very streetwise, and everything he said made perfect sense to me. Some days later, I saw the same guy, Roy, at another meeting. I didn't yet have an AA sponsor. (A sponsor is a fellow alcoholic who has many years of sobriety under his belt, and who knows the twelve-step programme intimately. Finding a sponsor is like finding someone to play chess with: you always get someone who is better than you, more experienced than you. Where I see thirty-two squares, he sees the whole sixty-four.) As the old Buddhist proverb goes: 'When the student is ready, the Teacher will come.' I suppose I was ready.

As Roy spoke to a few old-timers outside the meeting, I plucked up the courage and asked him would he be my sponsor.

He said, 'Sure, no problem.'

Another member told me afterwards that prior to the previous meeting, Roy hadn't shared in about two years.

I met up with Roy at my house to begin learning the twelve steps of Alcoholics Anonymous. Step four – where I had to make a searching and fearless moral inventory of myself – was a very hard one for me. I knew that in order to do it properly, I had to write down every wrong I'd ever done to another person. I procrastinated, frozen by various forms of fear and paranoia. I thought the police had my home bugged and were waiting for the right time to raid the house to get their hands on my statement. Also, I just didn't want to see on a single piece of paper the evidence of what and who I truly was. But Roy was all over me, and I knew in myself that there was no way around it. Finally, I did it – but I kept the document in a steel biscuit tin under my bed, with a tin of lighter fluid and a box of matches, so that I could burn it if the police raided the house.

The fifth step is where you reveal to yourself, to God and to another human being the exact nature of all your wrongs. In other words, I had to sit down with another human being, look that person in the eye and tell him or her every single thing I had ever done wrong. Roy made an appointment for me to do my fifth step with a Jesuit priest he knew, Fr Jim Smyth.

Shortly before my confession, my mobile phone rang. It was a detective from the Gardaí. He said that he'd heard I was in AA now and doing very well. He wondered if I'd pop into the station to do my fifth step with the police, to get everything off my chest? I told the detective in no uncertain terms what he could do with himself, and told him not to ring my phone again. But other detectives continued to ring me, coming across as very concerned about me and trying to coax me into doing my fifth step with them! I was fully aware that the only thing the police were concerned about was having me sent to prison for a very long time.

I was as nervous as hell about meeting Fr Jim and reading my fourth-step statement to him, and I was paranoid about the police following me. Driving into town to meet the priest was one of the most difficult things I've ever had to do. And all the more so, because I was sober. I had my statement in the biscuit tin – with the lighter fuel and matches, just in case.

When I got to the church, Fr Jim, a man in his eighties, showed me into a little room. We both got ourselves a mug of tea and sat facing each other. After a bit of chit-chat, I leaned down to pick up my fourth-step statement.

But Fr Jim said, 'Leave that where it is, Alan. You don't need that. I think you know what you need to talk about.'

He was right. But knowing what to say and actually saying it were two completely different things. I began talking about my childhood, my teenage years, my criminality, my journalistic career.

But I wasn't talking about my deepest and darkest secrets. I kept saying to myself, 'Alan, just say it, just say one sentence, just do it.' Eventually, I did. And soon everything that was buried deep within me came pouring out. I found myself looking this man right in the eye as I recounted all the stuff I thought I would have taken to the grave with me.

When I had finished, Fr Jim asked me to kneel. He said a prayer over my head, gave me absolution and ended with the words, 'God has forgiven you, now you must learn to forgive yourself. God loves you, Alan, and now God wants you to love yourself.' Before I left the church, Fr Jim asked me would I come back up to see him the following week and join him for lunch. I felt honoured to be asked, and I graciously accepted the invitation.

As soon as I left the church, I sat down on the pavement and set fire to my fourth-step statement. I watched as it burned and the wind scattered the ashes down the street.

A few days later, two detectives turned up at my door. They came into the house and told me that they wanted to advise me about a threat to my life. They talked me through a number of security precautions, and then I was handed an official Garda Information Message form. But they wouldn't tell me anything about who was making the threat. The police reiterated that if I wished to speak with them about anything, if there was anything on my mind, I could just ring them and they'd be there for me. I was pretty sure the police wanted to drive me off the rails so that they'd have a reason to arrest me and lock me up.

The following week, when I met Fr Jim for lunch, I was able to relax in a new and unfamiliar way. For the first time, I felt I could speak openly and honestly with another human being. This man knew every single cough and spit of my entire life; I didn't have to worry about censoring myself, and that gave me a great sense of freedom. To be able to sit with another human being and talk about anything that comes into your mind, or to share your deepest darkest secrets, is the greatest gift one can receive.

During our conversation I happened to mention that I had been in St Ita's, and Fr Jim asked me when that had been. I told him that my last stay there was in December 2007.

Fr Jim replied, 'Do you know what, Alan? I was only ever in Portrane once in my entire life, and that was in December of 2007. It was after being up in Beaumont Hospital, visiting a Travelling lady. I went up to her to give her a blessing, and she asked me would I go to Portrane to visit a young man who was just transferred down there.'

Father Jim

The hairs on the back of my neck stood up, and I got goosebumps all over – suddenly, I remembered. I said, 'I remember you, Father. I remember you in Portrane. You were wearing a long black mac, and you were carrying a small leather case, like an old gun case. And inside it was a cross – a big gold cross, with a lock on the end of it – and you blessed me with it.'

Fr Jim said, 'Yes, that was Father John Sullivan's cross, Alan. It's more than two hundred years old.' He went on to say, 'Alan, the man I saw sitting on the side of that bed had nothing but emptiness in his eyes. I thought to myself, "There's no hope for this young man." When I asked you did you want a blessing, you looked up at me and said two words: "Please, Father." I felt very sad for that young man.'

My head was in a spin; I was trying to make sense out of it all. It was a remarkable coincidence, and I felt that in some way I had been meant to meet Fr Jim, this man who had helped me so much.

Due to my hepatitis C and cirrhosis of the liver, I was still very unwell. I was still obese, and my feet, ankles and lower legs were huge due to the build-up of fluid. My doctors declined to put me on any medication, because my liver was so badly damaged.

But I didn't let any of this deter me. I continued to attend my AA meetings. I prayed every morning, asking for guidance. I tried not to harm anyone. Every night I gave thanks for the day that had just passed, regardless of how the day had been. I was regimental about opening my mind to God every morning, and giving thanks at night.

There were times when discouragement would set in, and I would think, 'Why on earth am I doing this? I'm just going to die very soon anyway.' But I was determined to die sober. That acceptance of my death and the determination to stay sober were what kept me going. I wanted to live. I wanted to be normal. I wanted to interact with people. I wanted to love and to care for others. I wanted to be human. I needed life!

After a while of going to AA, I knew I had to let go of my fear and get rid of my blade. Leaving home without it was a very hard thing for me to do; it was one of the most fearful challenges I have ever faced. Even as I write this now, I am full of fear. People reading this will know that I no longer carry a blade on my person: that is still terrifying to me.

19

The Miracle Man

I was spending a lot of time going in and out of hospital for check-ups, blood tests, a colonoscopy, ultrasound and MRI. I was also going to as many AA meetings as I could, trying to improve on my family relationships, to write my book and to develop scripts. I was aware that my liver could fail at any time. And I knew that to pass away from liver failure was one of the most painful deaths that one could go through.

On 17 August 2009, I was on one of my regular visits to my liver specialist, Dr Tariq Tajuddin, at the hepatology clinic at Beaumont Hospital. When I walked into his office, Dr Tajuddin turned to face me on his swivel chair.

He said, 'Ah, the miracle man!'

I asked him what he was talking about.

The doctor said, 'Alan, your hepatitis C – it's gone! I've had your bloods checked on three separate occasions since March, just to make sure, and it's gone.' He hit a few keys on his computer and got my bloods up on screen. 'Look,' said the doctor. 'There were your bloods eight months ago: all high where they should be low, and all low where they should be high. They're all over the place. Here they are today.' He hit a few more keys on his keyboard. 'All your bloods in your liver have completely normalised. I have to say, Alan, this is the first time in my entire career I have ever seen anything like this happen.'

I said, 'I want that in writing, Doctor!'

And the good doctor did give it to me in writing – on Beaumont Hospital headed paper.

I reviewed Alan in Professor Murray's hepatology clinic today. As you know, previously he had chronic hepatitis C, genotype 1, of unknown source. Interestingly, Alan spontaneously has cleared his hepatitis C virus, as shown on his most recently repeated PCR test on three occasions. Even more interestingly, his liver blood tests have completely normalised. His INR is now settling down to 1.3 from 2.17. Alan looks well, with no stigmata of chronic liver disease or its complications. Again, this is a quite unusual occurrence and difficult for me to understand how someone with advanced liver disease and presumed cirrhosis could clear the virus spontaneously, without treatment, years after infection.

It was impossible to get my head around it all. My weight rapidly dropped from 21st 4lbs to 16st; my yellow jaundice went; the fluid in my legs, ankles and feet reduced dramatically. Within weeks, I had fully recovered – with absolutely no explanation for it. I could make sense of it only as part of a sequence of events going back to 2007 when, after cutting my throat, I opened my heart to Jinny, the Traveller lady in Beaumont Hospital. Then in Portrane, unbeknownst to me, Fr Jim blessed me with the 200-year-old cross belonging to the late Fr John Sullivan. Shortly thereafter, I first felt clarity in my head, and was able to use empathy for the first time in a long while. With my new clarity I was able to deal effectively with the team of psychiatrists, and secure myself a place at Cuan Mhuire.

After that, I started going to AA meetings and was fortunate enough to meet Ray, who put me in touch with Fr Jim – who, as far as I was concerned, I had never met before. Through this sequence of events, it seemed to me, God had begun to make himself known to me. I saw God's hand, too, in the spontaneous clearance of my hepatitis C virus and the normalising of my liver function. And I see God in the many instances described in this book – plus several others I haven't mentioned – when I ought to have died: the car crashes, the stabbings and beatings, the drug overdoses, the suicide attempts.

Not long after my cure, I was faced with a challenge. In May of 2009, I was up at St Francis Xavier's Church, visiting Fr Jim, when he told me that he and his fellow Jesuits were wondering how I would feel about standing up at the altar and telling the parishioners about what had happened to me. I was flabbergasted: I could not believe that such an esteemed body of people had invited me to share my story from the altar. How could I say no?

On the day I was to share my story, I was seated up the front of the church. As I heard the droves of parishioners shuffling in, I started getting nervous. When Fr Donal opened the mass, I glanced over my shoulder and saw that the church was packed to the rafters: there must have been close to 500 people present. Then Fr Donal introduced me and mentioned the blessing of Fr John Sullivan's cross. I made my way to the altar, and I spoke for about twenty minutes. I was happy with how I carried it off: it felt great to express a message of hope.

What happened next was unexpected. I was asked to stand at the front of the altar, and the whole congregation formed a queue in front of me. Every single parishioner wanted to shake my hand. I recall one man saying to his two children as they stood in front of me, 'Say hello, and shake hands. This is a very special man.'

It was totally weird, but I was delighted to see people leaving the church with hope in their hearts.

I don't take my alcoholism lightly. It is a deadly disease. I know I have to maintain my contact with God. When I came into AA first, I was searching for peace of mind, searching for God; I was looking externally. Then I realised I never had to go looking for God – it's just that my mind was closed to him. When my mind began to open and I started to let a bit of light in, I realised that God had always been within me, right from the day I was born. Every morning I prayed, asking for help. I began to give back to the AA fellowship by doing service – preparing the tea and coffee before meetings, cleaning up at the end of meetings, doing secretarial work, and generally assisting in any way I could. I slowly began to stop judging other people, as that was only taking up negative room inside my head.

Many people associate alcoholism with the homeless wino, drunk and begging. I've been that homeless drunk. I've also been the alcoholic criminal, the alcoholic journalist, the alcoholic airport and holiday-rep employee, the sex-mad alcoholic, the suicidal alcoholic, the depressive alcoholic, the male-prostitute alcoholic, the isolated home-drinking alcoholic. The disease of alcoholism does not cherry-pick people; it has no friends.

With Fr John Sullivan's cross

I still have many fears – even a fear of success. When I write a script and send it off to the BBC, I think, 'My God, what if they commission me to write a number of episodes? Will I be able to see it through and live up to their expectations?' That's the 'alchy' thinking again – running off a hundred miles down the road, and the BBC haven't even tied their shoelaces yet.

Another part of me that I have to watch concerns affairs of the heart. I wear my heart on my sleeve. I respect and love women, but they can be my downfall. I have learned that walking away from something that is causing conflict in my life is not a sign of weakness, but rather a sign of strength. I learn from my mistakes – learn to improve myself.

My alcoholism, I understand now, is wrapped up with problems I've had around sex. For many years, I saw women as sexual objects, and I often used them for my own gratification. It was never about pleasing the woman – once I got what I wanted, I was happy. In relationships, I was jealous, possessive and controlling, and I thought that's what love was. I never examined why I was drawn to pornography, prostitution and the exploitation of women. With regard to my occasional attraction to men, I suffered from internalised homophobia, and probably still do. There was never any honesty in my thinking about sex.

Sex is rarely discussed at any AA meeting – at least, not in Ireland. Sometimes it seems as though everything *but* sex is talked about at AA meetings. For me, misdirected sex was a formidable threat to my sobriety, and the only way to deal with that was to discuss it and seek guidance, have the willingness to change and then ask God to remove it. So I did.

I suppose I always felt sexually inadequate, and I had always been troubled by fears of sexual incompetence and rejection. Oddly, this may have led to frenzied promiscuity. My sexual problems led me in a number of directions, but the result was always pain, misery, tension and guilt.

I have learned from all of that and more. I know how to love and appreciate women today. God has steered my life in a direction where I find myself helping women in addiction – aiding them, encouraging them, appreciating them and caring for them – whereas in the past, it was all quite the opposite. Don't get me wrong, I'm far from becoming a monk. But I do believe God will send the right person into my life, when I'm ready.

I continue to attend AA meetings at least two or three times a week – I want to, I need to. AA is to me what insulin is to a diabetic. The meetings keep me grounded, and they remind me of the life I left behind. I don't live in the past, but I will never shut the door on it either.

I still struggle with various kinds of bad behaviour: sulking, flattery, seeking praise for myself and withholding deserved praise from others. I can be manipulative. Road rage is a problem for me: taxi and bus drivers still drive me mental, so I know I need to work on that.

I hope to make amends to those I have hurt or harmed. It is a task that I will probably spend the rest of my life trying to complete. I have made amends to some: doing so scared the living shit out of me. I don't want to open up old wounds, and I don't want to hurt anyone. If the people I approach spit in my face, I will accept that. The most important factor I must remember is to ensure that I do not cause upset, hurt or harm to those I wish to approach. Because the making of amends is not about me – it is about the people I hurt.

With Glen, Ma, Declan and William

Well into my forties, I still live with my Ma, and I'll always be here for her. (My father left the family home years ago, after my parents' marriage broke down. Today he has his own little place, and my Ma and Da have divorced. They still talk to each other, and they can tolerate each other since he moved out. On occasion, I drop in to see him.) The way I see it, my mother was always there for me; she never gave up on me. Some may form the opinion that she was far too easy-going with me, and that is why I became a criminal. But I know that's not true. I know plenty of people who were stripped naked, whipped, beaten, kicked out from their homes, disowned by their loved ones. And they turned out much worse than me, God bless them. I look at my mother today and I can see the joy and relaxation written all over her face: she can put her head on her pillow at night and just sleep. She has no more pain, no more hidden fears, no more stress, no more court appearances, no more visits to prison, no more early-morning house raids.

As long as I'm above ground, I will always be there for my

mother. She most certainly will never end up in one of those old folks' homes – that is her biggest fear. At the time of writing, she is seventy-three years of age. She never drank, and she stopped smoking a long time ago. She cycles everywhere. She's been working since the age of fourteen, and she's still working today, in Croke Park. She sings in our local church choir, despite having suffered terrible abuse at the hands of the nuns when she was young. She'd do anything for anyone.

Whenever I am feeling tense, agitated, uneasy, restless, moody, upset, sad, lonely, disturbed, hopeless, helpless or haunted, there are four things that help.

Firstly, there's scripture. I pick up the Bible, flick through it, then just stop at a page and read it. The stories enlighten me and take me away from myself.

Secondly, I take my own inventory. I write down how I'm feeling, what I am going through, and when I read it back to myself aloud, the problem begins to lift. It is truly amazing how it works, but it does – the answer is in the question.

Thirdly, I have my music. I find the right song from my CD collection that identifies or explains what I am going through, and it lifts me from that mood.

And finally, there is the power of prayer. I lie back on my bed and have an open and deep conversation with God. I speak aloud and talk to God as if he was sitting right next to me. I explain in great detail the entire problem, and then I ask him a question. And the answer comes to me – it works, every time.

I couldn't ask for a better life than the one I have now. I'm in my sixth year of sobriety. As long as I don't drink, I know it will be a good day. I am so proud of my two little nephews, Robbie and Lee: they're really great kids, and I love them to bits. I do a lot of writing, and I swear no amount of cocaine could give me the natural high I get when working on a play or a script. I'll always write; it's all I know. If I don't ever get anything performed or produced, well, it certainly won't be for the want of trying. And I'll keep at it until the day I pass on.

My needs and wants in life today are not much. As long as I can keep my little twelve-year-old motor on the road, put a drop of petrol into it, tax it, pay the insurance and get it through the NCT, I feel fine, because I can get to AA meetings around the city and give lifts to others. I can bring my nephew Lee to his football training every Monday and Thursday, to his goalkeeping training on a Tuesday and his games on Sundays. I can drive my Ma to work or to the shops. And I get huge comfort and security from knowing that I have twenty or thirty euros in the bank. If an AA member asks me to join them for a coffee, or to go for a bit of lunch, it's great not to have that fear of not knowing if I've got any money.

There are still times when I don't have the guide of my inner compass. If you set your boat on a course for the North Pole, and you're even one degree off, you will not notice a change in your course right away. But eventually you'll find yourself sitting at a bar in the South Pole, thinking, 'How the fuck did I end up here?' When I feel an emptiness inside, with the loss of love and feelings, or I'm weighed down by the threat of insanity, I know I need to keep my eye on the compass.

I sometimes miss the madness attached to drinking and drugging. I sometimes ask myself, 'Will I give it a lash one more time before I die?' But then common sense kicks in, thank God. I must learn to live totally independently – to be strong, both internally and externally – not only for me but also for my family, friends, lovers and strangers. I am deeply contented with the simple life I have today. No more madness, no more criminality, no more deceiving, conning, using or hurting people.

I know I am going to die some day, and I have come to accept it. Until the day I die, I just want to do the right thing.